Frommer's®

P9-CDX-867

San Francisco
day BY day®

3rd Edition

by Matthew Poole

WILEY

John Wiley & Sons, Inc.

Contents

Published by:

John Wiley & Sons, Inc.

111 River St.
Hoboken, NJ 07030-5774

ISBN 978-1-118-02748-6 (paper); ISBN 978-0-470-44262-3 (ebk); ISBN 978-1-118-17551-4 (ebk); ISBN 978-1-118-17552-1 (ebk)

Editor: Stephen Bassman
Production Editor: Erin Amick
Photo Editor: Cherie Cincilla
Cartographer: Andrew Dolan
Production by Wiley Indianapolis Composition Services

For information on our other products and services or to obtain technical support, please contact our Customer Care Department within the U.S. at 877/762-2974, outside the U.S. at 317/572-3993 or fax 317/572-4002.

Wiley also publishes its books in a variety of electronic formats. Some content that appears in print may not be available in electronic formats.

Manufactured in China

5   4   3   2   1

A Note from the Editorial Director

Organizing your time. That's what this guide is all about.

Other guides give you long lists of things to see and do and then expect you to fit the pieces together. The Day by Day guides are different. These guides tell you the best of everything, and then they show you how to see it in the *smartest, most time-efficient way*. Our authors have designed detailed itineraries organized by time, neighborhood or special interest. And each tour comes with a bulleted map that takes you from stop to stop.

Hoping to relive the Summer of Love, or to hop on a cable car to the Fisherman's Wharf? Planning a drive across the Golden Gate Bridge, a hike up Telegraph Hill to Coit Tower, or a jaunt over to the best vineyards in the Napa Valley? Whatever your interest or schedule, the Day by Days give you the smartest route to follow. Not only do we take you to the top sights and attractions, but we introduce you to those special moments that only locals know about—those "finds" that turn tourists into travelers.

The Day by Days are also your top choice if you're looking for one complete guide for all your travel needs. The best hotels and restaurants for every budget, the greatest shopping values, the wildest nightlife—it's all here.

Why should you trust our judgment? Because our authors personally visit each place they write about. They're an independent lot who say what they think and would never include places they wouldn't recommend to their best friends. They're also open to suggestions from readers. If you'd like to contact them, please send your comments our way at feedback@frommers.com, and we'll pass them on.

Enjoy your Day by Day guide—the most helpful travel companion you can buy. And have the trip of a lifetime.

Warm regards,

Kelly Regan

Kelly Regan, Editorial Director
Frommer's Travel Guides

About the Author

Matthew Poole, a native Californian and San Francisco resident, has authored more than two dozen travel guides to California, Hawaii, and abroad, and is a regular contributor to radio and television travel programs. Before becoming a full-time travel writer and photographer, he worked as an English tutor in Prague, a ski instructor in the Swiss Alps, and a scuba instructor in Maui and Thailand. His other titles include *Frommer's San Francisco, Frommer's California, Frommer's Irreverent Guide to San Francisco,* and *Frommer's San Francisco Free & Dirt Cheap.* You can follow Matthew's weekly blog posts about travel adventures in California at LocalGetaways.com.

Acknowledgments

I would like to acknowledge the following people for their time and effort in helping me complete this 2012 edition: Katy Connor, Kristine Givas, Erika Lenkert, David Lytle, Kristin Luna, and my unflappable editor, Stephen Bassman.

— Matthew Poole

Advisory & Disclaimer

Travel information can change quickly and unexpectedly, and we strongly advise you to confirm important details locally before traveling, including information on visas, health and safety, traffic and transport, accommodations, shopping, and eating out. We also encourage you to stay alert while traveling and to remain aware of your surroundings. Avoid civil disturbances, and keep a close eye on cameras, purses, wallets, and other valuables.

While we have endeavored to ensure that the information contained within this guide is accurate and up-to-date at the time of publication, we make no representations or warranties with respect to the accuracy or completeness of the contents of this work and specifically disclaim all warranties, including without limitation warranties of fitness for a particular purpose. We accept no responsibility or liability for any inaccuracy or errors or omissions, or for any inconvenience, loss, damage, costs, or expenses of any nature whatsoever incurred or suffered by anyone as a result of any advice or information contained in this guide.

The inclusion of a company, organization, or website in this guide as a service provider and/or potential source of further information does not mean that we endorse them or the information they provide. Be aware that information provided through some websites may be unreliable and can change without notice. Neither the publisher nor author shall be liable for any damages arising herefrom.

Star Ratings, Icons & Abbreviations

Every hotel, restaurant, and attraction listing in this guide has been ranked for quality, value, service, amenities, and special features using a **star-rating system.** Hotels, restaurants, attractions, shopping, and nightlife are rated on a scale of zero stars (recommended) to three stars (exceptional). In addition to the star-rating system, we also use a **kids icon** to point out the best bets for families. Within each tour, we recommend cafes, bars, or restaurants where you can take a break. Each of these stops appears in a shaded box marked with a coffee-cup-shaped bullet 🍵.

The following **abbreviations** are used for credit cards:

AE	American Express	DISC	Discover	V	Visa
DC	Diners Club	MC	MasterCard		

Frommers.com

Now that you have this guidebook to help you plan a great trip, visit our website at **www.frommers.com** for additional travel information on more than 3,600 destinations. We update features regularly to give you instant access to the most current trip-planning information available. At Frommers.com, you'll find scoops on the best airfares, lodging rates, and car rental bargains. You can even book your travel online through our reliable travel booking partners. Other popular features include:

- Online updates of our most popular guidebooks
- Vacation sweepstakes and contest giveaways
- Newsletters highlighting the hottest travel trends
- Online travel message boards with featured travel discussions

A Note on Prices

In the "Take a Break" and "Best Bets" sections of this book, we have used a system of dollar signs to show a range of costs for 1 night in a hotel (the price of a double-occupancy room) or the cost of an entree at a restaurant. Use the following table to decipher the dollar signs:

Cost	Hotels	Restaurants
$	under $150	under $10
$$	$150–$250	$10–$20
$$$	$250–$350	$20–$30
$$$$	$350–$450	$30–$40
$$$$$	over $450	over $40

An Invitation to the Reader

In researching this book, we discovered many wonderful places—hotels, restaurants, shops, and more. We're sure you'll find others. Please tell us about them, so we can share the information with your fellow travelers in upcoming editions. If you were disappointed with a recommendation, we'd love to know that, too. Please write to:

Frommer's San Francisco Day by Day, 3rd Edition
John Wiley & Sons, Inc. • 111 River St. • Hoboken, NJ 07030-5774

20 Favorite **Moments**

20 Favorite **Moments**

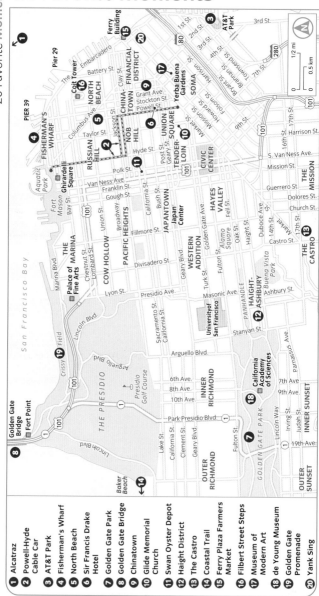

Previous page: The City by the Bay.

Most of the great cities of the world are best seen on foot, and San Francisco is no exception. Unlike some sprawling metropolises, San Francisco is constrained by bay and sea to a mere 7 square miles (18 sq. km) of increasingly coveted real estate. Yes, you'll have to walk up and down a few hills, but don't let that deter you from leisurely strolling this most walking-friendly city.

1 Do time on the Rock. Even if you loathe tourist attractions, you'll love Alcatraz. Just looking at the Rock from across the bay is enough to give you the heebie-jeebies. Heck, even the boat ride across the bay is worth the price. *See p 11.*

2 Catch an early morning cable car. Skip the boring California line and take the Powell-Hyde cable car down to Fisherman's Wharf—the ride is worth the wait. When you reach the top of Nob Hill, grab the rail in one hand and hold the camera with the other. This view of the bay will make you a believer. *See p 7.*

3 Watch the San Francisco Giants play at AT&T Park. If it's baseball season, then you *must* spend an afternoon or evening watching the National League's Giants play at one of the finest ballparks in America. For only $10, you can buy a bleacher-seat ticket on the day of a game. Even if the season's over, you can still take a guided tour of the stadium. *See p 135.*

4 Feast on Dungeness crab at San Francisco's Fisherman's Wharf. You'll find better Dungeness crab elsewhere, but eating it straight from the seafood vendors' boiling pots at the corner of Jefferson and Taylor streets is a quintessential San Francisco experience. *See p 7.*

5 Start your day with North Beach coffee. One of the most pleasurable smells of San Francisco is the aroma of roasted coffee beans wafting down Columbus Avenue in the early morning. Start the day with a cup of Viennese on a sidewalk table at **Caffè Trieste** followed by a walk down Columbus Avenue to the bay. *See p 30.*

6 Sipping a cocktail in the clouds. Some of the best ways to view the city are from top-floor lounges in the high-end hotels such as the **Sir Francis Drake,** the **Grand Hyatt San Francisco,** and **the Mark Hopkins InterContinental.** Drinks aren't cheap, but views are priceless. *See p 123.*

7 Skating through Golden Gate Park on a weekend. C'mon! When's the last time you've been skating? And if you've never tried skating before, there's no better place to learn than on the wide, flat main street through Golden Gate Park, which is closed to vehicles on weekends. *See p 88.*

8 A walk across the Golden Gate Bridge. Don your windbreaker and walking shoes and prepare for a wind-blasted, exhilarating journey across San Francisco's most famous landmark. It's simply one of those things you have to do at least once in your life. *See p 38.*

9 Stroll through Chinatown. Chinatown is a trip. I've been through it at least 100 times, and it has never failed to entertain me. Head straight for the food markets, where a cornucopia of critters sit in boxes waiting for the wok. *(Is that an armadillo?) See p 42.*

10 Spending a soul-stirring Sunday morning at Glide Church. The high-spirited singers and hand-clapping worshipers at Glide turn churchgoing into a spiritual party that leaves you feeling elated, hopeful, and at one with mankind. See p 133.

⓫ **Experience the Swan Oyster Depot.** My dad doesn't care much for San Francisco ("Too crowded!") but he loves having lunch at this beloved seafood institution, which has been serving up fresh fish since 1912. See p 113.

⓬ **Hang in the Haight.** Though the power of the flower has wilted, the Haight is still, more or less, the Haight: a sort of resting home for aging hippies, dazed ex-Deadheads, skate punks, and rather pathetic young panhandlers. Think of it as visiting a people zoo, with shopping and bars (don't neglect the Lower Haight's bar scene). See p 34.

⓭ **Cruise the Castro.** The most populated and festive street in the city isn't just for gays and lesbians. There are some great shops and cafes, but it's the abundance of positive energy that makes the trip here a must. And please make time to catch a flick (any flick, doesn't matter) at the **Castro Theatre.** See p 62.

⓮ **Hike the Coastal Trail.** Walk the forested coastal trail from the Cliff House to the Golden Gate Bridge and

You'll get a brief Wurlitzer concert before films at the Castro, one of the city's original movie houses.

you'll see why locals put up with living on a foggy fault line. Start at the parking lot just above Cliff House and head north. Dress warmly. See p 86.

⓯ **Graze at the Ferry Plaza Farmers Market.** We San Franciscans take our farmers markets very seriously. Arrive hungry at the Ferry Building (Embarcadero at Market St.) on Saturday, Sunday, Tuesday, and Thursday and join the locals (and local chefs) as they shop for America's finest organic produce, with free samples. See p 12.

⓰ **Climb the Filbert Street Steps.** San Francisco is a city of stairs, and the crème de la crème is the Filbert Street Steps, a 377-step descent that wends its way through flower gardens and some of the city's oldest and most varied housing. It's a beautiful walk down, and great exercise going up. See p 33.

⓱ **Visit the Museum of Modern Art.** Ever since the SFMOMA opened in 1995, it has been the best place to go for a quick dose of culture. Have a light lunch at Caffè Museo before, and afterwards stroll through the nearby Yerba Buena Gardens. See p 13.

⓲ **A day at the de Young.** It's a pleasure just to look at the de Young Museum in Golden Gate Park. Then catch a blockbuster exhibit or two inside. See p 90.

⓳ **Meander along the Marina's Golden Gate Promenade.** There's something about walking along the promenade that just feels right. The combination of beach, bay, boats, Golden Gate views, and cool breezes is good for the soul. See p 84.

⓴ **Dine on dim sum at Yank Sing.** If you like Chinese food, you'll love dim sum. At Yank Sing, you'll be wowed by the variety of dumplings and mysterious dishes that are carted past you. Just point at what looks good and dig in. See p 116. ●

1 The Best **Full-Day Tours**

The Best **in One Day**

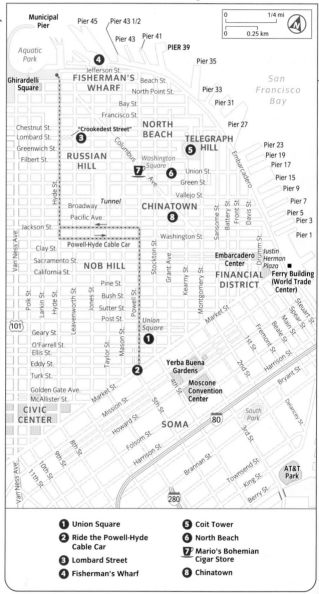

❶ Union Square	❺ Coit Tower
❷ Ride the Powell-Hyde Cable Car	❻ North Beach
❸ Lombard Street	❼ Mario's Bohemian Cigar Store
❹ Fisherman's Wharf	❽ Chinatown

Previous page: The beloved International Orange icon, the Golden Gate Bridge.

This full-day tour introduces you to San Francisco's best-known neighborhoods—Union Square to scenic Fisherman's Wharf, historic North Beach, and vibrant Chinatown. Once you arrive at Fisherman's Wharf, you can do the rest on foot, but public transportation options are listed, just in case. START: **BART/Muni at Powell or Montgomery. Bus no. 2, 3, 4, 38 to Powell Street or bus no. 30 or 45 to Geary Street. Cable car on Powell lines.**

❶ **Union Square.** Start your tour at the shopping and commercial hub of San Francisco. The square itself, named for a series of violent pro-union mass demonstrations staged here on the eve of the Civil War, is an oft-used art and music exhibition space. Restored for $25 million in 2002, all that remains from the old square is the 90-foot (27m) Victory Tower, dedicated by Theodore Roosevelt after the Spanish-American War. ⏱ *30 min; best before 9am. Union Sq. is btw. Post, Geary, Stockton & Powell sts. BART: Powell or Montgomery. Bus: 2, 3, 4, 38 to Powell St. or 30, 45 to Geary St. Cable car: Powell lines.*

❷ ★★ **kids** **Ride the Powell-Hyde cable car.** Head to the cable-car turnaround at Powell and Market streets and await the Powell-Hyde line. The first of these engine-less cars made its maiden voyage in 1873. The cable car will take you over Russian Hill. Pay attention as you crest Hyde Street at Greenwich Street: You'll catch your first breathtaking glimpse of the San Francisco Bay and Alcatraz Island. For details on how these cars work, see p 167. ⏱ *30 min; best before 9:30am. Powell & Market sts. $5 per ride.*

❸ ★ **Lombard Street.** "The crookedest street in the world" is in fact not even the crookedest street in San Francisco (Vermont St. btw. 20th and 22nd sts. in Potrero Hill is more crooked!). The zigzags were added in the 1920s, as the street's 27-degree pitch was too steep for cars. Cars are only permitted to descend, but pedestrians can take the stairs up or down on either side. ⏱ *30 min.; best weekday mornings. Lombard St. (btw. Hyde & Leavenworth sts.). Cable car: Powell-Hyde line.*

❹ ★★ **Fisherman's Wharf.** San Francisco's most-visited destination is filled with history and a multitude of activities. Although the wharf has plenty of tacky souvenir shops and overpriced restaurants, it offers

Riding a cable car is one of the best ways to see San Francisco up close.

some beautiful vistas that make a visit well worth it. The following minitour points you to the wharf's most scenic aspects and minimizes time in the crowds. ⏲ *90 min. Hyde & Beach sts. www.fishermanswharf.*

org. Bus: 10, 30, 47 to Van Ness Ave. & N. Point St. or 19 to Polk & Beach sts. Cable car: Powell-Hyde line to Fisherman's Wharf or Powell-Mason line to Taylor & Bay sts. Streetcar: F to Jones & Beach sts.

Fisherman's Wharf

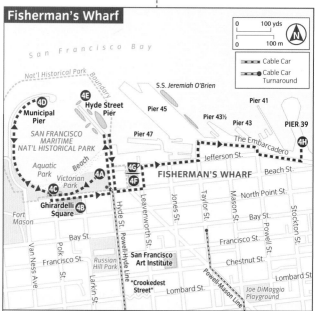

4A Victorian Park is where you'll alight from the cable car. You'll see arts and crafts for sale as you walk toward **4B Ghirardelli Square,** built in 1893 as Domingo Ghirardelli's chocolate factory. When the factory moved in the 1960s, the building became a National Historic Landmark and now houses a mall. **4C** The **Maritime Museum** (p 23) is a three-story Art Deco structure shaped like an ocean liner and filled with seafaring memorabilia. A walk along the **4D Municipal Pier** affords views of the Golden Gate Bridge. The **4E Hyde Street Pier** (p 22) holds

refurbished antique ships, including a 19th-century square-rigger. Walk to the end of the pier to take in the view of the Golden Gate Bridge. **4F** The **Cannery,** once a fruit-canning facility, now houses shops, restaurants, and the National Maritime Visitors Center. **4G Order a crepe** from the cart in the Cannery courtyard. Now fortified, you can brave the crowds at **4H PIER 39.** Look for the infamous sea lions that have lived by the pier since 1989. ⏲ *2–3 hr.; go in the morning to beat the crowds; bring a jacket—it can be chilly year-round.*

5 ★ **Coit Tower.** The 210-foot (64m) landmark atop Telegraph Hill was erected in 1933 with $125,000 bequeathed by local character Lillie Hitchcock Coit, who wished to add beauty to the city. Inside the tower's base are murals by several artists, many of whom studied under Diego Rivera. Commissioned as part of the New Deal's Works Project Administration, the murals have a pro-worker motif that caused a stir in their day. Pay the fee to climb the tower: A 360-degree city view awaits you. While on Telegraph Hill, look out for the flock of wild green parrots, descendants of escaped pets. ⏱ *45 min.* ☎ *415/362-0808. Admission to the top $5 adults, $3.50 seniors, $1.50 kids 6–12. Daily 10am–6pm. Bus: 39.*

6 ★★ **North Beach.** The immigrants from Genoa and Sicily who founded the Bay Area's fishing industry settled into North Beach in the 1870s—establishing a plethora of Italian restaurants, cafes, and bakeries. In the 1950s, the area's cafes and bars became a haven for writers and artists from the **Beat Generation** (p 49). Today the neighborhood is a combination of Mediterranean warmth and Bohemian spirit. For more on this area, see p 46. ⏱ *1–2 hr.; best Mon–Sat from 11am–4pm. Sun and early mornings shops are closed. Bus: 39 to Washington Sq.*

7 **Mario's Bohemian Cigar Store and Cafe.** Pick up sandwiches and enjoy them in Washington Square Park (p 47) across the street. *566 Columbus Ave. (at Union St.).* ☎ *415/362-0536. $.*

PIER 39's sea lions bathe, bark, and splash about—it's one of the best shows in town, and it's free.

8 **Chinatown.** The most densely populated neighborhood in San Francisco, Chinatown is also one of the most fascinating. Take a walk down Grant Street to find shops filled with creative, eclectic knick-knacks. Chinatown locals shop on Stockton Street, which is teeming with grocery stores, herb shops, and vendors of ceremonial items. *(See p 42 for a complete tour of this colorful neighborhood.)* ⏱ *1–2 hr.*

The Best **in Two Days**

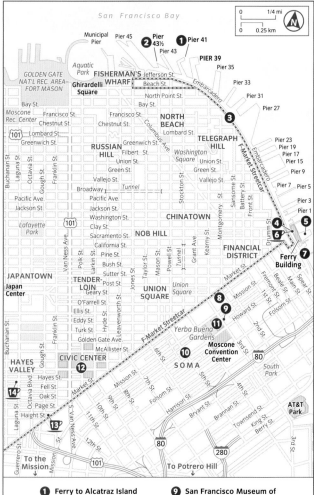

1. Ferry to Alcatraz Island
2. Red & White Fleet Bay Cruise
3. F-Market Streetcar
4. Ferry Building
5. Ferry Plaza Farmers Market
6. Gott's Roadside
7. Embarcadero Promenade
8. Garden Court
9. San Francisco Museum of Modern Art (SFMOMA)
10. SoMa
11. Yerba Buena Center for the Arts
12. Civic Center
13. Zuni Café
14. Suppenküche

If you have two days, take the one-day tour outlined above on the first day. For your second day, you should start by going to prison. For many, a visit to Alcatraz is a major highlight. However, pre-reserved tickets are required. If you're unable to get tickets ahead of time, I've listed an alternative bay cruise. Following Alcatraz (or the cruise), you'll get a taste for the city's epicurean underpinnings, as well as its rich artistic and cultural life, in SoMa and the Civic Center. You'll want the whole day for this tour. START: **Pier 41, Fisherman's Wharf. Cable car Powell-Mason. Bus no. 30. Streetcar F.**

❶ ★★★ Alcatraz Island. This tiny island, less than 1½ miles (2.4km) offshore, beckons onlookers taking in the vista of the SF Bay. It's hard to believe this scenic rock once housed the country's most hardened criminals, including Al Capone, "Machine Gun" Kelly, and Robert Stroud (the Birdman). Spanish for "pelican," Alcatraz was so named in 1775 for the birds that nested on its rocky shores. From the 1850s to 1933, the U.S. military used Alcatraz as a fort, and in 1934 the government converted it into a maximum-security prison. Given its sheer cliffs and surrounded by frigid waters with treacherous currents, Alcatraz was considered inescapable. However, the prison's upkeep cost a fortune, as all supplies had to come by boat. In 1962 three prisoners did escape; the prison was shut down the next year. The island remained unoccupied until 1969, when Native Americans seized it to publicize American Indian rights' issues. They were expelled in 1971. Today, the National Park Service manages Alcatraz. The boat trip to Alcatraz takes you over chilly waters away from the vibrant city; you arrive and walk uphill to the barren former prison. During the audio tour, former guards and inmates recount riveting tales of prison life and spectacular escape attempts. Two night tours (highly recommended) are also available, offering a more intimate and wonderfully spooky experience. ⏱ *2–3 hr., including ferry ride. Take the first ferry of the day, if possible. Wear a jacket & walking shoes; it's an uphill walk from the ferry landing to the prison (motorized carts carry visitors with disabilities). The ferry sells snacks, but there's no food on the island. Pier 41, Fisherman's Wharf.* ☎ *415/981-7625 to reserve tickets. www.alcatrazcruises.com or www.nps.gov/alcatraz. Admission (includes ferry trip and audio tour) $26 adults, $25 seniors 62 & older, $16 children 5–11. Night tours cost $33 adults, $31 seniors 62 & older, $20 children 5–11. Arrive at least 20 min. before departure time. Bus: 30. Cable car: Powell-Mason line. Streetcar: F.*

Take a daytime (or even better, nighttime) tour of Alcatraz (a.k.a. "The Rock"). Book ahead.

② ★ **Red & White Fleet Bay Cruise.** If you are unable to pre-reserve Alcatraz tickets, take a 1-hour bay cruise with audio narration. You'll travel under the Golden Gate Bridge and around Alcatraz while you take in dazzling views. ⏲ *1 hr. Pier 43½.* ☎ *415/673-2900. www.redandwhite.com. Tickets $24 adults, $16 seniors over 62 & kids 5–17, free for kids under 5. Check the website for discount fares. Bus: 30. Cable car: Powell-Mason line. Streetcar: F.*

③ ★ **F-Market Streetcar.** Several streetcars travel along Market Street, but the F line also heads along the scenic waterfront. Its streetcars are imported from around the world, including vintage cars from Europe and turn-of-the-20th-century trolleys from other U.S. cities. ⏲ *15 min.; avoid rush hour (Mon–Fri, before 9:30am & 4:30–6:30pm). Board at Beach & Stockton sts.; exit at the Ferry Terminal loop. Fare $2 adults, 75¢ seniors & kids 5–17.*

④ ★★ **Ferry Building.** This 1898 building reopened in 2003 after a 4-year, multimillion-dollar renovation. Outside, you'll see a 240-foot

Take a trip back in time on a vintage F-Market & Wharves line streetcar.

(72m) clock tower. Inside is a collection of restaurants and gourmet-food stores offering artisan cheese, handcrafted chocolates, and other specialty foods that will make your mouth water. Make your way to the back of the building for a look at the stately Bay Bridge. If you're lucky, you'll visit on a day the **Farmers Market** is being held. ⏲ *1 hr. 1 Ferry Building (at the Embarcadero & Market sts.). www.ferrybuilding marketplace.com. Mon–Fri 10am–6pm; Sat 9am–6pm; Sun 11am–5pm. Bus: 2, 14, 21 to Steuart & Market sts. Streetcar: F, any Market St. streetcar to the Ferry Bldg. or Embarcadero.*

⑤ ★★★ **Ferry Plaza Farmers Market.** On Saturday and Tuesday, local farmers and food producers set up booths around the Ferry Building. On Saturday mornings, the market teems with locals making their regular market trek to stock up on organic fruits and vegetables, naturally raised meats, fresh-baked goods, and so on. Saturdays also feature trailer cars out back, from which city restaurants serve gourmet breakfasts. Given the penchant for using local, organic, and naturally raised produce and meats at many San Francisco restaurants—not to mention homes—this market is a hallmark of city life. ⏲ *1 hr. 1 Ferry Building (at Embarcadero & Market sts.). Tues 10am–2pm; Sat 8am–2pm.*

⑥ **Gott's Roadside.** Order an all-natural Niman Ranch burger with sweet potato fries and sit at the outdoor tables. (See p 21 for full review.) *Ferry Building Marketplace.* ☎ *415/318-3423. $.*

⑦ ★★ **Embarcadero Promenade.** The city developed this scenic stretch of waterfront after the

1989 earthquake destroyed the ugly elevated freeway that once obscured the view. The wide sidewalk and bayside scenery make this a favored destination for pedestrians, bikers, and runners. Notice the Embarcadero Ribbon, a 2½-mile (4km) continuous line of glass encased in concrete, as well as the 13-foot-tall (4m) metal pylons and bronze plaques embedded in the sidewalk, which are imprinted with photographs, drawings, poetry, and historical facts about the waterfront. ⏱ *30 min.–1 hr.; avoid weekday afternoons 4–6pm when traffic is heavy. Return to Market St. to catch the F-Market streetcar to the Montgomery St. station, or walk.*

⑧ Garden Court. The extravagant Palace Hotel astounded San Franciscans and bankrupted its owner, who allegedly committed suicide a day before the grand opening in 1875. Three decades later the hotel was ravaged by fire following the 1906 earthquake. The hotel was restored and reopened in 1909, unveiling the magnificent Garden Court with its domed ceiling made from 80,000 panes of glass. After admiring the glass ceiling, step into the Pied Piper bar to admire the $2.5-million Maxfield Parrish painting of the same name. ⏱ *20 min. 2 New Montgomery St. (at Market St.).* ☎ *415/546-5089. www.sfpalace restaurants.com/gardencourt. Mon– Sat 6:30am–11am and 11:30am–2pm; Sun breakfast 6:30–9:30am; Sun brunch 10am–2pm; Sat tea 1–3pm. BART/Muni: Powell, Montgomery.*

⑨ ★★★ San Francisco Museum of Modern Art (SFMOMA). In 1995, SFMOMA moved into its $62-million home, designed by Swiss architect Mario Botta. The permanent collection includes more than 15,000 works by Henri Matisse, Jackson Pollock, Georgia O'Keeffe, and others. The first major museum to recognize photography as an art form, SFMOMA also has numerous excellent examples by Ansel Adams, Man Ray, and others. Not enough of the permanent collection is on display at any one time, but temporary exhibits are usually excellent. The **Caffè Museo,** to the right of the museum entrance, offers very good quality fresh soups, sandwiches, and salads. Be sure to visit the **MuseumStore,** which carries a

The glass ceiling of the Garden Court is a glittering masterpiece.

wonderful array of modern and contemporary art books, innovative design objects and furniture, jewelry and apparel, educational children's books and toys, posters, and stationery: It's one of the best gift shops in town. ⏱ *1½ hr.; weekdays are the best time to visit. 151 3rd St. (btw. Mission & Howard sts.).* ☎ *415/357-4000. www.sfmoma.com. Admission $18 adults, $9 seniors over 62, $9 students with ID, free for kids 12 and under. Half-price Thurs 6–9pm. Free to all 1st Tues of the month. Thurs 11am–8:45pm; Fri–Tues 11am–5:45pm. Closed Wed & major holidays. Bus: 15, 30, 45. BART/Muni: Montgomery St.*

⑩ ★★★ SoMa (South of Market). This former industrial area south of Market Street has become a major center for art and culture. While the SFMOMA and Yerba Buena Center for the Arts, detailed in bullets ⑨ and ⑪ respectively, are the cultural anchors of the neighborhood, you'll find numerous other museums and galleries here. I list my favorites in the minitour on the next page. ⏱ *2–4 hr. Visit any time during daylight hours, although SFMOMA is closed Wed.*

SFMOMA.

⑪ ★★★ kids Yerba Buena Center for the Arts (YBCA). The YBCA transformed an area once filled with dilapidated buildings into San Francisco's artistic center. Take a moment to stroll through the tranquil grounds and contemplate the soothing Martin Luther King, Jr. Memorial Fountain. From May to October, you might enjoy a free concert on the grassy Esplanade. Among the structures here, the galleries building designed by Pritzker Architecture Prize–winning architect Fumihiko Maki contains several exhibition spaces, while the theater building hosts dance, music, and theater performances. Kids will enjoy Yerba Buena's playground, ice-skating rink, bowling alley, and Zeum, a high-tech museum for children. ⏱ *1½ hr.; best time to come is during daylight hours.* ☎ *415/978-2787. www.ybca.org. Ice-skating & bowling center: 750 Folsom St.* ☎ *415/820-3532. www.skatebowl. com. Zeum: 701 Mission St.* ☎ *415/777-2800. www.zeum.com. Admission $10 adults, $8 students & seniors, $8 kids 3–18, free for kids under 3. Wed–Fri 1pm–5pm; Sat–Sun 11am–6pm.*

⑫ ★★ Civic Center. Less than a decade after the 1906 earthquake destroyed City Hall, San Francisco completed an ambitious new administrative and cultural center in grandiose, Beaux Arts style. It contains City Hall, with its 308-foot-tall (92m) dome; the homes of the San Francisco Symphony, Opera, and Ballet; the main public library; the Asian Art Museum; and other notable buildings. For more details on the Civic Center, see the neighborhood tour on p 57. ⏱ *1 hr.; best time to visit are weekdays during daylight hours. Most Civic Center buildings are bordered by Hayes, Franklin & Hyde sts. & Golden Gate Ave.*

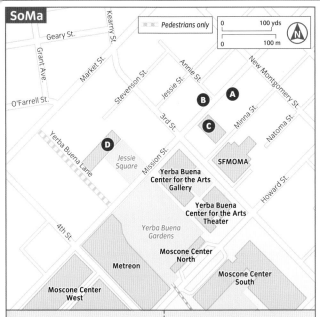

SoMa

Geary St.
Kearny St.
Grant Ave.
Market St.
O'Farrell St.
Stevenson St.
Jessie St.
Annie St.
New Montgomery St.
3rd St.
Minna St.
Natoma St.
Yerba Buena Lane
Mission St.
Howard St.
4th St.
Jessie Square
SFMOMA
Yerba Buena Center for the Arts Gallery
Yerba Buena Center for the Arts Theater
Yerba Buena Gardens
Moscone Center North
Metreon
Moscone Center South
Moscone Center West

Pedestrians only

0   100 yds
0   100 m

N

The **A California Historical Society** has artwork detailing California history, including photographs by Ansel Adams. *678 Mission St.* 415/357-1848. www.californiahistoricalsociety.org. *Admission $3 adults, $1 students & seniors, free for kids under 5. Wed–Sat noon–4:30pm.* Among the cool things at the **B Museum of the African Diaspora** is a three-stories-tall image of a young girl composed of thousands of photographs. *685 Mission St.* 415/358-7200. www. moadsf.org. *Admission $10 adults, $5 students & seniors, free for kids under 13. Wed–Sat 11am–6pm; Sun*

noon–5pm. The **C Contemporary Jewish Museum** opened in spring 2008 in an arresting building designed by Daniel Libeskind. *736 Mission St.* 415/655-7835. *www. thecjm.org. $10 adults, $8 seniors/ students, $5 Thurs after 5pm Fri–Tues 11am–5pm; Thurs 1pm–8pm.* The **D Museum of Craft and Folk Art** features folk art from around the world. *51 Yerba Buena Ln. (at Mission St. btw. 3rd & 4th sts.).* 415/227-4888. *www. mocfa.org. Admission $5 adults, $4 seniors, free under 18. Wed–Sat 11am–6pm.*

Treat yourselves to dinner at **13 Zuni Café** *(1658 Market St.;* 415/552-2522; *$$$; see p 116),* an SF institution and one of the first purveyors of innovative California

cuisine. For a festive—and cheaper—alternative, enjoy hearty German fare and refreshing beers at **14 Suppenküche** *(601 Hayes St.;* 415/252-9289; *$$; see p 113).*

The Best **in Three Days**

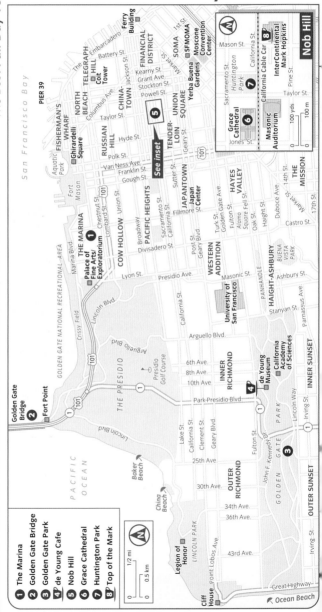

1. The Marina
2. Golden Gate Bridge
3. Golden Gate Park
4. de Young Cafe
5. Nob Hill
6. Grace Cathedral
7. Huntington Park
8. Top of the Mark

Nob Hill

7. California Cable Car
8. InterContinental Mark Hopkins
6. Grace Cathedral
Masonic Auditorium
Huntington Park

California St.
Mason St.
Sacramento St.
Taylor St.
Pine St.
Jones St.

100 yds
100 m

San Francisco Bay

Ferry Building
Embarcadero
The Embarcadero
Battery St.
Kearny St.
Grant Ave.
Stockton St.
Powell St.
Jackson St.
Columbus Ave.
Taylor St.
Hyde St.
Polk St.
Van Ness Ave.
Franklin St.
Gough St.
Market St.
1st St.

TELEGRAPH HILL
Coit Tower
NORTH BEACH
FINANCIAL DISTRICT
SOMA
SFMOMA
Moscone Convention Center
Yerba Buena Gardens
CHINA-TOWN
UNION SQUARE
TENDER-LOIN
RUSSIAN HILL
FISHERMAN'S WHARF
Ghirardelli Square
PIER 39

5. See inset

Aquatic Park
Fort Mason
Marina Blvd.
Chestnut St.
Lombard St.
Broadway
Sacramento St.
California St.
Fillmore St.
Divisadero St.
Post St.
Geary Blvd.
Union St.
Sutter St.
Turk St.
Golden Gate Ave.
Fulton St.
Oak St.
Haight St.
Duboce Ave.
Castro St.
14th St.
17th St.

THE MARINA
1. Palace of Fine Arts/Exploratorium
COW HOLLOW
PACIFIC HEIGHTS
JAPANTOWN
Japan Center
HAYES VALLEY
Alamo Square
WESTERN ADDITION
THE MISSION

Presidio Ave.
Lyon St.
Masonic St.
Ashbury St.
Stanyan St.
Parnassus Ave.
California St.

University of San Francisco
HAIGHT-ASHBURY
BUENA VISTA PARK
PANHANDLE

GOLDEN GATE NATIONAL RECREATIONAL AREA
Crissy Field
Lincoln Blvd.
Arguello Blvd.
THE PRESIDIO
Presidio Golf Course
Arguello Blvd.
Park-Presidio Blvd.
6th Ave.
8th Ave.
10th Ave.

INNER RICHMOND
4. de Young Museum
California Academy of Sciences
INNER SUNSET

GOLDEN GATE PARK
John F. Kennedy Dr.
Lincoln Way
Irving St.

Golden Gate Bridge
2. Fort Point

Baker Beach
China Beach
PACIFIC OCEAN

Lake St.
California St.
Clement St.
Geary Blvd.
Fulton St.
25th Ave.
30th Ave.
34th Ave.
36th Ave.
43rd Ave.

OUTER RICHMOND
OUTER SUNSET

Legion of Honor
LINCOLN PARK
Point Lobos Ave.
Cliff House
Ocean Beach
Great Highway
Irving St.

3. Golden Gate Park

0   1/2 mi
0   0.5 km

For those who can stay 3 days in the city, we recommend that you spend the third day visiting one of San Francisco's most celebrated landmarks, the Golden Gate Bridge. You'll take in breathtaking views from there, as well as from the de Young Tower in Golden Gate Park and again from the Top of the Mark in historic Nob Hill. Dress warmly. START: **Chestnut and Fillmore streets. Bus no. 22, 30.**

❶ ★ **The Marina.** Start your day in this mercifully hill-free San Francisco neighborhood, where parents pushing strollers share the sidewalk with young urbanites buying their lattes before hopping on the bus to work. Window-shop at the many boutiques before stepping into the Grove (p 55). Fortify yourselves with a good breakfast before trekking the bridge. For more on Chestnut Street, see p 55. ⏲ *45 min. Chestnut St., btw. Fillmore & Divisadero sts.*

❷ ★★★ **Golden Gate Bridge.** At any time of day, gleaming in sunshine or draped in wispy white fog, this imposing red structure spanning the narrow opening into the San Francisco Bay—with the wooded Presidio on one end and the golden Marin Headlands on the other—is a sight to behold. Crossing the bridge itself offers breathtaking views of the SF skyline, the bay flecked with picturesque sailboats, and the area's striking, hilly geography. If you don't want to walk all the way across, you can head part of the way and then return. You can also take a bus back. For more details, see p 39. ⏲ *1½–2 hr.; best in the morning or midday, before the wind picks up. Bus: 28. Catch bus westbound on Lombard St. and exit at south end of Golden Gate Bridge.*

❸ ★★★ **Golden Gate Park.** The park itself is the pride of San Francisco, but what really makes it special are the multitude of attractions located within it, such as the de Young Museum and California Academy of Sciences. Visit the de Young first, so you can grab lunch at the cafe (see next stop). Then check out the California Academy of Sciences in its new, very green home. After that, stroll through the serenely beautiful Japanese Tea Garden and the fascinating Conservatory of Flowers. For a complete description, see the Golden Gate Park tour on p 88. Don't miss the free trip up the de Young's observation tower for panoramic city, park, and Marin Headlands views. ⏲ *2–3 hr. Bus: 28. Catch bus southbound; exit on Presidio Park and Fulton St. and walk east 4 blocks to de Young entrance.*

Whether you drive, bike, or walk, you'll never forget the first time you cross the Golden Gate.

4 de Young Cafe. Grab a sandwich made with fresh local ingredients and enjoy it alfresco next to the resplendent sculpture garden. *50 Hagiwara Tea Garden Dr.* ☎ *415/750-2614. $.*

5 **Nob Hill.** This neighborhood is named for its once wealthy residents, or "nabobs" as the elite of San Francisco were known. The "Big Four" railroad barons of the Southern Pacific Railroad—Leland Stanford, Mark Hopkins, Charles Crocker, and Collis Huntington—built their ostentatious mansions here in the late 1870s. They were all destroyed in the fire following the 1906 quake. Today some of the city's most prestigious hotels occupy Nob Hill. 🕐 *20 min. Taylor & Sacramento sts. From GG Park, take bus 33 or 44 to California St., then take bus 1 to Nob Hill. You'll pass the Richmond & Pacific Heights neighborhoods along the way.*

6 ★ **Grace Cathedral.** Following the destruction of the Crocker mansion in 1906, Crocker's family donated the land to the Episcopal Church to build Grace Cathedral. Completed in 1964, it's built from reinforced concrete beaten to achieve a stonelike effect. The doors are stunning replicas of Ghiberti's bronze *Doors of Paradise* in the Baptistry of Florence; inside, the 1840 organ and the stained-glass windows impress. 🕐 *25 min. 1100 California St. (at Taylor St.)* ☎ *415/749-6300. www.gracecathedral.org. Free admission.*

7 **Huntington Park.** The mansion of David Colton, another Southern Pacific Railroad magnate, was here until he sold it to Collis Huntington in 1892. The mansion burned following the 1906 quake, and Huntington donated the lot to the city. The city used the land to create Huntington Park. Framed by the granite walls that were once part of the Colton estate, the park is an oasis in a very urban section of town. 🕐 *15 min. Taylor & California sts. Bus: 1. Cable car: all lines.*

8 **Top of the Mark.** Head to the 19th floor lounge at the Mark Hopkins Intercontinental, located on the site of a former Nob Hill mansion. Make a toast and admire the panoramic city view. *Number 1 Nob Hill. (at Mason & California sts.)* ☎ *415/392-3434. $$$.* ●

Flood Fountain is one of two fountains in Huntington Park.

San Francisco Waterfront

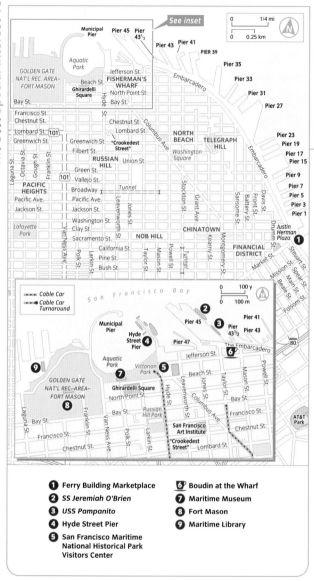

See inset

Municipal Pier
Pier 45 Pier 43½
Pier 43 Pier 41
PIER 39
Pier 35
Pier 33
Pier 31
Pier 27

Aquatic Park

GOLDEN GATE NAT'L REC. AREA– FORT MASON

Jefferson St.
FISHERMAN'S WHARF
Beach St.
Ghirardelli Square
North Point St.
Bay St.

Embarcadero

Bay St.

Francisco St.
Chestnut St.
Lombard St. 101
Greenwich St.

Chestnut St.
Lombard St.
Greenwich St. "Crookedest Street"
Filbert St.

NORTH BEACH
Washington Square
TELEGRAPH HILL

Pier 23
Pier 19
Pier 17
Pier 15

RUSSIAN HILL
Green St.
Union St.

Pier 9

PACIFIC HEIGHTS
Pacific Ave.
Jackson St.

101
Vallejo St.
Broadway
Pacific Ave.
Jackson St.
Washington St.
Clay St.
Sacramento St.

Tunnel

Pier 7
Pier 5
Pier 3
Pier 1

NOB HILL
California St.
Pine St.
Bush St.

CHINATOWN

FINANCIAL DISTRICT

Justin Herman Plaza ❶

Lafayette Park

Market St.

Cable Car
Cable Car Turnaround

San Francisco Bay

0   100 y
0   100 m

❷
Municipal Pier
Hyde Street Pier ❹
Pier 45
Pier 47
❸ Pier 43½ Pier 43
Pier 41

Aquatic Park
Victorian Park ❺
Jefferson St.
The Embarcadero ❻

❾

GOLDEN GATE NAT'L REC. AREA– FORT MASON
❽

Ghirardelli Square
North Point St.
❼

Beach St.

Russian Hill Park

Powell St.

Bay St.
Bay St.
Francisco St.
Chestnut St.

AT&T Park

Francisco St.
Chestnut St.

San Francisco Art Institute
"Crookedest Street" Lombard St.

❶ Ferry Building Marketplace
❷ SS Jeremiah O'Brien
❸ USS Pampanito
❹ Hyde Street Pier
❺ San Francisco Maritime National Historical Park Visitors Center
❻ Boudin at the Wharf
❼ Maritime Museum
❽ Fort Mason
❾ Maritime Library

Previous page: Catch a view from a cable car, the first system of its kind in the world when it debuted in 1873.

Flanked by the Pacific Ocean to the west and the San Francisco Bay to the north and east, San Francisco possesses a rich seafaring past. It became a trading post in the early 1800s and harbored hundreds of ships after the discovery of gold. During 20th-century global conflicts, the city served as an embarkation point for Pacific-bound servicemen. Take 4 to 5 hours to enjoy this scenic walk through history, and don't forget to bring a sweater. If your schedule allows, take this tour on a Tuesday or Saturday morning, when the Ferry Plaza Farmers Market, a San Francisco favorite, takes place at your first stop—the Ferry Building Marketplace. START: **Ferry Building (at the Embarcadero & Mission St.). Streetcar F to Ferry Terminal. Bus no. 2, 7, 14, 21, 66, 71 to Steuart & Market streets.**

① ★★ **Ferry Building Marketplace.** Stroll through this gourmet market inside the **Ferry Building** (p 12), where tenants sell the best of Northern California's bounty, from award-winning cheeses and pasture-raised beef to exotic mushrooms and artisanal chocolates. Then head outside to watch the ferries depart to Angel Island, Marin County, Oakland, and Alameda. Before the Bay and Golden Gate bridges were constructed, the ferry system included hundreds of boats shuttling both people and goods. If you are lucky enough to be here during the alfresco **Ferry Plaza Farmers Market** (Tues and Thurs 10am–2pm; Sat 8am–2pm, just outside the main doors of the marketplace; for more details, see p 12), you'll want to add an extra hour to mingle with the locals and check out the stands hawking farm-fresh produce, flowers, and ready-made snacks by local restaurants. ⏱ *25 min. 1 Ferry Building (at the Embarcadero & Mission St.). Streetcar: F to Ferry Terminal; bus: 2, 7, 14, 21, 66, 71 to Steuart & Market sts. After you explore the marketplace, hop on the F streetcar westbound toward Fisherman's Wharf. Exit at Jones and Beach sts. and walk 2 blocks to Pier 45.* **Note:** *Be sure to have your camera out— the streetcar ride takes you along the scenic waterfront.*

② ★★ **SS Jeremiah O'Brien.** During World War II, the U.S. ramped up production of warships, revolutionizing building methods by prefabricating several parts at a time in various shipyards. The new technique allowed the U.S. to make ships faster than Germany could

Get to the Ferry Plaza Farmers Market early enough on a Saturday, and you'll shop for the area's best produce alongside local chefs.

sink them. One such "Liberty Ship" was the *O'Brien,* which participated in both the 1944 D-day invasion and the anniversary celebrations 50 years later. You can tour almost the entire ship—don't miss the flying bridge, the cozy captain's quarters, and the impressive engine room with its *massive steam pipes.* ⏱ *30 min. Pier 45.* ☎ *415/544-0100. www.ssjeremiahobrien.org. Admission $10 adults, $5 seniors, $5 kids 6–14, free for military with ID & kids under 6, $25 for family with 2 adults & up to 4 kids 17 and under. Daily 10am–4pm.*

❸ ★ USS Pampanito. On its six Pacific tours in WWII, this submarine sank six Japanese ships and damaged four others, and also helped save 73 British and Australian prisoners of war. The intriguing 20-minute audio tour through the cramped quarters, narrated by former crew members, is well worth the extra $2. ⏱ *45 min. Pier 45* ☎ *415/775-1943. www.maritime.org. Admission $10 adults, $6 seniors, $4 children 6–12, $20 for family with 2 adults & up to 4 kids 17 and under. Audio tour $2. Winter Sun–Thurs 9am–6pm, Fri–Sat 9am–8pm; summer daily 9am–8pm.*

❹ ★★★ Hyde Street Pier. This lovely pier houses eight historic, refurbished ships, three of which you can tour. The majestic *Balclutha,* one of the few remaining square-riggers, took its maiden voyage from Cardiff, Wales, in 1887, and over the course of its working life, carried coal, wheat, lumber, and canned salmon from Alaska. In retirement it appeared in the film *Mutiny on the Bounty.* The captain's quarters, with the picture of his daughter, Inda Francis (born onboard on a trip from India to San Francisco), are particularly compelling. The 1890 steam ferryboat *Eureka* was the last of 50 paddlewheel ferries that regularly plied the bay, making its final trip in 1957. The restored 300-foot-long (90m) sidewheeler is loaded with deck cargo, including a sizable collection of antique cars and trucks. The third boat currently on display is the 1907 oceangoing tugboat *Hercules.* ⏱ *25 min. Jefferson & Hyde sts.* ☎ *415/447-5000. www.nps.gov/safr. Free admission to walk on pier; admission to board all ships $5 adults, free for kids 15 and under. Daily 9:30am–5pm; summer until 5:30pm.*

Tour the ships docked at the Hyde Street Pier.

5 San Francisco Maritime National Historical Park Visitors Center. Take a moment to step inside this intriguing visitors center, housed in a refurbished wing of the Cannery, once the site of a major canning facility that packed up California produce bound for export. The visitor center contains wooden models of the Hyde Street pier boats and hosts delightful art exhibits with nautical themes. ⏱ *15 min.* ☎ *415/561-6662. www. maritime.org. Free admission. Daily 9:30am–5pm; summer until 7pm. Closed major holidays.*

6 ★ Boudin at the Wharf. About 3,000 loaves a day are baked within the glass-walled bakery (you'll smell it before you see it). After devouring a Boudin chowder bowl, spend some time browsing the excellent free historical museum. *160 Jefferson St. (btw. Taylor and Mason sts.).* $ ☎ *415/ 928-1849. www.boudinbakery.com. Daily 10am–7pm.*

7 ★ Maritime Museum. This three-story structure shaped like a bright white Art Deco ship is an impressive remnant of the Depression-era Works Progress Administration (WPA). Maritime park officials say the recent restoration has cleaned up old WPA artwork and unveiled murals once hidden by false walls. In addition, you'll find plenty of exhibits devoted to maritime history as well as a replica of a ship's radio communications room where you can have a seat and play with all the knobs and buttons. ⏱ *30 min. 900 Beach St. (at Polk St.)* ☎ *415/561-7100. www.maritime. org. Free admission. Daily 10am–5pm. Closed major holidays.*

The USS Balclutha *is one of the ships permanently docked at the National Maritime Historical Park.*

8 ★ Fort Mason. Walk east toward the Municipal Pier. At the start of the pier, take the path heading uphill on your left. This collection of piers and buildings belonged to the U.S. military until 1972; during World War II and the Korean War, it served as the point of departure for well over a million American service personnel. ⏱ *30 min. Marina Blvd. (at Buchanan St.).*

9 Maritime Library. If you'd like to soak up more maritime history, come here for books, magazines, oral histories, ships' plans, and some 250,000 photos on the subject. Admission is by appointment, but if you arrive appointment-less on a quiet afternoon, the librarians can usually accommodate you. ⏱ *15–30 min. Building E, 3rd floor, Fort Mason Center.* ☎ *415/561-7040. Free admission. By appointment Mon–Fri and 3rd Sat of the month 1–4:30pm. Closed all federal holidays.*

Romantic San Francisco

1 The Embarcadero
2 Filbert Steps
3 Coit Tower
4 Washington Square
5 XOX Truffles
6 Angel's Flowers
7a Café Jacqueline
7b L'Osteria del Forno

0   200 yds
0   200 m

::::::: Stairway

ith its dazzling vistas and intimate restaurants, San Francisco is made for lovers. This tour takes you from the tranquil waterfront through one of San Francisco's most enchanting hidden neighborhoods into sultry North Beach, with a scenic sunset stop along the way. Best to begin at 3 or 4pm and end with a romantic dinner. START: **The Embarcadero at Pier 17. Streetcar F to Green Street.**

1 ★★ The Embarcadero. Enjoy the lovely views of the Bay Bridge, Treasure Island, and the East Bay. ⏱ *15 min. The Embarcadero at Pier 17. Streetcar: F to Green St.*

2 ★★ Filbert Steps. In this captivating corner of town, the street becomes too steep for cars. As you head uphill, you'll pass lush, flower-bedecked gardens decorating Carpenter Gothic homes (characterized by steeply sloped roofs, pointed arches over windows, and "gingerbread" detailing on the facades) dating from as early as 1870. ⏱ *30 min. Steps start at Filbert & Sansome sts.*

3 ★★ Coit Tower. Catch a glorious sunset over the City by the Bay. If you make it here before 6pm, ascend to the top of the pillar for a dazzling panorama. ⏱ *30 min.* ☎ *415/362-0808. Admission to the top $5. Daily 10am–5pm. See p 9.*

4 ★ Washington Square. Stroll through this welcoming park, one of the oldest in the city, which has the feel of an old-world town square. Saints Peter and Paul Church, a local landmark in front of which Joe DiMaggio and Marilyn Monroe famously posed after their marriage in 1957, serves as a stately backdrop. ⏱ *15 min. Filbert & Stockton sts.*

5 ★ XOX Truffles. After climbing Telegraph Hill, you've earned a stop at this luscious store. Sinful delicacies come in flavors like cognac, and you must try Casimira's Favorite. What is it? I'll let you be surprised. ⏱ *15 min. 754 Columbus*

Ave. ☎ *415/421-4814. www.xox truffles.com. Mon–Sat 9am–6pm; Sun 10:30am–6pm.*

6 ★ Angel's Flowers. Buy your loved one a rose at this friendly local florist. ⏱ *15 min. 1554 Stockton St.* ☎ *415/397-5356. www. angelsflowersbyamy.com. Mon–Sat 10am–7pm.*

For an indulgent culmination to your evening, dine at **7 ★★ Café Jacqueline** *(1454 Grant Ave., btw. Green & Union sts.;* ☎ *415/981-5565; $$$; p 101),* a purveyor of fine soufflés. A moderately priced alternative is **8 ★★ L'Osteria del Forno** *(519 Columbus Ave., btw. Union & Green sts.;* ☎ *415/982-1124; $$; p 108),* a cozy Italian favorite.

Catch panoramic views of the city from the top of Coit Tower.

Downtown Galleries

1 49 Geary
2 251 Post St.
3 John Berggruen
4 Café de la Presse
5 Caldwell Snyder Gallery
6 Hang Gallery

0   100 yds
0   100 m

San Francisco has long been on the cutting edge of the American art scene, and the city's downtown galleries provide a rich look at the depth of SF's artistic offerings, including works by masters of the past century, edgy contemporary pieces, and superb photographic prints. Most galleries carry the bimonthly "San Francisco Bay Area Gallery Guide," which lists current exhibits. **Note:** Most galleries open around 10:30am (noon on weekends) and close around 5:30pm, but on the first Thursday of each month, galleries stay open later and many serve wine and cheese. Best Tuesday through Saturday. START: **Bus no. 16, 17, 49. Streetcar F. BART/Muni at Powell Street.**

1 ★★★ 49 Geary. This nondescript building houses several galleries. Take the elevator to the fifth floor and then walk the stairs down to each level. Your first stop off the elevator should be the **Robert Koch Gallery** (☎ 415/421-0122; closed Sun–Mon), where the photographs are worth a few thousand words—and cost as many dollars. The **Stephen Wirtz Gallery** (☎ 415/433-6897; closed Sun–Mon) features contemporary works and splendid photography exhibits. *49 Geary St. (btw. Grant Ave. & Kearny St.).*

2 ★ 251 Post St. You'll find a handful of galleries in this building, among them the **Meyerovich Contemporary Gallery** (☎ 415/421-7171; closed Sun), which features well-known contemporary artists and counts among its collection works on paper by masters like Chagall, Matisse, Miró, and Picasso. *251 Post St., 4th Floor (btw. Grant & Stockton sts.).*

3 ★★★ John Berggruen. This exclusive, spacious gallery showcases only two or three artists at a time, whose work is usually well worth admiring. It also occasionally exhibits art by some of the biggest names of the 20th century. *228 Grant Ave. (btw. Post & Sutter sts.).* ☎ 415/781-4629. Closed Sun.

4 Café de la Presse. Sip an espresso at this bustling, Parisian-inspired cafe. *352 Grant Ave. (at Bush St.).* ☎ 415/398-2680. $.

5 Caldwell Snyder Gallery. Works from cutting-edge American, European, and Latin American artists are exhibited in a striking, 9,000-square-foot space. *341 Sutter St. (btw. Grant Ave. & Stockton St.).* ☎ 415/392-2299. Closed Sun.

6 ★★★ Hang Gallery. Hang features arresting pieces by yet-to-be-discovered artists for purchase, or rent (!), at reasonable prices. Check out the Hang Annex across the street, too. *556 & 557 Sutter St. (btw. Powell & Mason sts.).* ☎ 415/434-4264. Open daily.

Explore the avant-garde collection at the Hang Gallery.

San Francisco Literati

1 John's Grill
2 29 Russell St.
3 Sterling Glade
4 Macondray Lane
5 Ina Coolbrith Park
6 Caffé Trieste

7 City Lights Bookstore
8 The Beat Museum
9 Former residence of Allen Ginsberg
10 Montgomery Block/ Transamerica Pyramid
11 Vesuvio

Mystery writers, poets, authors of nonfiction, social commentators, and many others with a gift of the pen have long made their home in San Francisco. This tour takes you on a historical journey through the city's literary past. START: **Union Square area. Streetcar F. BART/Muni at Powell Street.**

1 John's Grill. Start your tour at Dashiell Hammet's favored hangout. Although his fictional character Sam Spade ordered chops and a baked potato, don't come for the food, but for the great 1940s vibe and to enjoy a drink at the bar. Be sure to check out the Maltese Falcon room upstairs. Then jump on the Powell-Hyde cable car around the corner. *63 Ellis St. (btw. Stockton & Powell sts.).* 415/986-0069. *Streetcar F. BART/Muni: Powell St.*

When Kerouac wasn't on the road, he lived at 29 Russell Street, off Hyde Street.

2 29 Russell St. Jack Kerouac lived in the attic of this unassuming cottage with Neal Cassady and Cassady's wife for 6 months in 1952. Kerouac revised *On the Road* here, a stream-of-consciousness novel based on his travels across the country with Cassady, and wrote parts of *Visions of Cody.* The house is now a private residence. *10 min. 29 Russell St. (off Hyde St., btw. Green & Union sts). Exit the cable car at Green St.*

3 ★ Sterling Glade. In 1872 poet George Sterling founded San Francisco's Bohemian Club, a club of influential newspapermen, novelists, and poets that included nature writer John Muir and Sterling's good friend Jack London. Sterling's seminal poem "A Wine of Wizardry" appeared in the 1907 issue of *Cosmopolitan,* with a forward by Ambrose Bierce, who compared Sterling to Milton and Keats. Sadly, Sterling committed suicide in 1926 at the age of 57. Two years later, the city dedicated this hilltop green space in his name. Enjoy lovely

Relive the 1940s at John's Grill.

A peek through the trees in Ina Coolbrith Park reminds you you're still in the city.

views of the Golden Gate Bridge from the northwest corner of the park. ⏱ *15 min. Larkin St. (btw. Greenwich & Lombard sts.).*

④ Macondray Lane. Many people believe this steep alley, accessible only to pedestrians, was the model for Barbary Lane, the Russian Hill residence for the characters in Armistead Maupin's *Tales of the City,* which in 1994 was made into a widely acclaimed public television miniseries. ⏱ *15 min. Off Jones St. (btw. Union & Green sts.).*

⑤ Ina Coolbrith Park. Josephine Donna Smith, a niece of Mormon founder Joseph Smith, arrived in San Francisco in 1862 as a 21-year-old divorcée and changed her name to Ina Coolbrith. Already a published poet, she joined a circle of writers that included Mark Twain and Ambrose Bierce and became librarian of the Oakland Public Library in 1873. It was there that she introduced a young, poor Jack London to classic literature and inspired him to write. (He would eventually earn fame with such stories as *Call of the Wild* and *White Fang.*) In 1899 she became the only woman named honorary member of the Bohemian Club (see Sterling Glade entry

above) and according to the plaque at the top of this steep park, Coolbrith was named the first poet laureate in the country by the state legislature in 1919. Your hike up the many steps to reach the plaque will be rewarded with sweeping North Beach views. ⏱ *15 min. Taylor & Vallejo sts.*

⑥ ★ Caffé Trieste. The West Coast's first espresso house, still owned by the same family, was a popular hangout of the beatniks, whose photos fill the walls. Best for a cappuccino or a thick pizza slice. *609 Vallejo St. (btw. Columbus & Grant aves.).* ☎ *415/392-6739.*

⑦ ★ City Lights Bookstore. Founded in 1953 and owned by Lawrence Ferlinghetti, one of the first Beat poets to arrive in San Francisco, City Lights is now a city landmark, a literary mecca, and one of the last of the Beat-era hangouts in operation. An active participant in the Beat movement, Ferlinghetti established his shop as a meeting place where writers and bibliophiles could (and still do) attend poetry readings and other events. This vibrant part of the literary scene and

Caffé Trieste.

The mural on the wall outside Vesuvio's, a favorite Beat hangout.

well-stocked bookshop prides itself on its collection of art, poetry, and social and political paperbacks. ⏱ *30 min. 261 Columbus Ave. (at Broadway).* ☎ *415/362-8193. www.citylights.com. Daily 10am–midnight.*

8 The Beat Museum. This tiny museum houses relics of San Francisco's beatnik generation: Ginsberg's typewriter, Ferlinghetti's paintings, a rare copy of *Howl,* numerous photos, books, and even Kerouac bobbleheads. *540 Broadway (btw Columbus Ave. and Kearny St.) 800/KER-OUAC (537-6822). Free admission. Mon–Fri 8am–5pm; Sat 10am–2pm.*

9 Former residence of Allen Ginsberg. It was here in 1955 where Ginsberg, a central figure in the Beat movement, wrote his controversial poem *Howl,* an uncensored examination of modern life. ⏱ *5 min. 1010 Montgomery St. (at Broadway).*

10 Montgomery Block/Transamerica Pyramid. The landmark Transamerica Pyramid sits on the site of the former Montgomery Block, which in 1853 was, at four stories, the tallest building in the American West. Among the many writers who lived in the block-long building were Mark Twain, Ambrose Bierce, Jack London, and George Sterling. The lobby was the center of SF society, and its unusual construction atop redwood logs allowed it to withstand even the 1906 earthquake. The Montgomery Block building was demolished in 1959. Next to the Transamerica building you'll find a peaceful redwood forest—right in the middle of the city. ⏱ *15 min. Columbus Ave. & Montgomery St.*

11 ★ Vesuvio. This excellent example of pressed-tin architecture was the preferred watering hole for the Beats. Order a "Jack Kerouac," made with rum, tequila, orange/cranberry juice, and lime, or a bohemian coffee, made with brandy, amaretto, and a lemon twist. Opened in 1949, Vesuvio's still maintains its original bohemian atmosphere. *255 Columbus Ave. (at Jack Kerouac St.).* ☎ *415/362-3370.* *See p 121.*

A Day with a View

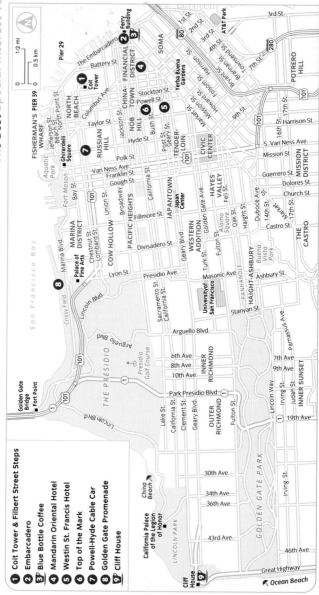

1. Coit Tower & Filbert Street Steps
2. Embarcadero
3. Blue Bottle Coffee
4. Mandarin Oriental Hotel
5. Westin St. Francis Hotel
6. Top of the Mark
7. Powell-Hyde Cable Car
8. Golden Gate Promenade
9. Cliff House

If you're the Type A traveler who wants to capture the entire city on camera, this is your tour. Completed, you will see just about all of San Francisco's 7 square miles, from numerous high vantage points. Plan a full day for this, and bring walking shoes and extra memory for your camera. If you have a car and want the ultimate view, don't miss the top of Twin Peaks. START: **Coit Tower.**

1 ★★ Coit Tower & Filbert Street Steps. Start at the top of Coit Tower (bus no. 39), then head east (toward Berkeley) on the Filbert Street Steps to the Embarcadero. *1 Ferry Building.*

2 ★★ Embarcadero. Walk south on the Embarcadero to the Ferry Building Marketplace.

3 ★★★ Blue Bottle Coffee. Sit at the counter within the Ferry Building Marketplace and fuel up. *1 Ferry Building.* ☎ *510/653-3394.*

4 ★★★ Mandarin Oriental Hotel. Secret View Spot: Walk into the hotel like you own it, and head to the 46th floor. Turn left out of the elevator and . . . "Oh my!" *222 Sansome St. (btw. Pine and California sts.). Bus: All Market St. buses. Streetcar: J, K, L, M to Montgomery.*

5 Westin St. Francis Hotel. The elevators are located in the 32-story Tower Building. Push "32" and prepare for a 30-second, 1,000-feet-per-minute rush to the top—the fastest elevators in the city. The views are absolutely beautiful on a clear day. *335 Powell St. (btw. Geary and Post sts.). Bus: 2, 3, 4, 30, 38, 45, 76. Cable car: Powell-Hyde or Powell-Mason lines.*

6 ★★★ Top of the Mark. Walk up, up, up Powell St. to Nob Hill and the InterContinental Mark Hopkins Hotel. Take the elevator to the Top of the Mark for a drink. *1 Nob Hill (at California and Mason sts.). Bus: 1. Cable car: California St., Powell/ Market line (direct stop).*

Enjoy a view of downtown while perched atop Coit Tower.

7 ★★★ Powell-Hyde Cable Car. Take the Powell-Hyde Cable Car to Fisherman's Wharf. The view of Alcatraz and the bay is phenomenal at Hyde and Lombard Streets.

8 ★ Golden Gate Promenade. Hop off the cable car and head west toward the Golden Gate Bridge via Fort Mason and Marina Green (keep the bay to your right).

9 ★★★ Cliff House. Almost done! Either take Bus 28 at the bridge's Visitor Center to Geary Blvd., then switch to Bus 38 heading west (cheap but tiresome), or taxi to Cliff House (quick but pricey). A picturesque meal by the Pacific awaits. ***Note:*** If it's foggy or dark, views are limited. This is also a great brunch spot. *1090 Point Lobos (at Merrie Way). Bus: 18, 38.*

Hippie Haight

1. Buena Vista Park
2. Janis Joplin's former residence
3. Magnolia Pub & Brewery
4. Haight Street
5. Intersection of Haight and Ashbury streets
6. Former residence of the Grateful Dead
7. Ashbury Tobacco Center
8. Distractions
9. Free Medical Clinic
10. Former residence of Charles Manson
11. Evolutionary Rainbow Mural
12. Amoeba Music

During the 1967 "Summer of Love," thousands of young people flooded Haight-Ashbury (simply the Haight to locals) in search of free love, drugs, and music. As *the* center of hippie culture in the 1960s, this neighborhood captured the world's imagination. Nonconformity is the rule here: A few years back public ire forced the closing of a Gap store not long after it opened. The Victorian townhouse–lined streets where the Dead, Janis Joplin, Jefferson Airplane, and Timothy Leary lived contain a mix of clean-cut residents, hipster 20-somethings, homeless people, and colorful characters (or lost souls, depending on your point of view) like tie-dye-wearing former Deadheads and aging flower children. This tour is a must for anyone fascinated by San Francisco's role in the psychedelic '60s. Some stops are private homes or working businesses (not museums); they serve to remind you of the Haight's historical past. START: **Buena Vista Park. Bus no. 6, 7, 66, 71.**

① ★ **Buena Vista Park.** Climb the pathway and head uphill to get a beautiful view of the venerable Victorian buildings surrounding the park and the city. In 1867 this forest was set aside as the first of SF's city parks. The retaining wall (added in 1930) contains broken marble from an old city cemetery; look around and you'll see some headstone inscriptions. ⏲ *30 min. Bus: 6, 7, 66, 71.*

② ★ **Janis Joplin's former residence.** You won't hear anyone belting out "Me and My Bobby McGee" in this nondescript multiunit complex where Janis lived during the Summer of Love, but it is worth swinging by for pure nostalgia and to admire the neighboring Victorian homes boasting intricate woodwork details. ⏲ *15 min. 122 Lyon St.*

③ ★ **Magnolia Pub & Brewery.** Relax with a pint of Blue Bell Bitter or Prescription Pale Ale (brewed in the basement). Before it was a brewpub, this historic building had an endlessly colorful array of previous incarnations, but in the 1960s it housed the Drogstore Café (a

You'll still find hippies and hippie icons celebrated on Haight Street.

Make a right and step back into the 1960s.

famous hippie gathering spot—NOT named Drugstore, but Drogstore) and former-dancer turned curiously shaped, dessert-creator Magnolia Thunderpussy and her Ice Cream Parlor (people still talk about her inimitable desserts like Montana Banana). Ah, only in the Haight. *1398 Haight St.* ☎ *415/864-7468. www.magnoliapub.com. $$.*

④ ★ **Haight Street.** This block epitomizes the Haight's free-spirited past. Few chain stores or tacky T-shirt shops blot this block. You'll find shops like **Dreams of Kathmandu** (1352 Haight St.; ☎ 415/255-4968), where a turquoise facade gives way to a lovely array of Tibetan prayer rugs, tapestries, masks, and Buddha statues. Funky rave shop **Ceiba** (1463 Haight St.; ☎ 415/437-9598), which advertises "Fashion, Music, Art," is just a few steps away, and across the street is **Recycled Records** (1377 Haight St.; ☎ 415/626-4075), which holds an impressive collection of old LPs and 45s. Particularly notable is **Pipe Dreams** (1376 Haight St.; ☎ 415/431-3553), aka "The Oldest Smoke

Shop in San Francisco." Hundreds of water pipes share shelf space with T-shirts, lighters, and incense. Another intriguing stop is **Bound Together Bookstore** (1369 Haight St.; ☎ 415/431-8355), a not-for-profit, volunteer-run bookseller otherwise known as an "Anarchist Collective." Titles here include works by Che Guevarra, Henry David Thoreau, and Noam Chomsky, as well as "The Anarchist Yellow Pages." ⏲ *25 min. Haight St. (btw. Central & Masonic aves.); most stores open btw. 11am & 8pm.*

⑤ **Intersection of Haight and Ashbury streets.** The corner of Haight and Ashbury streets is the center of the neighborhood. You've seen the ubiquitous photo of the crisscrossed street signs—here is your chance to take a shot of your own. ⏲ *5 min. Haight at Ashbury.*

⑥ **Former residence of the Grateful Dead.** The Grateful Dead lived here from June 1966 until October 1967, when the police raided the house and arrested everyone inside for marijuana possession. Jerry Garcia was out shopping at the time. Within a few weeks, the band moved to Marin County—but their memory still lives on in the hearts and minds of many Haight hippies and in T-shirts and memorabilia found in local curio shops. Today a private residence, the attractive Victorian shows little trace of its colorful past, with the exception of occasional notes left behind by mourning fans. ⏲ *15 min. 710 Ashbury St.*

⑦ **Ashbury Tobacco Center.** This store, allegedly the inspiration for Jimi Hendrix's song "Red House," sells 1960s paraphernalia, lava lamps, and an assortment of smoking and tobacco accessories. ⏲ *15 min. 1524 Haight St. (at Ashbury St.).* ☎ *415/552-5556. Daily 10am–9:30pm.*

⑧ Distractions. This head shop will truly leave you agape with its collection of paraphernalia including water pipes, incense, glow sticks, stickers, and disco lights. ⏱ *15 min. 1552 Haight St.* ☎ *415/252-8751. Mon–Fri 11am–8pm; Sun 11am–7pm.*

⑨ Haight Ashbury Free Clinic. This clinic was set up in 1967 with a mission and philosophy to provide free (and nonjudgmental) medical care. In the beginning, many patients sought help coming down from LSD overdoses. Today the clinic offers everything from help for homeless youths to drug-detox programs. ⏱ *15 min. 558 Clayton St.* ☎ *415/746-1950.*

⑩ Former residence of Charles Manson. The serial murderer lived in this house throughout 1967. It was here that he recruited confused young people into his cult. ⏱ *15 min. 636 Cole St.*

⑪ Evolutionary Rainbow Mural. Just north of Haight Street is a bright, vivid mural depicting the story of evolution painted in 1967 by artist Yana Zegri. She still returns from Florida to touch it up from time to time. ⏱ *15 min. Haight & Cole sts.*

This lovely Victorian house served as home base for the Grateful Dead in the 1960s.

⑫ Amoeba Music. If you're looking for the latest from Britney, this might not be the store for you (though they *do* have everything), but if you're into interesting music that's not necessarily on every station all the time, check this place out. You can buy, sell, and trade in this cavernous, loud Haight Street hot spot. ⏱ *30 min Haight St. (btw. Shrader and Stanyan sts.).* ☎ *415/831-1200. Mon–Sat 10:30am–10pm; Sun 11am–9pm.*

The clinic still offers progressive, no-cost healthcare to the public, just as it did 40 years ago.

Crossing the Golden Gate Bridge

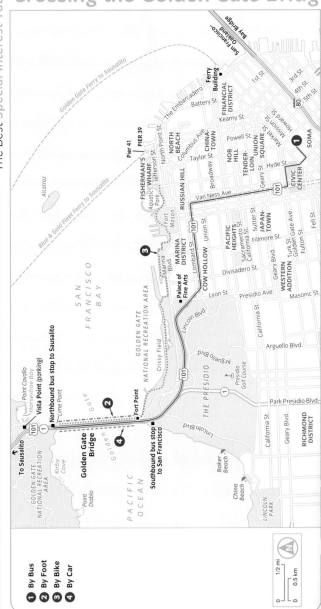

San Francisco–Oakland Bay Bridge

Golden Gate Ferry to Sausalito

Blue & Gold Fleet Ferry to Sausalito

Ferry Building

FINANCIAL DISTRICT

The Embarcadero

Battery St.

Kearny St.

1st St.

3rd St.

4th St.

5th St.

80

Howard St.

Mission St.

Market St.

SOMA

Pier 41

FISHERMAN'S PIER 39 WHARF

Aquatic Park

Fort Mason

North Point St.

Jefferson St.

Columbus Ave.

NORTH BEACH

CHINA-TOWN

Powell St.

Taylor St.

Broadway

NOB HILL

TENDER-LOIN

UNION SQUARE

Geary St.

Hyde St.

CIVIC CENTER

101

Alcatraz

SAN FRANCISCO BAY

Van Ness Ave.

RUSSIAN HILL

101

MARINA DISTRICT

Marina Blvd.

Lombard St.

Union St.

PACIFIC HEIGHTS

Sutter St.

Sacramento St.

California St.

Fillmore St.

JAPAN-TOWN

WESTERN ADDITION

Turk St.

Geary Blvd.

Golden Gate Ave.

Fulton St.

Fell St.

Palace of Fine Arts

COW HOLLOW

Lyon St.

Presidio Ave.

Divisadero St.

Masonic St.

GOLDEN GATE NATIONAL RECREATION AREA

Crissy Field

Lincoln Blvd.

Arguello Blvd.

Arguello Blvd.

THE PRESIDIO

Presidio Golf Course

Park Presidio Blvd.

California St.

Geary Blvd.

RICHMOND DISTRICT

To Sausalito

101

1

Golden Gate Bridge

GOLDEN GATE NATIONAL RECREATION AREA

Point Diablo

Kirby Cove

Point Bonita

Horseshoe Bay

Point Cavallo

Vista Point (parking)

Lime Point

Northbound bus stop to Sausalito

Fort Point

Southbound bus stop to San Francisco

Golden Gate

PACIFIC OCEAN

Baker Beach

China Beach

LINCOLN PARK

Lincoln Blvd.

N

1/2 mi

0.5 km

0

0

1 By Bus
2 By Foot
3 By Bike
4 By Car

The brilliant, International Orange–colored Golden Gate Bridge, often half-veiled by San Francisco's trademark rolling fog, spans tidal currents and ocean waves, connecting the City by the Bay with Marin County to the north. The trek across this awe-inspiring expanse is a fitting part of a visit to the city. This tour should take 2 to 3 hours (depending on how you decide to cross), or all day if you opt to take an excursion to **Sausalito** (p 152). In summer be sure to visit after 10 or 11am (after the morning fog has burned off); all other seasons, visit anytime. And *always* bring a jacket—this bridge makes its own weather. **Note:** If you choose to walk or ride across the bridge, this tour may be combined with "The Golden Gate Promenade" tour, p 84.

1 **By bus.** To reach the Golden Gate Bridge via public transportation, take a northbound (Marin County–bound) Golden Gate transit bus and return on a southbound (SF-bound) bus. Or consider continuing on a northbound bus to **Sausalito** (p 152). ⏱ *35 min. Golden Gate transit.* ☎ *415/923-2000. www.golden gatetransit.org. One-way fare $3.65 adults, $1.80 seniors & kids 6–18, free for kids 5 & under. All northbound (Marin County–bound) buses stop at the bridge. While most lines head north only in afternoon commuter hours, bus 10 runs approx. once per hr. Call for exact schedules. Bus 10 departs from Folsom & 7th sts., stopping at Mission & 1st sts., Market & 7th sts., the Civic Center & along Geary St. **Note:** If you continue on to Sausalito, you can exit the bus on the south side, walk across the bridge & hop on a Sausalito-bound bus (no. 2 or 10) at the bus stop on the north side of the bridge. To return to SF by bus, you must take it from the bus stop on the south side of the bridge (the bus stop on the north side is only for northbound buses). From the Marina or Presidio, take Muni bus 28, 29.*

2 **By foot.** Walking across the bridge isn't exactly peaceful (it is usually windy and cold, and the bridge vibrates with traffic). But it's worth it for the awe-inspiring vistas. ⏱ *45 min. one-way.*

3 **By bike.** The best way to cross the bridge is on two wheels. Rent bikes at **Blazing Saddles** at Pier 41 and ride along the scenic SF waterfront of the Golden Gate Promenade (see detailed tour p 84) and along the well-marked bike path up to the Golden Gate Bridge. Return back over the bridge. If you choose to

Angel Island.

One of the best days you'll have on your trip: A bike ride across the Golden Gate to Sausalito. Catch the ferry back.

continue on the bridge's northern side along U.S. 101, it's an easy ride downhill to **Sausalito** (p 152), where you can catch a ferry back to Pier 41. ⏱ *2–3 hr. one-way;* ⏱ *3–4 hr. including Sausalito & ferry; see p 152. Bike rentals from Blazing Saddles North Beach location 1995 Columbus (at Francisco St.); Fisherman's Wharf locations Pier 41, Pier 43½, 2715 Hyde St., & 465 Jefferson St.* ☎ *415/202-8888. www.blazing saddles.com. $32/day.*

❹ **By car.** The fastest way to grasp the immense structure's sheer size is by car. If you drive, cross over the bridge and pull over at the first exit in Marin County (marked VISTA POINT) for breathtaking views of San Francisco. Consider stopping at the parking lot before driving across and walk across the bridge a short distance. After you cross and visit the bridge, consider continuing north with a side trip to **Sausalito** (p 152). ⏱ *5 min. From downtown, drive north on Van Ness Ave. Turn left at Lombard St., which becomes Hwy. 101 N. $5 bridge toll when driving south.* ●

The Golden Gate Bridge

Defying the popular notion that such a bridge could not be built, chief engineer Joseph Baerman Strauss spent $35 million and 4½ years constructing this mammoth project. On May 27, 1937, the Golden Gate Bridge (www.goldengatebridge.org) opened to pedestrian traffic (it opened the next day to vehicular traffic). A crowd of over 200,000 proud San Franciscans and others crossed the 1¾-mile-long (2.8km) bridge on foot. Named for the 400-foot-deep (120m) Golden Gate Strait that it spans, the bridge's towers rise 746 feet (224m), and the 4,200-foot (1,260m) distance between them remained the longest of any suspension bridge for 27 years. The bridge is also designed to withstand strong winds, able to swing up to 27 feet (8m) in the unlikely event of a 100-mph (160kmph) gale.

3 The Best
Neighborhood Walks

Chinatown

1. **The Dragon's Gate**
2. **Grant Avenue**
3. **St. Mary's Square**
4. **Old St. Mary's Cathedral**
5. **Waverly Place**
6. **Tin How Temple**
7. **Golden Gate Fortune Cookies Co.**
8. **Stockton Street**
9. **Chinese Historical Society**
10. **Bank of Canton**
11. **Portsmouth Square**
12. **R&G Lounge**

Previous page: Chinatown street lanterns.

Teeming with vibrant colors, exotic grocers, and surprising alleyways, Chinatown is endlessly fascinating. Its first residents arrived in the 1800s to work as servants; many more came during the gold rush—fleeing war and famine at home. By 1851, 25,000 Chinese were working in California, most of them living in SF's Chinatown. But life was tough. First employed in the gold mines and later on the railroads, Chinese laborers were essentially indentured servants who faced constant prejudice. The 1906 earthquake and fire destroyed much of Chinatown, and Chinese refugees swamped relief camps outside the city center. An effort by city officials to permanently relocate them failed, and Chinatown continued to grow and thrive, in part because Chinese people were not allowed to buy homes elsewhere until 1950. Today it remains a complete community where residents shop, socialize, attend school, exercise, worship, and play. START: **Bush and Grant streets. Bus no. 2, 3, 4, 15, 30, 45 to BART/Muni at Montgomery Street.**

❶ The Dragon's Gate. Chinatown's best-known entryway mirrors traditional gateway arches found in many Chinese villages. The stone lions on either side of the arch are meant to protect against evil spirits. The dragons and fishes on the pagoda atop the arch signify prosperity. *Bush & Grant sts. Bus: 2, 3, 4, 15, 30, 45. BART/Muni: Montgomery St.*

❷ Grant Avenue. This bustling street lined with shops whose wares—from Chinese calligraphy pens to jewelry—overflow onto sidewalk tables is the main thoroughfare. Look up at the vibrant colors of the banners strung over the street like an urban canopy. The predominant red is for good luck, gold is for prosperity, and green for longevity. *Grant Ave. (btw. Bush & Jackson sts.).*

❸ St. Mary's Square. Italian-born sculptor Beniamino Bufano created the imposing stainless-steel statue of Sun Yat-Sen, the first president of the Republic of China. Sun Yat-Sen traveled the world to raise money and support for the overthrow of the Qing dynasty in

Silk lanterns hang high above the streets of Chinatown.

mainland China. It is believed that he wrote a new constitution for his country while living in San Francisco in 1911. *East of Grant Ave. (btw. Pine & California sts.).*

④ Old St. Mary's Cathedral. The first cathedral in California was built in 1854 by Chinese laborers using Chinese granite. The interior was destroyed by fire following the 1906 earthquake and rebuilt 3 years later. Today the church has an active congregation and many outreach programs. *660 California St. (at Grant Ave.).* ☎ *415/288-3800. www. oldsaintmarys.org. Mass Mon–Fri 8:30am & 12:05pm; Sat 12:05 & 5pm; Sun 8:30 & 11am.*

⑤ Waverly Place. This alley between Sacramento and Washington streets is also known as the "Street of Painted Balconies," where everything from verandas to fire escapes is rendered in vivid shades of red, yellow, and green. Here you'll also find many fascinating shops, including the **Clarion Music**

Look up or you'll miss the Buddhist Tin How Temple.

Center (816 Sacramento St., at Waverly Place; ☎ 415/391-1317), selling musical instruments from all over the world, and **Bonsai Villa** (825 Clay St., at Waverly Place; ☎ 415/837-1688), filled with (what else?!) miniature trees in tiny pots. Several clinics offer traditional Chinese remedies including acupuncture. *East of Grant Ave. (btw. Sacramento & Washington sts.).*

⑥ Tin How Temple. Climb three flights of stairs to one of the oldest Chinese temples in America. Established in 1852—it moved to this location in 1911—it has an elaborate altar holding a statue of Tin How, or Tien Hou, Queen of the Heavens and Goddess of the Seven Seas. You're likely to see people here meditating or praying. Admission is free, but consider giving a donation or buying incense. No picture taking inside the temple. ⏲ *30 min. 125 Waverly Place (btw. Clay & Washington sts.). Free admission; donation suggested.*

⑦ Golden Gate Fortune Cookies Co. Grab a bag of freshly made fortune cookies in this tiny, low-tech factory. Enjoy them like the locals do: unfolded and fortuneless. Take another moment to enjoy the murals of typical Chinatown life in the alley. *56 Ross Alley (btw. Washington & Jackson sts.).* ☎ *415/781-3956. $.*

⑧ Stockton Street. While Grant Street may appeal to tourists, this is where Chinatown locals do their shopping. In grocery stores, pigs hang from hooks and crates overflow with exotic vegetables and fruits. Live frogs, turtles, eels, and other sea creatures are also available. Also on this street are traditional herb shops selling dried

Dried sea horses are just one of the many remedies used in traditional Chinese medicine.

plants and animal parts, for use in prescriptions written by traditional Chinese healers. Still other stores sell ceremonial "money" and paper goods to be burnt as offerings to ancestors. Even DVD players and washing machines made out of paper are sold for burning purposes, as no one knows for sure what's needed in the afterlife. *Stockton St. (btw. Sacramento St. & Broadway).*

9 Chinese Historical Society of America. Founded in 1963 to record and disseminate information about the history and contributions of America's Chinese immigrants, the society displays documents, photographs, and artifacts such as clothing from the earliest immigrants, traditional herbs, and the original Chinatown telephone book. ⏱ *30 min. 965 Clay St. (btw. Stockton & Powell sts.).* ☎ *415/391-1188. Admission $3 adults, $2 college students & seniors, $1 kids 6–17, free for kids under 6; free for all 1st Thurs of the month. Tues–Fri noon–5pm; Sat 11am–4pm.*

10 Bank of Canton. Dating from 1909, this colorful pagoda-like structure is the oldest Asian-style edifice in Chinatown. Until 1949 it housed the China Telephone Exchange, which was famous for its operators who were fluent in five Chinese dialects and English, and who knew (by heart!) the phone number of virtually every Chinatown resident. *743 Washington St. (btw. Grant Ave. & Kearny St.).*

11 Portsmouth Square. Captain John B. Montgomery of the USS *Portsmouth* raised a flag here in 1846 to declare San Francisco part of the United States. A year later, California's first public school was opened on the plaza, and just a year after that, Sam Brannan announced the discovery of gold in the state. Today the square is an important communal center for Chinatown residents, who practice tai chi, gamble over cards, or bring children to frolic here. *Next to Kearny St., btw. Washington & Clay sts.*

12 R&G Lounge. Is your stomach growling for an authentic Cantonese meal but you're overwhelmed by so many choices on each block? Try this local favorite. *631 Kearny St. (at Commercial St.)* ☎ *415/982-7877. $$. See p 111.*

Russian Hill & North Beach

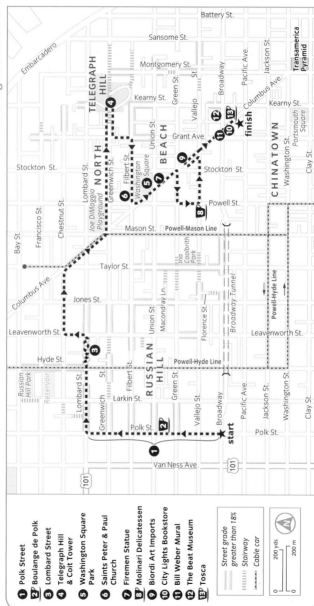

1 Polk Street
2 Boulange de Polk
3 Lombard Street
4 Telegraph Hill & Coit Tower
5 Washington Square Park
6 Saints Peter & Paul Church
7 Firemen Statue
8 Molinari Delicatessen
9 Biordi Art Imports
10 City Lights Bookstore
11 Bill Weber Mural
12 The Beat Museum
13 Tosca

Street grade greater than 18%
Stairway
Cable car

0   200 yds
0   200 m

Stroll through the vibrant urban landscape of North Beach (otherwise known as San Francisco's Italian Quarter) and Russian Hill, and follow the steep curves of Lombard Street, with its lush gardens and breathtaking views. Take your time enjoying these neighborhoods like a local: indulging in simple luxuries like sitting and people-watching at sidewalk cafes. ***Note:*** This tour involves trekking up and down steep hills. START: **Bus no. 19. Cable car Powell-Hyde lines.**

1 Polk Street. This is the main drag on Russian Hill, so named for the Russian seamen who sailed south from Alaska to hunt sea otters for their skins. Those who died on the expeditions are reputedly buried on the top of this hill at Vallejo Street, but no trace of the graves exists today. Polk Street's young, urban, and European feel helps define the hill today, though it's less trendy than Pacific Heights (p 50) or the Marina (p 54). *Polk St. (btw. California & Chestnut sts.). Bus: 19. Cable car: Powell-Hyde lines.*

2 Boulange de Polk. This excellent cafe serves croissants as good as any in Paris, plus a fine café au lait. *2310 Polk St.* ☎ *415/345-1107. $.*

3 Lombard Street. Although locals don't understand why tourists will wait in 3-block-long car lines (on summer weekends) to drive here, the windy curves and stately homes of Lombard Street do have their charm. Take my advice: Walk this street, don't drive it. Vibrant hydrangeas are in bloom each spring, and year-round you'll take in a brilliant view of Coit Tower and the Bay Bridge. *Lombard St. (btw. Hyde & Leavenworth sts.).*

4 ★ Telegraph Hill & Coit Tower. Named for a semaphore that was installed here in 1850 to alert residents of ships' arrivals, this steep-sided hill was once home to various immigrant groups, from Chileans and Peruvians to Irish, and later

to Italians. When the fire of 1906 came to Telegraph Hill, its Italian residents saved many homes by dousing the flames with 500 barrels of red-wine-soaked blankets and burlap bags. The crown of the hill is the quirky cylindrical landmark, **Coit Tower** (p 9). If your feet tire, catch bus no. 39 at Union Street and Columbus Avenue, which heads up to the tower.

5 Washington Square Park. This land was designated a public park in 1847, making it one of the oldest parks in the city. Feeling like an old-world town plaza, it draws residents of all stripes who come to sun themselves on the lawn, read a book on a park bench, or watch their children play in the playground on the northwest corner. Notice, however, that it's not really a square. *Columbus & Filbert sts.*

Lombard Street is known as the Crookedest Street in the World. Drive down slowly, or take the stairs.

The interior of Coit Tower contains murals painted by local artists as part of a WPA project in the 1930s.

6 Saints Peter & Paul Church. This ornate church is the religious center of the neighborhood's Italian community. Since the Italians who came to North Beach in the 1870s were primarily fishermen, it became known as "the Church of the Fishermen," and yearly processions to bless the fishing fleet still start out here. Inside, check out the elaborate altar carved by Italian craftsmen, the decorative columns, and the stained-glass windows. Today masses are given in English, Italian, and Chinese. *660 Filbert St. (btw. Powell & Stockton sts.).* ☎ *415/421-0809. www.sts peterpaul.san-francisco.ca.us. Mass in English Sun 7:30am, 8:45am, 1 & 5pm; Mass in Chinese Sun 10:15am;* *Mass in Italian Sun 11:45am; Mass in Latin 1st Sun of the month.*

7 Firemen Statue. This bronze statue of three firemen and a damsel in distress was created in 1933 at the bequest of local character Lillie Hitchcock Coit, who was saved from a tragic fire as a young girl and became devoted to firemen. Upon her death in 1929, she endowed one-third of her estate to the SF Board of Supervisors "for the purpose of adding beauty to the city." The city used money to build Coit Tower (p 9), which contrary to popular belief is not meant to resemble a fire hose—it is simply a fluted column. *Columbus Ave. (btw. Union & Filbert sts.).*

8 Molinari Delicatessen. This shop has been supplying the city with imported and house-made Italian foods since 1896. ***Beware:*** The mouthwatering Italian sandwiches are enormous! *373 Columbus Ave.* ☎ *415/421-2337. $.*

9 ★ Biordi Art Imports. Biordi has been importing fine pottery from central Italy since 1946. The elegant ceramic plate ware is gorgeous. *412 Columbus Ave. (btw. Green & Vallejo sts.)* ☎ *415/392-8096. See p 76.*

10 ★ City Lights Bookstore. This legendary bookstore is one of

Washington Square Park, flanked by Saints Peter & Paul Church.

Leave lots of time to browse at the City Lights Bookstore.

the last Beat-era hangouts in operation, owned by famed beatnik Lawrence Ferlinghetti. *261 Columbus Ave.* ☎ *415/362-8193. www.citylights.com. Daily 10am–midnight. See p 72.*

⑪ Bill Weber Mural. This attention-grabbing mural, restored in 2004, covers two sides of a residential building. It depicts the history of North Beach and Chinatown with icons like jazz musicians, Italian fishermen, the Imperial Dragon, and Herb Caen, whose *San Francisco Chronicle* columns, always at the epicenter of local politics and society, were a facet of SF life for nearly 6 decades. *Broadway & Columbus sts.*

⑫ The Beat Museum. This tiny museum houses relics of San Francisco's beatnik generation: Ginsberg's typewriter, Ferlinghetti's paintings, a rare copy of *Howl*, numerous photos, books, and even Kerouac bobbleheads. *540 Broadway (btw. Columbus Ave. & Kearny St.) 800/KER-OUAC (537-6822). Free admission. Mon–Fri 8am–5pm; Sat 10am–2pm.*

⑬ ★ Tosca. One of the city's oldest cafes, dating from 1919, has for years attracted politicians and socialites. Order a "house cappuccino," really a hot chocolate with brandy. *242 Columbus Ave.* ☎ *415/986-9651. $.*

The Parrots of Telegraph Hill

If you're walking around San Francisco—especially Telegraph Hill or Russian Hill—and you suddenly hear lots of loud squawking and screeching overhead, look up. You're most likely witnessing a fly-by of the city's famous green flock of wild parrots. These are the scions of a colony that started out as a few wayward house pets—mostly cherry-headed conures, which are indigenous to South America—who found each other and bred. Years later, they've become hundreds strong, traveling in chatty packs through the city, and stopping to rest on tree branches to delight residents who have come to consider them part of the family. Check out the book *The Wild Parrots of Telegraph Hill,* or see the heartwarming movie of the same name.

Pacific Heights & Cow Hollow

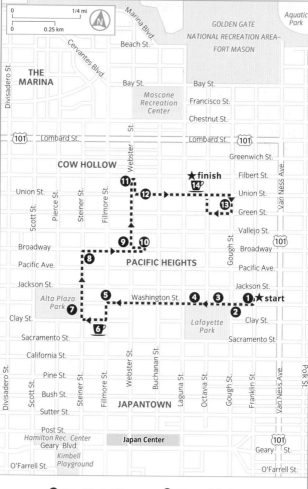

1 Haas-Lilienthal House
2 Gough Street
3 Spreckels Mansion
4 Mary Phelan Mansion
5 Fillmore Street
6 The Coffee Bean and Tea Leaf
7 Alta Plaza Park
8 *Mrs. Doubtfire* house
9 Schools of the Sacred Heart
10 The Hamlin School
11 Vedanta Temple
12 Union Street
13 Octagon House
14 Ottimista Enoteca-Café

Majestic Victorian homes, steep hillsides, charming commercial streets, and sweeping bay vistas permeate this upscale section of San Francisco. Even before residents such as Nancy Pelosi became U.S. Speaker of the House and Danielle Steel penned her first romance novel, Pacific Heights drew the attention of Hollywood. Movies filmed in Pacific Heights include *Basic Instinct*, *The Princess Diaries*, and *The Wedding Planner*. **Note:** A few stops in the residential sections are private homes (not museums)—they serve to showcase famous residences and striking examples of Victorian architecture. START: **Franklin Street (at Washington St.). Bus no. 1, 12, 19, 27, 47, 49, 83. Cable car California line.**

❶ Haas-Lilienthal House. Built in 1886, this flamboyant example of a Queen Anne house features architectural frills like dormer windows, flying cupolas, ornate trim, and a winsome turret. San Francisco Architectural Heritage now maintains it as a museum (the only one of its kind in SF) and offers guided tours. Neighborhood walking tours are also available on Sat and Sun; call for details. ⏱ *1 hr. 2007 Franklin St. (at Washington St.).* ☎ *415/441-3004. www.sfheritage.org. 1-hr. guided tours $8 adults, $5 seniors & kids under 12. Tours start every 20–30 min. Wed & Sat noon–3pm;*

The Haas-Lilienthal House is a prime example of the city's Victorian architecture.

Sun 11am–4pm. Bus: 1, 12, 19, 27, 47, 49. Cable car: California line.

❷ Gough Street. The Victorians on this block, all built in 1889, are particularly stately. Numbers 2004 to 2010 are in the Queen Anne style, while no. 2000 is in the Queen Anne–Eastlake style (marked by elaborate woodwork). *Gough St. (btw. Washington & Clay sts.).*

❸ Spreckels Mansion. Romance novelist Danielle Steel's home is one of the most extravagant in town—built in 1913 for Adolph Spreckels, heir to the sugar empire of German-American industrialist Claus Spreckels, who made his fortune refining California sugar beets and Hawaii sugar cane. Houses were razed or physically moved to make room for the mansion, which occupies an entire city block. The original house featured an indoor pool and a circular Pompeian room with a fountain. Despite the home's grand size, it can't fit all of Ms. Steel's more than 20 cars, which are parked all over the neighborhood. *2080 Washington St. (btw. Octavia & Gough sts.).*

❹ Mary Phelan Mansion. James Phelan, SF mayor from 1894 to 1902 and U.S. senator from 1915 to 1921, commissioned this house for his sister Mary, after hers was destroyed in the 1906 earthquake. *2150 Washington St.*

5 ★ Fillmore Street. One of the lovelier lanes to stroll along in San Francisco, Fillmore Street is lined with fashionable boutiques and several cafes. For more on shopping here, see chapter 4. *Fillmore St., btw. Jackson & Sutter sts.*

6 The Coffee Bean and Tea Leaf. Grab a traditional coffee drink or a specialty tea concoction like a Moroccan Mint Latte and chill out at an outdoor table. *2201 Fillmore St.* ☎ *415/447-9733. $.*

7 ★ Alta Plaza Park. Originally a rock quarry, this park boasts wide views of downtown, grand staircases, a children's playground, and intricate terraced landscaping with stately pine trees and flower gardens. Barbra Streisand drove down the steps in front of Pierce and Clay streets in the 1972 movie *What's Up Doc?*—chips made by this stunt are still visible on the steps (the movie's

Victorian architecture is generally more ornate than the Edwardian homes you'll also find throughout the city.

producers refused to pay for repairs). ***Fun tip:*** If you stand at the top of the steps and start walking down, you'll feel like you're stepping off a cliff. *Btw. Steiner, Scott, Clay & Jackson sts.*

8 *Mrs. Doubtfire* house. Remember the film *Mrs. Doubtfire*? Robin Williams played a divorced father who disguised himself as a nanny to spend more time with his kids at this cream-colored Victorian with conical spires. *2640 Steiner St. (btw. Pacific St. & Broadway Ave.).*

9 Schools of the Sacred Heart. This ornate mansion was built for James Leary Flood, son of millionaire James Flood, one of the original "Bonanza Kings" who struck it rich with the Comstock Lode, an enormous silver strike in Nevada. Completed in 1915, it offered a prime view of the Panama-Pacific Exposition held that year. In 1939, Mrs. Flood donated it to the Society of the Sacred Heart; today it's the main building for separate boys' and girls' elementary schools. *2222 Broadway (btw. Fillmore & Webster sts.).*

10 The Hamlin School. On the next block you'll find another mansion that belonged to James Leary Flood. Flood's sister Cora Jane Flood, who never married, lived here for several years after her brother and his wife moved across the street. Like its neighbor, this mansion is also now a private K-8 school. Director Garry Marshall shot a portion of *The Princess Diaries* here. *2120 Broadway (btw. Webster & Buchanan sts.).*

11 Vedanta Temple. This structure, built from 1905 to 1908, is a temple for the Northern California Vedanta Society, a branch of Hinduism. Its astounding combination of several types of architecture—including Moorish columns, onion domes, and medieval

All faiths are welcome at the Hindu Vedanta Temple.

turrets—reflects the Hindu idea that there are numerous paths (or many religions) to reach the same place. *2963 Webster St. (at Filbert St.).* ☎ *415/922-2323.*

⑫ **Union Street.** This lengthy lane is the commercial heart of Cow Hollow, so named for the 30 dairy farms that existed here in the 1860s. The street draws locals and visitors for leisure shopping at its swank boutiques. For more on shopping here, see chapter 4.

⑬ **Octagon House.** This unusual, eight-sided, cupola-topped house built in 1861 is maintained by the National Society of Colonial Dames of America. The small museum contains Early American furniture and artifacts. Historic documents include signatures of 54 of the 56 signers of the Declaration of Independence. ⏱ *30 min. 2645 Gough St.* ☎ *415/441-7512. Free admission; donation suggested. Open 2nd Sun & 2nd & 4th Thurs of the month noon–3pm. Closed Jan & holidays.*

⑭ **Ottimista Enoteca-Café.** Sip a glass of pinot nero, nosh on pastry-baked olives, and view the Union Street scene from your outdoor table at this Italian-inspired wine bar (see p 127 for more details). *1838 Union St.* ☎ *415/674-8400. $$.*

Queen Anne Architecture

Queen Anne homes dominated Victorian residential architecture from 1880 to 1910. In fact, this style is virtually synonymous with the phrase *Victorian house*. Typical characteristics of a Queen Anne home include projecting bay windows, wraparound porches, towers, turrets, balconies, elaborate banisters and spindles, stained glass, decorative trim, and patterned shingles.

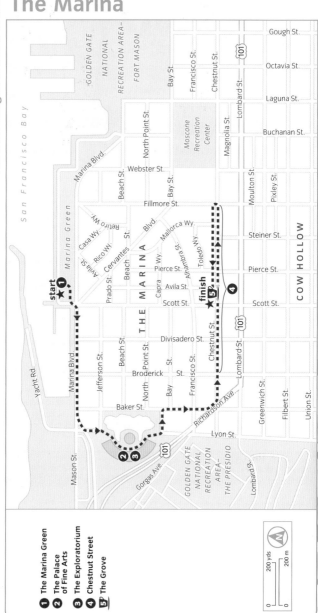

The Marina

1. The Marina Green
2. The Palace of Fine Arts
3. The Exploratorium
4. Chestnut Street
5. The Grove

It is difficult to believe today's swank and wealthy Marina District (nicknamed simply "the Marina") was once home to mud flats. The flats were filled in for the Panama-Pacific Exposition of 1915, held to celebrate the completion of the Panama Canal. This same exposition also left behind the glorious Palace of Fine Arts, a delightful stop on a SF visit. Today the Marina is popular with trendy singles and stroller-pushing parents (grateful for the lack of hills). An address along its patch of green (the Marina Green, your first stop on this tour) is highly coveted for its front-seat views of the bay, the Golden Gate Bridge, Angel Island, and the yacht-filled private marinas that give the neighborhood its name. START: **Marina Boulevard. (btw. Fillmore & Scott sts.). Bus no. 22.**

① ★★ **The Marina Green.** This stretch of lawn is a popular place to stroll, run, or bike. Check out the musical sculpture called the Wave Organ (p 85). On a typically windy afternoon, you'll see people flying colorful and acrobatic kites. *Marina Blvd. (btw. Fillmore & Scott sts.). Bus: 22.*

② ★★ **The Palace of Fine Arts.** Most of the Panama-Pacific Exposition structures were built of temporary materials. Only this one was left intact and rebuilt in the 1960s. It now houses the Exploratorium (see next stop). The classical rotunda with curved colonnades, inspired by classic Greek and Roman ruins, is topped with a dramatic dome and situated around a lovely pond, home to many ducks and geese. *3601 Lyon St. (at Marina Blvd.).*

③ ★★★ **The Exploratorium.** Described by *Scientific American* magazine as the "the best science museum in the world" (I agree!), this hangarlike hall holds over 650 interactive exhibits that enthrall both kids and adults. 🕐 *90 min. Best weekday afternoons (to avoid school tours) and weekend mornings. 3601 Lyon St., in the Palace of Fine Arts.* ☎ *415/397-5673. www.exploratorium.edu. Admission $15 adults; $12 seniors, students & kids 13–17; $10 kids 4–12;* free for kids under 4. Free for all 1st Wed of the month. Tues–Sun 10am–5pm. Closed Mon except MLK Day, President's Day, Memorial Day & Labor Day.

④ **Chestnut Street.** A stroll along the Marina's upscale retail quarter is a fun way to end your tour. *Chestnut St. (btw. Fillmore & Broderick sts.).*

⑤ **The Grove.** Grab an outdoor table and people-watch as you sip a cup of java. *2250 Chestnut St. (at Avila St.).* ☎ *415/474-4843. $.*

The Exploratorium in the Palace of Fine Arts makes science fun for kids (and adults).

The Best Neighborhood Walks

Civic Center & Hayes Valley

1 San Francisco Main Library
2 Asian Art Museum
3 Civic Center Plaza
4 City Hall
5 Veterans Building
6 War Memorial Opera House
7 Louise M. Davies Symphony Hall
8 Hayes Valley
9 Arlequin
10 Christopher Elbow Artisanal Chocolates
11 Hayes Street
12 Alamo Square Historic District
13 Postcard Row

The Civic Center area, the southwestern section of Market Street, contains the notable Civic Center Plaza and several museums and buildings worth a visit for their architectural splendor. After the Civic Center, you'll continue through hip Hayes Valley—where you'll discover the city's highest concentration of Painted Ladies (SF's famous Victorian houses), one cluster of which is reproduced so often on SF postcards it has been nicknamed Postcard Row. *Note:* The Civic Center area has its fair share of homeless residents so come during daylight hours. START: **100 Larkin St. (at Grove St.). BART/Muni at Civic Center.**

1 ★ San Francisco Main Library. San Francisco's 376,000-square-foot (112,800-sq.-m) main library opened in 1996; its facade of Sierra White granite came from the same quarry that provided the stone for other Civic Center buildings, built 8 decades earlier. Step inside to appreciate the library's calm atmosphere, the five-story atrium, and the interesting bridges that connect the floors. The four-story staircase travels up along a panel featuring 200 small glass shades, upon each of which fiber-optic light beams display the name of famed authors. ⏱ *30 min. 100 Larkin St. (at Grove St.).* ☎ *415/557-4400. www.sfpl.org. Mon & Sat 10am–6pm; Tues–Thurs 9am–8pm; Fri noon–6pm; Sun noon–5pm.*

2 ★★★ Asian Art Museum. With one of the Western world's largest collections of Asian art, covering 6,000 years and including world-class sculptures, paintings, and ceramics from regions of south Asia, west Asia, Southeast Asia, the Himalayas, China, Korea, and Japan, there's never enough time to take it all in. Take a moment to admire the space itself; Milanese architect Gae Aulenti, who turned a Paris train station into the Musée d'Orsay, transformed SF's former Main Library into this world-class museum with 37,500 square feet (11,250 sq. m) of exhibition space. ⏱ *1–2 hr.*

200 Larkin St. (at Fulton St.). ☎ *415/581-3500. www.asianart.org. Admission $12 adults, $8 seniors, $7 students & kids 13–17, free for kids under 12. $5 for all after 5pm every Thurs; free for all 1st Sun of every month. Tues–Wed & Fri–Sun 10am–5pm; Thurs 10am–9pm.*

3 Civic Center Plaza. From the middle of the plaza, take a moment to appreciate the neoclassically styled buildings (inspired by the turn-of-the-20th-century "City Beautiful" idea—see "Beaux Arts Architecture," below) that surround you. Today the entire Civic Center is designated a National Historic Landmark District. *Btw. Polk, McAllister & Grove sts. & Van Ness Ave.*

4 ★ City Hall. The impressive 308-foot (92m) dome on this 1915 building is taller than the one on the U.S. Capitol and is one of the largest

The Asian Art Museum has more than 15,000 objects of art.

domes in the world. City Hall, another prime example of Beaux Arts architecture, is adorned by real gold leaf on portions of the dome and much of the exterior. The interior rotunda is made of oak and limestone, and has a monumental marble staircase. Public tours are offered weekdays at 10am, noon, and 2pm. *400 Van Ness Ave. (btw. McAllister & Grove sts.). ☎ 415/554-4933. www. sfgov.org/cityhall. Mon–Fri 8am–5pm.*

⑤ Veterans Building. This 1932 structure was designed by Arthur Brown, the architect of City Hall and the War Memorial Opera House, as a tribute to World War I veterans. Today the theater hosts cultural events and classical-music recitals. *401 Van Ness Ave. (btw. McAllister & Grove sts.). ☎ 415/621-6600. Mon–Fri 8am–5pm.*

⑥ War Memorial Opera House. The home of the San Francisco Opera was built in remembrance of fallen World War I soldiers. It was also the site of the signing of the U.S.-Japan peace treaty in 1951, marking the formal end of World War II. *301 Van Ness Ave. (at Grove St.). ☎ 415/621-6600.*

⑦ Louise M. Davies Symphony Hall. This curved, modern structure, named for one of its benefactors, was completed in 1980. A $10-million renovation in 1992 improved the acoustics, and today the symphony is an integral part of SF cultural life. *201 Van Ness Ave. (at Grove St.). ☎ 415/552-8000.*

⑧ Hayes Valley. This vibrant, hip neighborhood is one of the most dynamic in the city. Once known for its homeless population, it has

transformed itself since the 1989 earthquake destroyed two noisy freeway on-ramps that kept pedestrians away. In place of the old ramps you'll find an open space and grassy park. In turn, the nearby streets have filled with hip furniture shops, clothing stores highlighting local designers, galleries, restaurants, and cafes.

Opened by longtime Hayes Valley restaurateurs, **⑨ Arlequin Cafe** *(384B Hayes St. btw. Gough and Franklin sts.; ☎ 415/626-1211; $)*, boasts "food to go," but in fact you should enjoy your gourmet sandwich on the premises—specifically, in the peaceful garden out back. If you're not hungry, hopefully you're still thirsty, because at **⑩ Christopher Elbow Artisanal Chocolates** *(401 Hayes St. at Gough St.; ☎ 415/355-1105; $)*, you'll find the best hot chocolate in the sleekest surroundings anywhere.

⑪ ★ Hayes Street. The area's main shopping drag features eclectic and unique shops carrying everything from funky backpacks to ultramodern furniture and fine Italian shoes (see chapter 4 for details on stores in this area). Or stop by some of the galleries, including **Octavia's Haze Gallery** *(498 Hayes St.; ☎ 415/255-6818)*, with handblown art glass from Italy, Seattle, and the Bay Area; and **Polanco** *(393 Hayes St.; ☎ 415/252-5753)*, which highlights Mexican art. *Hayes St. (btw. Franklin & Buchanan sts.).*

The gold adorning City Hall's dome is a fine example of the Beaux Arts—detail displayed in the Civic Center buildings.

A view from Alamo Square of the city and its "Painted Ladies."

⓬ Alamo Square Historic District. San Francisco's most remarkable Victorian homes perished in the 1906 post-earthquake fires, which swept through downtown. To prevent the fires from spreading westward, firemen dynamited the mansions along Van Ness Avenue. Although the fire did cross Van Ness in some places, many homes west of the thoroughfare were spared. A small area around Alamo Square has such a great concentration of these homes that it has been designated a historic area. *Historic District (btw. Divisadero, Webster & Fell sts. & Golden Gate Ave.).*

⓭ ★ Postcard Row. SF's ornate Victorians are fondly referred to as "Painted Ladies." Of these, the most famous lie on the south end of Alamo Square, with a backdrop of the San Francisco skyline providing a striking contrast. Take a look at (and your own shot of) the oft-photographed view from atop Alamo Park. *Hayes St. (btw. Steiner & Scott sts.).*

Beaux Arts Architecture

From about 1885 to 1920, Beaux Arts architecture flourished in America's wealthier cities. Architects trained at Paris's Ecole des Beaux-Arts designed grandiose structures combining classic Greek and Roman forms with French and Italian Renaissance styles. The penchant for massive stone buildings festooned with columns, garlands, and similar ornamental flourishes was best suited to government and other public buildings. The architects were part of the "City Beautiful" movement. The creation of more inviting city centers was expected to inspire civic pride and put American cities on par with their European counterparts. Following the devastating 1906 earthquake, the rebuilding of SF's entire city center in the Beaux Arts style marked a deliberate effort to lift the city's spirits and proclaim its resilience.

Japantown

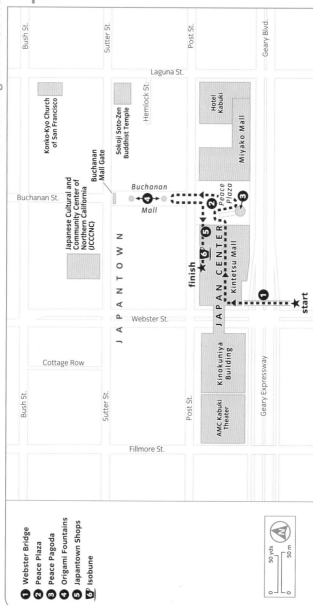

1 Webster Bridge
2 Peace Plaza
3 Peace Pagoda
4 Origami Fountains
5 Japantown Shops
6 Isobune

Konko-Kyo Church
of San Francisco

Sokoji Soto-Zen
Buddhist Temple

Japanese Cultural and
Community Center of
Northern California
(JCCCNC)

Buchanan
Mall Gate

Hotel
Kabuki

Miyako Mall

Buchanan

Mall

*Peace
Plaza*

J A P A N T O W N

finish

J A P A N   C E N T E R

Kintetsu Mall

start

Cottage Row

Kinokuniya
Building

AMC Kabuki
Theater

Geary Expressway

Bush St.

Sutter St.

Post St.

Geary Blvd.

Laguna St.

Hemlock St.

Buchanan St.

Webster St.

Sutter St.

Post St.

Fillmore St.

Bush St.

50 yds

50 m

0

0

Japantown once housed more than 100,000 Japanese-American residents. When they were forcibly interned in camps during World War II, other settlers moved in, among them African Americans recruited to work in the shipyards. Today less than 15,000 Japanese Americans remain in San Francisco. Although few of them live here, Japantown remains their cultural center. START: **Webster Street and Geary Boulevard. Bus no. 2, 3, 4, 22, 38.**

1 Webster Bridge. Built in the style of Japanese pedestrian bridges, this arched walkway spans several lanes of traffic over the city's widest thoroughfare, Geary Boulevard. Its height provides a good overview of Japantown, which today covers just 6 square blocks, down from over 40 blocks in the 1930s. *Webster St. & Geary Blvd. Bus: 2, 3, 4, 22, 38.*

2 Peace Plaza. The Japan Center, a collection of Japanese shops and restaurants, was opened in 1968. It seemed very modern at the time, but looks less impressive today. The serenely empty space between the two buildings is the Peace Plaza. Take a moment to examine the unusually austere fountain, where water cascades horizontally across a hard-edged cement surface. *Btw. Fillmore, Laguna & Posts sts. & Geary Blvd.*

3 Peace Pagoda. This concrete structure was designed by Japanese architect Yoshiro Taniguchi as a gesture of goodwill from the people of Japan. *Peace Plaza.*

4 Origami Fountains. Noted Japanese-American sculptor Ruth Asawa designed these bronze sculptures in the style of the traditional Japanese art of paper folding. The airy, delicate sculptures, reminiscent of paper fans,

contrast with the heavy stone benches that encircle them. The benches are a good place to relax and observe the water rippling through the "folds" in the sculptures to the ground below. *Nihonmachi Pedestrian Mall, Buchanan St. (btw. Post & Bush sts.).*

5 Japantown Shops. Explore the array of Japanese shops selling bonsai, kimonos, handmade Japanese paper, ceramics, and even pop culture effects. For excellent bargains on Japanese tableware, head to the basement of **Soko Hardware** (p 77). *Many shops in the Japan Center or adjacent to it on Post St.*

6 Isobune. Pluck California rolls or maguro tuna sushi off little boats that cruise by on an aquatic conveyor belt in front of you. Come at lunch or dinnertime, when the sushi is fresh; in off hours it sails around the loop one too many times. *1737 Post St. (in the Japan Center).* ☎ *415/563-1030. $$.*

The five-tiered Peace pagoda was a gift from the people of Japan.

The Mission & the Castro

1. Mission Cultural Center
2. 24th Street
3. Balmy Alley
4. Garfield Square
5. Precita Eyes Mural Arts Center
6a. La Palma Mexicatessen
6b. Dominguez Mexican Bakery
7. St. Peter's Church
8. Galeria de la Raza
9. Discolandia
10. Mission Dolores Park
11. Mission Dolores
12. The Basilica Parish of Mission Dolores
13. Ike's Place
14. Gayest Corner in the World
15. Harvey Milk Plaza

As one of the last somewhat-affordable-for-San-Francisco places to live in town, the dynamic Mission draws many Latin-American immigrants and young, alternative types who call this neighborhood home. In addition to charming Latino markets and colorful Victorian-era homes, there are hundreds of vivid murals brightening up the sides of buildings and storefronts with religious, historical, political, or playful motifs. Next door is the Castro, a vibrant, politically active (and largely gay) neighborhood with a strong sense of community. START: **Bart at 24th Street.**

1 Mission Cultural Center. This nonprofit organization promotes Latino cultural arts and offers dance, painting, and folk-art classes. Note the mural above the entrance, which depicts Aztec gods, dancing skeletons, and seemingly destitute farmers in a desert. ⏱ *30 min. 2868 Mission St. (at 25th St.)* ☎ *415/643-5001. www.missionculturalcenter. org. Gallery hours vary. Call for details. BART: 24th St.*

2 24th Street. This leafy street lined with Mexican bakeries and other distinctly Latino stores is the neighborhood's commercial heart. Among the many colorful murals you'll see here is one on the corner of South Van Ness Avenue entitled *Carnaval*, depicting the city's Latin residents celebrating the Carnaval

SF festival that occurs yearly the last weekend in May. *24th St. (from Mission to York sts.).*

3 ★★ **Balmy Alley.** This year-round outdoor gallery is a high point of a visit to the Mission. The murals first appeared some 3 decades ago, but in 1984 a group called PLACA began painting them everywhere—fences, garage doors, and the backs of the homes that flank this tiny alley. Some murals are political, some philosophical, some silly—but all are great fun to contemplate. *Balmy Alley (btw. 24th & 25th sts.).*

4 Garfield Square. Visitors are drawn here for the many murals, such as the Primal Sea on 26th Street or the 1973 Diego Rivera mural with Mayan and Aztec

The Precita Eyes Mural Arts Center gives tours of the murals in Balmy Alley.

themes, on Harrison Street. Be sure also to check out the brightly decorated homes, including those across the street from the Rivera mural. *Btw. 25th, 26th & Harrison sts. & Treat Ave.*

5 Precita Eyes Mural Arts Center. This group is responsible for many of the local murals, including the *Primal Sea.* Precita Eyes sponsors mural contests and teaches art classes. Inquire inside this cheerful center about new murals in the area. *2981 24th St. (btw. Harrison & Alabama sts.).* ☎ *415/285-2287. www.precitaeyes.org.*

Pick up a Mexican snack or meal (tortillas are handmade on-site!) at **6A La Palma Mexicatessen** *(2884 24th St. at Bryant St.;* ☎ *415/ 647-1500; $),* a local, take-out-only favorite, or try pan dulce (sweet bread) from **6B Dominguez Mexican Bakery** *(2951 24th St. at Alabama St.;* ☎ *415/821-1717; $).*

7 St. Peter's Church. The impassioned mural adorning this church depicts Aztec gods, Spanish conquistadors, and ravaged native peoples. *24th St. (at Florida St.).*

8 Galeria de la Raza. Dedicated to fostering public appreciation of Chicano/Latino art and culture, this small gallery holds captivating exhibitions and performances. Its gift shop, filled with Latin-American imports, is also worth visiting. *2857 24th St. (at Bryant St.).* ☎ *415/826-8009. www. galeriadelaraza.org.*

9 Discolandia. Step inside this popular Latin-American CD shop and don't be surprised if you find yourself doing a little shake to a salsa beat. *2964 24th St. (at Alabama St.).* ☎ *415/826-9446.*

10 Mission Dolores Park. Take a stroll and admire the sublime city views. Established in 1905, the park served as a refugee camp for more than 1,600 families made homeless by the 1906 earthquake and subsequent fire. Today, students sun themselves while pretending to study, and locals play fetch with their dogs. *Dolores St. (btw. 18th & 20th sts.).*

11 ★★ Mission Dolores. Welcome to SF's oldest building, survivor of many earthquakes! Officially known as Mission of San Francisco de Assisi, this was the 6th of 21 California missions built on the

The handmade tortillas at La Palma Mexicatessen are a local favorite.

San Francisco's oldest building, Mission Dolores.

California coast. The mission itself was established in 1776 by Father Junipero Serra, but the structure was built 15 years later, using a combination of indigenous and Spanish building techniques. Note the vegetable-dye-painted ceiling with its Native-American tribal pattern, and the graveyard, dating from 1830. While some of the wooden tombstones are no longer legible, reading the names of early pioneers is stirring. (***Fun fact:*** Hitchcock filmed scenes for *Vertigo* here.) ⏱ *40 min. 3321 16th St. (Dolores St.)* ☎ *415/621-8203. www.mission dolores.org. Free admission; suggested donation $3 adults, $2 children, seniors & students. May–Oct daily 9am–4:30pm; Nov–Apr daily 9am–4pm.*

⑫ The Basilica Parish of Mission Dolores. This church, completed in 1918, replaced a former church destroyed in the 1906 earthquake. The coat of arms with the papal insignia on the altar symbolizes the church's special status as a basilica, so designated in 1952. The stained-glass windows depict the city's patron saint, St. Francis of Assisi, and California's 21 missions. *3321 16th St. (at Dolores St.)* ☎ *415/621-8203. Daily 8am–noon & 1–4pm.*

Stand in line for a drippy, warm, and deee-licious sandwich that you have to taste to believe at **⑬ Ike's Place** *(2247 Market St. at Sanchez St.;* ☎ *415/553-6888; $).* The line often snakes around the block of this little shop started up by native San Franciscan Ike Shehadeh, so call ahead. Call at 10am for a noon pickup. See www.hiddenmenu.com for off-menu options.

⑭ Gayest Corner in the World. This proud moniker for the intersection of 18th and Castro streets highlights the Castro's difficult history and proud resilience. No plaque proclaims this to be the

Rent the documentary The Life and Times of Harvey Milk *before your visit to the city.*

The intersection of 18th Street and Castro.

gayest intersection on earth, but most Castro residents will affirm that it is and may point to the profusion of rainbow flags as proof. During the 1970s, the gay community moved into this working-class neighborhood, fixing up homes and establishing openly gay businesses. With the election to the community board of openly gay resident Harvey Milk, acceptance by the wider community seemed assured. Milk's assassination and the AIDS epidemic a decade later fueled the community's political activism. *Corner of 18th & Castro sts.*

⓯ Harvey Milk Plaza. Named after the first openly gay politician elected to public office in the U.S., this plaza is the starting point for the city's many gay marches and rallies. Milk, who was on the city board of supervisors, and liberal mayor George Moscone, were both assassinated at City Hall in 1978 by conservative ex-supervisor Dan White. White's so-called Twinkie defense resulted in a mere 7-year prison sentence. Shocked by the verdict, both the gay and heterosexual communities stormed **City Hall** (p 57) during the White Night Riot on May 21, 1979. In 1997, on the 20th anniversary of Milk's election victory, then-mayor Willie Brown raised a rainbow flag on the plaza's flagpole. Several plaques are here: One at the base lists the names of past and present openly gay or lesbian state and local officials. *Castro St. (at Market St.).* ●

Shopping Best Bets

Best Take-Home Gifts
★★ Canton Bazaar, *616 Grant Ave. (p 76)*

Best Shoe Store
★★ Gimme Shoes, *416 Hayes St.; 2358 Fillmore St. (p 78)*

Best Wine Shop
★★ The Wine Club San Francisco, *953 Harrison (p 80)*

Best Scotch & Champagne Store
★★ D&M, *2200 Fillmore St. (p 79)*

Best Gallery of Local Artists
★★ Hang Art, *556 & 557 Sutter St. (p 71)*

Best Glassware
★★ Gump's, *135 Post St. (p 77)*

Best Toy Store
★ Ambassador Toys, *2 Embarcadero Center (p 82)*

Best Used Books
★ Green Apple Books and Music, *506 Clement St. (p 72)*

Most Outrageous Clothes & Accessories
★ Piedmont, *1452 Haight St. (p 82)*

Best Museum Shop
★★ SFMOMA MuseumStore, *151 3rd St. (p 77)*

Best Vintage-Clothing Store
★ Held Over, *1543 Haight St. (p 82)*

Best Designer Discounts
★★ Jeremy's, *2 S. Park St. (p 73)*

Best Music Store
★★ Amoeba Music, *1855 Haight Street (p 78)*

Best Cheese Shop
★★ Cowgirl Creamery's Artisan Cheese Shop, *Ferry Building Marketplace (p 79)*

Best Jeans Store
★★ A-B Fits, *1519 Grant Avenue (p 74)*

The famous red-heel-clad legs loom over the entrance to Piedmont on Haight Street. Previous page: Cable car souvenirs.

Shopping East of Van Ness Ave.

UNION SQUARE
(see inset map)

Apple Store
  San Francisco 15
Barneys New York 14
Crocker Galleria 8
Discount Cameras 10
49 Geary 13
Gump's 7
Lang Antiques & Estate
  Jewelry 4
Loehmann's 5
Macy's 11
Maiden Lane 9
Margaret O'Leary 6
Métier 3
Neiman Marcus 12
Saks Fifth Avenue 1
Wilkes Bashford 2

A-B Fits 4
Ambassador Toys 14
Biordi Art Imports 7
Bloomingdale's 21
Book Passage 19
The Cannery 2
Canton Bazaar 18
Chinatown Kite Shop 16
City Lights Bookstore 9

Cowgirl Creamery's Artisan
  Cheese Shop 19
Crown Point Press 23
Ghirardelli Square 1
Golden Gate Fortune Cookies
  Co. 10
Good Vibrations 15
Grand Central Station
  Antiques 26
Hang Art 20

Jeremy's 24
Kathleen Taylor,
  The Lotus Collection 13
Molinari Delicatessen 8
Nordstrom 21
Nordstrom Rack 27
Patagonia 2
Puppets on the Pier 3
Recchiuti Confections 19
SFMOMA MuseumStore 22
San Francisco Antique & Design
  Mall 28
Tai Yick Trading Company 6
Ten Ren Tea Company 5
Westfield San Francisco Centre 21
William Stout Architectural
  Books 12
The Wine Club 25
The Wok Shop 17

Shopping West of Van Ness Ave.

Shopping **A to Z**

Antiques

Grand Central Station Antiques SOMA   A vast collection of inexpensive antique European and American furniture. *333 9th St. (btw. Folsom & Harrison sts.).* ☎ *415/252-8155. www.gcsantiques. com. DISC, MC, V. Bus: 12, 19. Map p 69.*

Kathleen Taylor, the Lotus Collection FINANCIAL DISTRICT The place for decorative antique textiles, including tapestries, wall hangings, pillows, and table covers. *445 Jackson St. (btw. Sansome & Montgomery sts.).* ☎ *415/398-8115. www.ktaylor-lotus.com. AE, MC, V. Bus: 10, 12, 15. Map p 69.*

★★ **Lang Antiques & Estate Jewelry** UNION SQUARE   An impressive collection of vintage engagement rings, antique timepieces, lockets, and brooches. *323 Sutter St. (btw. Stockton St. & Grant Ave.)* ☎ *415/982-2213. www.lang antiques.com. AE, DC, DISC, MC, V. Bus: 2, 3, 4, 30, 45. Map p 69.*

★ **San Francisco Antique & Design Mall** POTRERO HILL   Over 100 antiques specialists show their stuff at this huge warehouse space. *701 Bayshore Blvd.* ☎ *415/656-3530. www.sfantique.com. AE, DISC, MC, V. Bus: 9. Map p 69.*

★ **Woodchuck Antiques** PRESIDIO HEIGHTS   Fashionable SF homeowners head here for 19th- and early-20th-century lamps, chandeliers, and bronzes. *3597 Sacramento St. (at Locust St.).* ☎ *415/922-6416. www.woodchuckantiques.com. AE, MC, V. Bus: 1, 2, 4. Map p 70.*

Art

★ **Crown Point Press** SOMA   Excellent etchings from U.S. and

An early-18th-century Italian silk floss embroidered panel from Kathleen Taylor, the Lotus Collection.

international artists, usually priced from $1,000 to $5,000. *20 Hawthorne St. (off Howard St., btw. 2nd & 3rd sts.).* ☎ *415/974-6273. www. crownpoint.com. MC, V. Bus: 15, 30, 45. Map p 69.*

★★ **49 Geary Street** UNION SQUARE   You'll find several top galleries here and on Sutter and Post streets. *49 Geary St. (btw. Grant Ave. & Kearny St.). Bus: 2, 3, 4, 30, 45. Streetcar: F. Map p 69.*

★★ **Hang Art** UNION SQUARE   Hang and the Hang Annex across the street feature lesser-known, but very talented, local artists—at exceptional prices. *556 & 557 Sutter St. (btw. Powell & Mason sts.).* ☎ *415/434-4264. www.hangart.com. AE, DC, DISC, MC, V. Bus: 2, 3, 4, 76. Cable car: Powell lines. Map p 69.*

Books

★ **Book Passage** FINANCIAL DISTRICT   This independent bookseller stocks books on cooking, sustainable agriculture, ecology, local history, and regional travel. *Ferry Building*

Marketplace, the Embarcadero (at Market St.). ☎ 415/835-1020. www.bookpassage.com. AE, DISC, MC, V. Streetcar: F. BART/Muni: Embarcadero. Map p 69.

★ **Books Inc.** PRESIDIO HEIGHTS, MARINA, CIVIC CENTER, AND CASTRO   The oldest independent bookseller in town has spot-on customer service. 3515 California St. (at Locust St.). ☎ 415/221-3666. Bus: 1, 2, 4. 2251 Chestnut St. (at Avila St.). ☎ 415/931-3633. Bus: 22 or 30. 601 Van Ness (at Golden Gate Ave.). ☎ 415/776-1111. Bus: 47, 49. 2275 Market St. (at Noe St.). ☎ 415/864-6777. Streetcar: F. www.booksinc.net. AE, DISC, MC, V. Map p 70.

Browser Books PACIFIC HEIGHTS This cozy, independent neighborhood bookstore has a wide selection of books and a knowledgeable staff. 2195 Fillmore St. (btw. Sacramento & California sts.). ☎ 415/567-8027. www.browserbookstore.com. AE, MC, V. Bus: 1, 3, 22. Map p 70.

★ **City Lights Bookstore** NORTH BEACH   Founded by Lawrence Ferlinghetti in 1953, this landmark shop still stocks avant-garde and alternative literature. 261 Columbus Ave. (at Broadway St.). ☎ 415/362-8193. www.citylights.com. AE, DISC, MC, V. Bus: 15, 30, 41. Map p 69.

★ **Green Apple Books and Music** RICHMOND   SF's best used-book store has more than 60,000 new and 100,000 used books, including rare graphic comics, an enticing cookbook selection, and art books. 506 Clement St. (at 6th Ave.). ☎ 415/387-2272. www.greenapplebooks.com. DISC, MC, V. Bus: 1, 2, 38. Map p 70.

★ **William Stout Architectural Books** FINANCIAL DISTRICT   You could lose yourself amid the glossy books devoted to architecture and design. 804 Montgomery St. (at Jackson St.). ☎ 415/391-6757. www.stoutbooks.com. MC, V. Bus: 12, 15, 30, 41. Map p 69.

Department Stores

★ **Barneys New York** UNION SQUARE   The hip, posh bastion to consumerism has arrived in SF—and all the top designers are represented. The basement is full of luscious creams, candles, and perfumes in beautiful packaging—you'll find a perfect gift for someone special. 77 O'Farrell St. (at Stockton St.). ☎ 415/268-3500. www.barneys.com. AE, MC, V. Bus: 2, 3,4, 30, 45. Streetcar: F. Cable car: Powell lines. Map p 69.

City Lights contains an impressive selection of art, poetry and political paperbacks.

★ **Bloomingdale's** SOMA This chic anchor of the Westfield Shopping Center has it all—be it a stunning handbag, designer kids' jeans, or a stylish European coffeemaker—if you can afford the designer price tag. *845 Market St. (btw. 4th & 5th sts.).* ☎ *415/856-5300. www. bloomingdales.com. AE, DISC, MC, V. Bus: 14, 27, 30, 45. Streetcar: F. Cable car: Powell lines. Map p 69.*

Macy's UNION SQUARE This abundantly stocked behemoth is the largest store on Union Square. The men's store is across the street. *170 O'Farrell St. (btw. Powell & Stockton sts.).* ☎ *415/397-3333. www.macys. com. AE, MC, V. Bus: 2, 3, 4, 30, 45. Streetcar: F. Cable car: Powell lines. Map p 69.*

Neiman Marcus UNION SQUARE Most items here are mercilessly expensive, but the third floor occasionally has good sales on items by lines/designers like Theory and Marc Jacobs. *150 Stockton St. (at Geary St.).* ☎ *415/362-3900. www.neiman marcus.com. AE. Bus: 30, 38, 45. Streetcar: F. Cable car: Powell lines. Map p 69.*

★ **Nordstrom** UNION SQUARE An excellent shoe department, knowledgeable service, and clothing for the whole family are some of the bonuses of this well-run department store. *865 Market St. (at 5th St.).* ☎ *415/243-8500. www.nordstrom. com. AE, DC, DISC, MC, V. Bus: 27, 30, 45. Streetcar: F. Cable car: Powell lines. Map p 69.*

Saks Fifth Avenue UNION SQUARE You'll find only top designers here, at top prices. The men's store is down the street. *384 Post St. (at Powell St.).* ☎ *415/986-4300. Men's store: 220 Post St.* ☎ *415/986-4300. www.saksfifth avenue.com. AE, DC, DISC, MC, V. Bus: 2, 3, 4, 38. Cable car: Powell lines. Map p 69.*

Neiman Marcus offers great views of Union Square in addition to great shopping.

Discount Shopping

★★ **Jeremy's** SOMA You'll find an astonishing array of top designer fashions, from shoes to suits, at rock-bottom prices. *2 S. Park St. (btw. Bryant & Brannan sts.)* ☎ *415/ 882-4929. www.jeremys.com. AE, MC, V. Bus: 10, 12. Map p 69.*

Loehmann's UNION SQUARE The national discount designer chain has a convenient location in downtown SF. *222 Sutter St. (btw. Grant Ave. & Kearny St.)* ☎ *415/982-3215. www.loehmanns.com. AE, DISC, MC, V. Bus: 2, 3, 4, 15, 30, 45. Map p 69.*

Nordstrom Rack SOMA If you have the patience to sift through the racks, you'll find designer jeans, shoes, dresses, you-name-it for peanuts. *555 9th St. (at Brannan St.)* ☎ *415/934-1211. www.nordstrom. com. AE, DC, DISC, MC, V. Bus: 10, 19, 27, 47. Map p 69.*

Electronics

★ **Apple Store San Francisco** UNION SQUARE/MARINA This is

one beautiful store brought to you by the makers of very hip electronics. The Chestnut Street location is less crowded, but you will still need an appointment for service on your iPhone (or other product). *1 Stockton St. (at Market St.).* ☎ *415/392-0202. Bus: 30 or 38. Streetcar: F. 2125 Chestnut St. (at Steiner St.).* ☎ *415/848-4445. Bus: 22, 30.* www.apple.com. *AE, DC, DISC, MC, V. Streetcar: F. Map p 69.*

Discount Cameras UNION SQUARE   An authorized dealer for all major brands of photographic, digital, and video equipment. Most repairs done in 3 to 5 days. *33 Kearny St. (btw. Geary & Post sts.).* ☎ *415/392-1103.* www.discount camera.com. *AE, DC, DISC, MC, V. Bus: 38. Streetcar: F. Map p 69.*

Fashion
A-B Fits NORTH BEACH   If you are searching for the perfect pair of denims, stop by this shop for expert advice on the best fit for your body. Choose from a hip collection of shirts, belts, and accessories to complete your look. *1519 Grant Ave. (btw. Union & Filbert sts.)* ☎ *415/982-5726. AE, MC, V. Bus: 30, 41, 45. Map p 69.*

Add some Calder style to your home with a mobile from SFMOMA's gift store.

Ambiance COW HOLLOW, HAIGHT-ASHBURY, NOE VALLEY   There is something for every taste at this chain of women's boutiques, from designer labels to affordable clothes, shoes, and accessories. *1864 & 1858 Union St. (btw. Octavia & Laguna sts.)* ☎ *415/923-9797. Bus: 41, 45. 1458 Haight St. (btw. Masonic & Ashbury sts.)* ☎ *415/552-5095. Bus: 43, 71. 3985 & 3989 24th St. (btw. Sanchez & Noe sts.)* ☎ *415/647-7144. Bus: 24, 48.* www.ambiancesf.com. *AE, MC, V. Map p 70.*

Bryan Lee COW HOLLOW   A swank shop that will prepare ladies and gents for a night on the town or a day at the office. *1840 Union St. (at Octavia St.)* ☎ *415/923-9923. AE, DC, DISC, MC, V. Bus: 22, 41, 45. Map p 70.*

★ **Giggle** MARINA   You'll find only the best for your baby here, from organic cotton pj's to the most stylish strollers. *2110 Chestnut St. (btw. Steiner & Pierce sts.)* ☎ *415/440-9034.* www.giggle.com. *AE, MC, V. Bus: 22, 30. Map p 70.*

Heidi Says PACIFIC HEIGHTS   This stylish but pricey boutique has three stores on Fillmore Street: Collections features fine designer clothing; Casual, two doors down, offers a selection of trendy shirts and dresses; and Shoe Salon has the latest in heels and accessories. *2126 Fillmore St.* ☎ *415/749-0655, 2416 Fillmore St.* ☎ *415/749-1144 (btw. Washington & Jackson sts.) 2105 Fillmore St. (btw. Sacramento & California sts.)* ☎ *415/409-6850.* www.heidisays.com. *AE, MC, V. Bus: 1, 3, 22. Map p 70.*

★ **Honeys & Heroes** PRESIDIO HEIGHTS   Find unique, well-priced clothes for boys and girls up to age 14 who want to set themselves apart from the Gap-pack. *3366 Sacramento St. (btw. Walnut St. & Presidio Ave.)*

Marc by Marc Jacobs is one of the designer boutiques along Maiden Lane.

☎ 415/567-6780. www.honeys andheroes.com. AE, DISC, MC, V. Bus: 1, 2, 3, 4. Map p 70.

MAC Modern Appealing Clothing HAYES VALLEY   Hip, affordable clothes—including tailored suits and fashionable separates—from designers like Paul Smith and Laurie B. *387 Grove St. (at Gough St.)* ☎ *415/863-3011. AE, MC, V. Bus: 21. Map p 70.*

★★★ **Maiden Lane** UNION SQUARE   Top designers like Marc Jacobs have boutiques on this pedestrian alley. Prada, Louis Vuitton, Kate Spade, and others are nearby. Major upscale designers without their own SF store can be found at Barneys, Bloomie's, Saks, or Neiman Marcus (see "Department Stores"). *Maiden Ln., off Stockton St. Bus: 30, 38, 45. Map p 69.*

★★ **Margaret O'Leary** PACIFIC HEIGHTS/FINANCIAL DISTRICT   Irish-born O'Leary began knitting elegant sweaters in SF in 1987. Now she has several swanky boutiques, which also carry accessories from other designers. *2400 Fillmore St. (at Washington St.).* ☎ *415/771-9982. Bus: 1, 12, 22. 1 Claude Ln. (off Sutter St., btw. Grant Ave. & Kearny St.)* ☎ *415/391-1010. (Claude Ln. location*

closed Sun–Mon). Bus: 2, 3, 4, 15, 30, 45. www.margaretoleary.com. AE, DISC, MC, V. Map p 69, 70.

★★ **Métier** UNION SQUARE   For classic, and pricey, attire from European ready-to-wear lines and designers, plus exquisite jewelry from LA designer Cathy Waterman, head to Métier. *355 Sutter St. (btw. Stockton St. & Grant Ave.)* ☎ *415/989-5395. www.metiersf.com. AE, MC, V. Closed Sun. Bus: 2, 3, 4, 30, 45. Map p 69.*

Mudpie PACIFIC HEIGHTS   This refined store stocks elegant baby and kids' clothes, accessories, and children's furniture, but prices are extreme. *2185 Fillmore St. (btw. Sacramento & California sts.)* ☎ *415/771-9262. AE, MC, V. Bus: 1, 22. Map p 70.*

Nomads HAYES VALLEY   Distressed and vintage trousers, shirts, and leather jackets from European and American designers. *556 Hayes St. (btw. Laguna & Octavia sts.)* ☎ *415/864-5692. www.nomads-sf. com. AE, DC, DISC, MC, V. Bus: 21. Map p 70.*

RAG HAYES VALLEY   If you want to add some truly unique San Francisco designs to your closet, head to this co-op shop where local,

Canton Bazaar.

emerging designers showcase their latest creations. *541 Octavia St. (btw. Hayes & Grove sts.)* ☎ *415/621-7718. www.ragsfem.com. MC, V. Bus: 21. Map p 70.*

★ **Sunhee Moon** PACIFIC HEIGHTS, COW HOLLOW, AND MISSION   Celebrated local designer Sunhee Moon creates clean, structured pieces you can wear—and look great in—every day. Her clothes have been spotted in top shops in NY, LA, and Japan; get them right in her own SF stores. *3167 16th St. (at Guerrero St.)* ☎ *415/355-1800. Muni: J. Bus: 22. 1833 Fillmore St. (btw. Bush & Sutter sts.)* ☎ *415/928-1800. Bus: 2, 3, 4, 22. 2059 Union St. (btw. Webster & Buchanan sts.).* ☎ *415/922-1800. www.sunheemoon.com. Bus: 22, 41, 45. AE, V, MC. Map p 70.*

★★ **Wilkes Bashford** UNION SQUARE   SF's most enduring men's clothing store. SF resident and comedian Robin Williams is among the high-profile customers who shop here for the finest European fashions. *375 Sutter St. (at Stockton St.)* ☎ *415/986-4380. www.wilkes bashford.com. AE, DC, DISC, MC, V. Bus: 2, 3, 4, 30, 45. Map p 69.*

Gifts & Souvenirs

★ **Biordi Art Imports** NORTH BEACH   Beautiful examples of hand-painted Majolica dishes and serving pieces nearly too pretty to use. *412 Columbus Ave. (at Vallejo St.).* ☎ *415/392-8096. www.biordi. com. AE, DC, DISC, MC, V. Bus: 15, 30, 41. Map p 69.*

★★ **Canton Bazaar** CHINATOWN   This multilevel store carries Chinese porcelain, jade, antiques, and hand-carved furniture. *616 Grant Ave. (btw. California & Sacramento sts.).* ☎ *415/362-5750. AE, DISC, MC, V. Bus: 1, 15, 30, 45. Map p 69.*

★ **Cliff's Variety** CASTRO   This only-in-SF shop is loaded with amusing, useful, necessary, and just plain fun items, among them art supplies. *479 & 471 Castro St. (at 18th St.).* ☎ *415/431-5365. www.cliffsvariety. com. AE, DC, DISC, MC, V. Muni: L, K, M. Streetcar: F. Map p 70.*

★★ **Flax Art & Design** MISSION   Flax carries just about every art and design supply you can think of, plus crafts, children's art supplies, frames, and calendars. *1699 Market St. (at Valencia St.).* ☎ *415/552-2355. www.flaxart.com. AE, DISC, MC, V. Bus: 6, 7, 26, 71. Streetcar: F. Map p 70.*

Good Vibrations MISSION AND NOB HILL   This straightforward, lay-person's sex-toy, book, and video emporium is geared mostly toward women, but not exclusively. *603 Valencia St. (at 17th St.).* ☎ *415/522-5460. Bus: 22, 26. BART: to 16th St. 1620 Polk St. (at Sacramento St.).* ☎ *415/345-0400. Bus: 1 or 19. Cable car: California line. www.goodvibes. com. AE, DISC, MC, V. Map p 70.*

★★ **Kiehl's** PACIFIC HEIGHTS   You can't go wrong with the personal-care products from this over-150-year-old company. Everyone loves to

Family-owned Flax Art & Design has been fostering creativity in SF for more than 60 years.

be pampered. *1971 Fillmore St. (at Pine St.).* ☎ *415/359-9260. www.kiehls.com. AE, DC, MC, V. Bus: 1, 22. Map p 70.*

★★ SFMOMA MuseumStore

SOMA   With an array of artistic books, jewelry, and intelligent toys, this is one of the more clever gift shops around. *151 3rd St. (btw. Mission & Howard sts.).* ☎ *415/357-4035. www.sfmoma.com. AE, DISC, MC, V. Bus: 9, 15, 30, 45. Map p 69.*

Tai Yick Trading Company CHINATOWN   This is a real find for tiny china tea sets, miniature Chinese bowls, and all kinds of porcelain and pottery. *1400 Powell St. (at Broadway St.).* ☎ *415/986-0961. www.taiyick.com. AE, DC, DISC, MC, V. Bus: 12, 15, 30, 45. Cable car: Powell-Mason. Map p 69.*

Housewares & Furnishings

★★ Gump's UNION SQUARE

Founded in 1861, this SF institution offers tasteful home accessories including fine crystal, elegant tableware, and other artful items, along with superlative service. *135 Post St. (btw. Grant Ave. & Kearny St.).* ☎ *415/982-1616. www.gumps.com.*

AE, DISC, MC, V. Bus: 2, 3, 4, 15, 30, 45. Map p 69.

★ Soko Hardware JAPANTOWN

A great selection of ceramic plates, tea sets, sake cups, and more at bargain prices. *1698 Post St. (at Buchanan St.).* ☎ *415/931-5510. MC, V. Bus: 2, 3, 4, 38. Map p 70.*

The Wok Shop CHINATOWN This shop has every conceivable implement for Chinese cooking, including woks, brushes, and oyster knives. It also sells plenty of kitchen utensils. *718 Grant Ave. (at*

Gump's department store feels like a chic museum you can shop in.

Amoeba Music carries CDs alongside a massive selection of LPs.

Sacramento St.). ☎ 415/989-3797 or 888/780-7171. www.wokshop.com. AE, DC, DISC, MC, V. Bus: 1, 30, 45. Map p 69.

Jewelry

★ **Gallery of Jewels** PACIFIC HEIGHTS, COW HOLLOW, AND NOE VALLEY   The name is not very appealing, but it's accurate: Various jewelry artists are represented here, offering a variety of lovely, limited-edition items—from intricately beaded necklaces to simple pendants or delicate drop earrings. *2115 Fillmore St. (at California St.).* ☎ *415/771-5099. Bus: 1, 12, 22. 2101 Union St. (at Webster St.).* ☎ *415/929-0259. Bus: 22, 41, 45. 4089 24th St. (at Castro St.).* ☎ *415/ 285-0626. Bus: 48. Muni: J. AE, DISC, MC, V. Map p 70.*

★★ **Ruby's Artist Cooperative** MISSION   As the name suggests, Ruby's provides a venue for local jewelry makers to show their delightful, one-of-a-kind creations. *3602 20th St. (at Valencia St.).* ☎ *415/550-8052. Bus: 12, 27. Muni: J. BART: to 16th or 24th St. 1431 Haight St. (btw. Ashbury & Masonic sts.).* ☎ *415/554-0555. www.rubygallery.com. MC, V. Map p 70.*

★ **Union Street Goldsmith**
COW HOLLOW   A showcase for Bay Area goldsmiths, this exquisite shop sells a contemporary collection of fine custom-designed jewelry in platinum and gold. *1909 Union St. (at Laguna St.).* ☎ *415/776-8048. www.unionstreetgoldsmith.com. AE, DC, DISC, MC, V. Bus: 22, 41, 45. Map p 70.*

Music & Musical Instruments
★★ **Amoeba Music** HAIGHT
The music store for young San Franciscans, with a huge collection of LPs, plus CDs and cassettes. *1855 Haight St. (btw. Shrader & Stanyan sts.).* ☎ *415/831-1200. www. amoeba.com. DISC, MC, V. Bus: 6, 7, 66, 71. Map p 70.*

Shoes & Bags
Brook's Shoes for Kids PRESIDIO HEIGHTS   Stylish European and American brands are sold by a knowledgeable and friendly staff. *3307 Sacramento St. (at Presidio Ave.).* ☎ *415/440-7599. www. brooksshoesforkids.com. AE, DISC, MC, V. Bus: 1, 3, 4. Map p 70.*

★★ **Gimme Shoes** HAYES VALLEY AND PACIFIC HEIGHTS   This über-fashionable, sparse store has the coolest designer shoes in town. *416 Hayes St. (at Gough St.).* ☎ *415/864-0691. Bus: 21. 2358 Fillmore St. (btw. Washington & Clay sts.).* ☎ *415/441-3040. Bus: 1, 22. www.gimme shoes.com. AE, DISC, MC, V. Map p 70.*

★★ **Rabat** MARINA AND NOE VALLEY   The minimalist surroundings perfectly match the stylish footwear. You'll find plenty of fabulous separates here, as well. *2080 Chestnut St. (at Mallorca Way).* ☎ *415/929-8868. Bus: 22 or 30. 4001 24th St. (at Noe St.).* ☎ *415/282-7861. Streetcar: J. BART: to 24th St. then bus 48.*

www.rabatshoes.com. AE, DISC, MC, V. Map p 70.

Shoe Biz HAIGHT, NOE, AND MISSION   Teens and 20-somethings will appreciate the funky shoes—like tennis shoes, skate shoes, and bright red leather boots—at moderate prices. *1446 Haight St. (btw. Ashbury St. & Masonic Ave.)* ☎ *415/864-0990. Shoe Biz II: 1553 Haight St.* ☎ *415/861-3933. Super Shoe Biz: 1420 Haight St.* ☎ *415/864-0990. Bus for Haight St. locations: 6, 7, 43, or 71. 3810 24th St. (btw. Church & Blanche sts.).* ☎ *415/821-2528. Bus: 48. Muni: J. 877 Valencia St. (at 20th St.).* ☎ *415/550-2528. BART: to 24th St. then bus 48. www.shoebizsf. com. AE, DISC, MC, V. Map p 70.*

Shopping Centers & Complexes

The Cannery FISHERMAN'S WHARF   Several tourist-oriented shops are in this charmingly restored former fruit-canning facility. *2801 Leavenworth St. (at Jefferson St.).* ☎ *415/771-3112. www.delmonte square.com. Bus: 10, 30. Cable car: Powell-Hyde. Streetcar: F. Map p 69.*

Crocker Galleria FINANCIAL DISTRICT   This glass-domed pavilion features several high-end shops selling expensive and classic designer creations. *50 Post St. (btw. Kearny & Montgomery sts.).* ☎ *415/393-1505. www.shopatgalleria.com. Bus: 2, 3, 4, 15, 30, 45. Map p 69.*

★ Ghirardelli Square FISHERMAN'S WHARF   Along with the quaint gift shops at this former chocolate factory comes a priceless view. This is a perfect spot to shop for SF's famous chocolate: Ghirardelli's flagship store, the Ghirardelli Soda Fountain & Chocolate Shop (p 80), is here. *900 North Point St. (at Larkin St.).* ☎ *415/775-5500. www.ghirardellisq.com. Bus: 10, 30. Cable car: Powell-Hyde. Map p 69.*

Westfield San Francisco Centre SOMA   Anchored by Bloomingdale's and Nordstrom, this is allegedly the largest city mall in America. It actually has some lovely stores and a huge basement food court. *865 Market St. (at 5th St.).* ☎ *415/512-6776. www.westfield. com/sanfrancisco. Bus: 27, 30, 45. Streetcar: F. Cable car: Powell lines. Map p 69.*

Specialty Foods, Wines & Liquors

★★ Cowgirl Creamery's Artisan Cheese Shop EMBARCADERO   Top-notch domestic and international cheeses, in addition to award-winning selections from Cowgirl Creamery's own Point Reyes facility, plus cheese tools, boards, and books about cheese. *Ferry Building Marketplace, 1 Ferry Building on the Embarcadero at Mission St.* ☎ *415/362-9354. www.cowgirlcreamery. com. MC, V. Streetcar: F. BART/Muni: Embarcadero. Map p 69.*

★★ D&M Wines and Liquors PACIFIC HEIGHTS   This unassuming shop boasts amazing champagnes and French brandies, plus one of the

The Westfield is the perfect place to explore on a cold, foggy afternoon.

The amazing cheeses at Cowgirl Creamery are a local foodie favorite.

world's best single-malt scotch selections. *2200 Fillmore St. (at Sacramento St.).* ☎ *415/346-1325. www.dandm.com. AE, MC, V. Bus: 1, 22. Map p 70.*

Ghirardelli Soda Fountain & Chocolate Shop FISHERMAN'S WHARF See "Ghirardelli Square," above.

★ **Golden Gate Fortune Cookies Co.** CHINATOWN Buy fortune cookies hot off the press at this tiny, alley-side Chinatown shop. Bring your own messages and watch them being folded into the cookies. *56 Ross Alley (btw. Washington & Jackson sts.).* ☎ *415/781-3956. No credit cards. Bus: 30, 45. Cable car: Powell-Mason. Map p 69.*

★ **Molinari Delicatessen** NORTH BEACH Since 1896, Molinari has been supplying SF with imported meats, cheeses, wines, and canned goods at moderate prices. *373 Columbus Ave. (at Vallejo St.).* ☎ *415/421-2337. MC, V. Bus: 12, 15, 30, 41. Map p 69.*

★ **Recchiuti Confections** EMBARCADERO Dreamy boxed chocolates, fleur de sel caramels, and extra-bitter chocolate sauce are some of the out-of-this-world offerings. *Ferry Building Marketplace, 1 Ferry Building, on the Embarcadero at Mission St.* ☎ *415/834-9494. www.recchiuti.com. AE, MC, V. Streetcar: F. BART/Muni: Embarcadero. Map p 69.*

★ **Ten Ren Tea Company** CHINATOWN In addition to a selection of 50 varieties of tea, you'll be offered a steaming cup of tea when you walk in. *949 Grant Ave. (btw. Washington & Jackson sts.).* ☎ *415/362-0656. www.tenren.com. AE, DC, MC, V. Bus: 1, 15, 30, 45. Map p 69.*

★★ **The Wine Club San Francisco** SOMA The largest wine merchant in the West offers bargain-basement prices. *953 Harrison St. (btw. 5th & 6th sts.).* ☎ *415/512-9086. www.thewineclub.com. AE, MC, V. Bus: 12, 19, 27. Map p 69.*

Sporting Goods: Clothing & Equipment

Patagonia FISHERMAN'S WHARF An excellent source for high-quality fleece and outerwear. *770 North Point St. (btw. Hyde & Leavenworth sts.).* ☎ *415/771-2050. www. patagonia.com. AE, DC, DISC, MC,*

Specialty tea from Ten Ren Tea Co. is a fun, inexpensive, and light gift to tote home.

Shop & Spa: The City's Best Day Spas

Kabuki Springs & Spa, 1750 Geary Blvd. (☎ 415/922-6000; www. kabukisprings.com), the Japan Center's most famous tenant, was once an authentic, traditional Japanese bathhouse. The Joie de Vivre hotel group bought and renovated it, however, and it's now more of a Pan-Asian spa with a focus on wellness. The deep ceramic communal tubs—at a very affordable $22 to $25 per person—private baths, and shiatsu massages remain. The spa is open from 10am to 9:45pm daily; joining the baths is an array of massages and ayurvedic treatments, body scrubs, wraps, and facials, which cost from $60 to $150.

Spa Radiance, 3011 Fillmore St. (☎ 415/346-6281; www.spa radiance.com), is an utterly San Francisco spa experience due to its unassuming Victorian surroundings and its wonderfully luxurious treatments such as facials, body treatments, massages, manicures, pedicures, Brazilian waxing, spray-tanning, and makeup application by in-house artists.

A more posh and modern experience is yours at **International Orange,** 2044 Fillmore St., second floor (☎ 888/894-8811; www. internationalorange.com). The self-described spa yoga lounge offers just what it says in a chic white-on-white space on the boutique-shopping stretch of Fillmore Street. They've also got a great selection of clothing and face and body products, including one of my personal favorites, locally made In Fiore body balms.

In the St. Regis Hotel, **Remède Spa,** 125 3rd St. (☎ 415/284-4060; www.remede.com), has two whole floors dedicated to melting away all your cares, worries, kinks, and knots—not to mention primping. Expect wonderful massages, facials, manis and pedis, waxes, and more. A few doors down in the W Hotel is the city's outpost of New York's **Bliss Spa,** 181 3rd St., fourth floor (☎ 415/281-0990; www.blissworld.com). The hip version to St. Regis's chic, it offers a similar spa menu, including wedding specialties.

Opened in 2003, **Tru,** 750 Kearny St. (☎ 415/399-9700; www. truspa.com), is a sleek, modern day spa with options that go way beyond your average hot stone massage. Signature treatments include oxygen facials and the world's only tropical rainforest water treatment room—a full-immersion experience involving steam, tropical rain storms, and a 100-gallon-a-minute waterfall. It's located inside the Hilton Hotel, between Union Square and the Financial District.

V. Bus: 10, 30. Cable car: Powell-Hyde. Map p 69.

★★ **Sports Basement** PRESIDIO/ POTRERO HILL   No fancy displays here. Sports equipment and attire is displayed on stacked crates, boxes, and anything else that's inexpensive. Manufacturers' overstocks and extras are a big part of the inventory, and you won't pay full price for anything. *610 Mason St. (in the Presidio).*

415/437-0100. Bus: 28, 29, 76. 1590 Bryant St. (btw. 15th & 16th sts.). 415/437-0100. Bus: 27, 33, 53. www.sportsbasement.com. AE, DC, DISC, MC, V. Map p 70.

Toys

★ **Ambassador Toys** FINANCIAL DISTRICT   Classic European dolls, wonderful wooden toys, clever games, and books are among the great playthings at this delightful store. *2 Embarcadero Center (at Sacramento St. btw. Front & Davis sts.).* 415/345-8697. www.ambassador toys.com. AE, DISC, MC, V. Bus: 1, 41. Cable car: California line. Map p 69.

Chinatown Kite Shop CHINA-TOWN   From world-class stunt fliers to more modest models, an awesome array of kites is on display here. *717 Grant Ave. (at Sacramento St.).* 415/989-5182. www.china townkite.com. AE, DC, DISC, MC, V. Bus: 1, 15, 30, 45. Cable car: California line. Map p 69.

Puppets on the Pier FISHER-MAN'S WHARF   Kittens, bunnies, dragons, and even cockroaches are just some of the amazing puppets here. *PIER 39, on the Embarcadero at Grant Ave., Fisherman's Wharf.* 415/781-4435. www.puppet dream.com. AE, DISC, MC, V. Bus: 10, 15. Streetcar: F. Map p 69.

Travel Goods

Flight 001 HAYES VALLEY   Jet-setters will find hip travel accessories like sleek luggage, "security-friendly" manicure sets, and other mid-air must-haves. *525 Hayes St. (btw. Laguna & Octavia sts.).*

415/487-1001. www.flight001. com. AE, DISC, MC, V. Bus: 21. Map p 70.

Vintage Clothing

Buffalo Exchange HAIGHT AND MISSION   This groovy shop is crammed with old and new attire from the 1960s, 1970s, and 1980s. It's a good place to espy the latest street fashions. *1555 Haight St. (btw. Clayton & Ashbury sts.).* 415/431-7733. 1210 Valencia St. (at 23rd St.). www.buffaloexchange.com. MC, V. Bus: 6, 7, 66, 71. Map p 70.

★ **Held Over** HAIGHT   Vintage clothing–hunters will love this large and well organized collection of dresses, suits, and accessories at reasonable prices. *1543 Haight St. (btw. Ashbury & Clayton sts).* 415/864-0818. Bus: 6, 7, 66, 71. MC, V. Map p 70.

Good Byes PRESIDIO HEIGHTS   This consignment shop offers excellent deals on high-quality attire and shoes for men and women. *3464 & 3483 Sacramento St. (btw. Laurel & Walnut sts.).* 415/346-6388. www.goodbyessf.com. DISC, MC, V. Bus: 1, 3, 4. Map p 70.

★ **Piedmont** HAIGHT   Absolutely outrageous women's garments and accessories—sold mostly to men. If in your heart of hearts you've ever coveted any of the gaudy get-ups you've seen on drag queens, this is the place to find them. The giant fishnet legs over the entrance are *so* totally the Haight. *1452 Haight St. (at Ashbury).* 415/864-8075. www.piedmontsf.com. AE, DISC, MC, V. Bus: 21. Map p 70. ●

5 The **Great Outdoors**

The Golden Gate Promenade

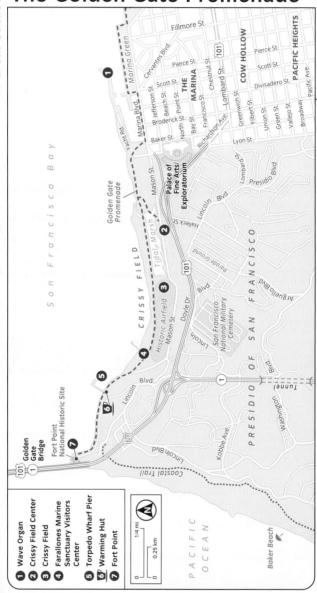

San Francisco Bay

Golden Gate Promenade

Tidal Marsh

CRISSY FIELD

Historic Airfield

PRESIDIO OF SAN FRANCISCO

San Francisco National Military Cemetery

PACIFIC OCEAN

Coastal Trail

Baker Beach

1 Wave Organ
2 Crissy Field Center
3 Crissy Field
4 Farallones Marine Sanctuary Visitors Center
5 Torpedo Wharf Pier
6 Warming Hut
7 Fort Point

1/4 mi
0.25 km

Golden Gate Bridge

Fort Point National Historic Site

Previous page: You'll have stunning views along China Beach, even moreso further up at nudist-friendly Baker Beach.

The Golden Gate Promenade is a 3.5-mile (5.6km) paved trail hugging San Francisco Bay. Not only is it the city's most scenic biking, jogging, and walking path, but it is also refreshingly flat. Come at any time of the day, but note that in summer the mornings may be foggy, while the late afternoon is usually windy. *Note:* This tour can be done on foot or by bike (see p 39 for bike rental info), and may be combined with the "Crossing the Golden Gate Bridge" tour (p 38). START: **Bus no. 30 to Broderick and Beach streets.**

❶ ★ kids **Wave Organ.** This is an amazing (and musical) piece of environmental art. Listen to strange humming sounds of the ocean currents, captured by tubes that emerge from the water below and pass through the concrete and rock structure. *Marina Breakwater, Baker St. & Marina Blvd. Bus: 30 to Broderick & Beach sts.*

❷ **Crissy Field Center.** Stop here to pick up maps and information about Crissy Field. Volunteers from this community-run facility also lead walks through the area. ⏱ *15 min. 1199 E. Beach St. (at Mason St.).* ☎ *415/561-7690. www.crissyfield center.org. Daily 9am–5pm.*

❸ ★★★ kids **Crissy Field.** This 100-acre (40ha) site contained what was a military airstrip until 1936. It lay abandoned until 1996, when individuals and civic organizations worked to put in more than100,000 native plants and restored the natural ecosystem. Today it contains a tidal marsh, beaches, and marvelous winding paths. *Old Mason & Baker sts.*

❹ kids **Farallones Marine Sanctuary.** This small house offers information and imaginative exhibits on the local marine wildlife. ⏱ *15 min. Presidio Building 991.* ☎ *415/ 561-6625. www.farallones.org. Free admission. Wed–Sun 10am–4pm.*

❺ **Torpedo Wharf Pier.** Walk to the end of this pier for brilliant views of the Golden Gate and Alcatraz.

❻ **Warming Hut.** Order organic gourmet sandwiches and explore the ecologically correct gift shop while you wait. Consider eating at the outdoor picnic tables. Warming Hut is open daily from 9am to 5pm. *Presidio Building 983.* ☎ *415/561-3040. $.*

❼ ★ **Fort Point.** Hastily completed by the U.S. Army Corps of Engineers at the onset of the Civil War, this formidable brick fortress at the foot of the Golden Gate Bridge was used as a base of operations to build the bridge and was manned by soldiers during World War II. ⏱ *15 min.* ☎ *415/556-1693. www.nps.gov/fopo. To continue with the "Crossing the Golden Gate Bridge" tour (p 38), follow the signs to the walking and biking trails leading to the Golden Gate Bridge.*

Fort Point sits under the Golden Gate Bridge.

Land's End

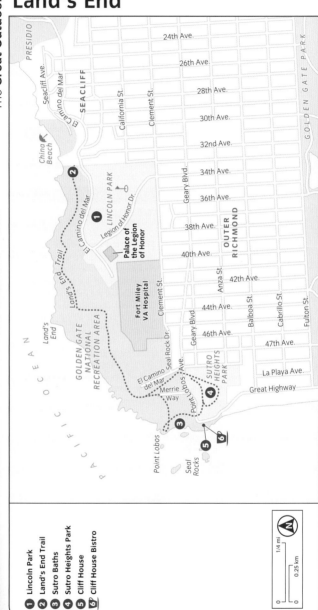

This rocky point, poetically named "Land's End," juts out into the wide expanse of the Pacific. This dramatic and striking section of the coast boasts rugged views of the violent surf and will make you feel like you're standing at the edge of the world. You'll marvel that these wild cliffs are contained within urban San Francisco. It's generally chilly and windy here, so dress warmly. START: Bus no. 1, 38 to Clement Street and 33rd Avenue.

❶ Lincoln Park. This 275-acre (111ha) park boasts Monterey cypresses and contains the ★★ **California Palace of the Legion of Honor,** an exact replica of the Legion of Honor Palace in Paris. Its collection spans 4,000 years, with European paintings by Monet and Rembrandt, and several Rodin sculptures. *Clement St. & 33rd Ave. Museum: Clement St. & 34th Ave.* ☎ *415/863-3330. www.famsf.org. Admission $10 adults, $7 seniors 65 & over, $6 kids 13–17, free for kids under 13. Price includes same-day admission to de Young Museum (p 90). Free admission to all 1st Tues of the month. Tues–Sun 9:30am–5:15pm. Bus: 18.*

Bundle up if you plan to check out the rock formations at chilly Ocean Beach, reachable via the N-Judah train.

❷ ★★★ Land's End Trail. Spectacular views of the Pacific's waves crashing against the cliffs, twisted cypress trees, and unusual rock formations accompany you on this 1.5-mile (2.4km) trek. *Eagle's Point. www.parksconservancy.org.*

❸ Sutro Baths. Check out the ruins of what were once astounding megapools, opened in 1897 by SF millionaire Adolph Sutro. Seven pools of various temperatures held 1.7 million gallons of water and could accommodate up to 10,000 people at a time. The baths were destroyed in a fire in 1966.

❹ Sutro Heights Park. Savor the expansive view of 3½-mile-long (5.6km) Ocean Beach and the hills beyond it from this woodsy park atop a bluff. Adolph Sutro, a Prussian émigré who created the Sutro Tunnel to reach the Comstock silver lode, and also served as mayor of San Francisco, once lived here. *La Playa Ave. & Geary Blvd.*

❺ Cliff House. An 1863 home on this site was destroyed by fire; later, Adolph Sutro's palatial 1869 structure also burned. The third Cliff House, now belonging to the National Park Service, was remodeled in 2004. Its viewing decks look out to Seal Rocks, home to a colony of sea lions and marine birds. Its restaurants, upscale Sutro's and the Cliff House Bistro (see below), boast breathtaking ocean views. *1090 Point Lobos (Geary St., west of 48th Ave.).* ☎ *415/386-3330. www.cliffhouse.com. Mon–Sat 9am–9:30pm; Sun 8:30am–9:30pm.*

☕ Cliff House Bistro. This casual, old-fashioned sandwich-and-salad spot in the Cliff House provides a warm respite from the wind. The view is worth the inflated prices. *In Cliff House, 1090 Point Lobos (Geary St., west of 48th Ave.).* ☎ *415/386-3330. $$.*

Golden Gate Park

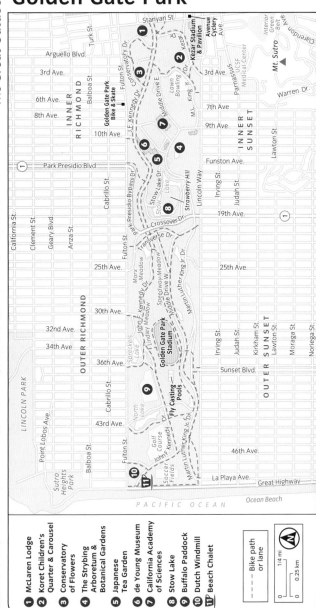

1 McLaren Lodge
2 Koret Children's Quarter & Carousel
3 Conservatory of Flowers
4 The Strybing Arboretum & Botanical Gardens
5 Japanese Tea Garden
6 de Young Museum
7 California Academy of Sciences
8 Stow Lake
9 Buffalo Paddock
10 Dutch Windmill
11 Beach Chalet

- - - Bike path or lane

0 — 1/4 mi
0 — 0.25 km

Golden Gate Park is the jewel of San Francisco. This narrow strip of green stretches inland from the Pacific Ocean, creating a magical 1,017-acre (412ha) rectangle containing a myriad of treasures. Take a day to explore this outdoor wonder at leisure. **Note:** If your schedule allows, visit on a Sunday, when one of the main throughways (JFK Dr.) is closed to car traffic. Also, see bullet ⑧ to explore the park by bike. START: **Fell and Stanyan streets. Bus no. 5, 21.**

① **McLaren Lodge and Park Headquarters.** This entry to the park honors John McLaren, park superintendent from 1890 to 1943, who transformed the barren land into a lush urban retreat. He did so by developing a new strain of grass to hold the sandy soil, windmills to pump water for irrigation, and a natural wall to prevent erosion from the ocean. Stop by for detailed park information. ⏱ *30 min. Fell & Stanyan sts.* ☎ *415/831-2700. www. sfrecpark.org. Free admission. Bus: 5, 21.*

② ★ kids **Koret Children's Quarter & Carousel.** Built in 1887 as the first public children's playground in the U.S., it was reopened in 2007 after a major renovation with huge slides, a super wave climbing wall, and a decorative 1912 carousel. ⏱ *30 min. 320 Bowling Green Dr. (at 1st Ave.). Carousel $2 per ride adults, $1 per ride kids 6–12, free for kids under 6 with paying adult.*

③ ★★ **Conservatory of Flowers.** This striking glass structure, an 1878 public conservatory, showcases rare orchids, carnivorous flora, and plants from five continents. ⏱ *1 hr. Off John F. Kennedy Dr., near Stanyan St. entrance.* ☎ *415/831-2090. www. conservatoryofflowers.org. Admission $7 adults; $5 seniors 65 & over, students & kids 12–17; $2 kids 5–11. Tues–Sun 9am–5pm.*

④ **San Francisco Botanical Gardens at Strybing Arboretum.** More than 6,000 species of

The lovely Conservatory of Flowers is the oldest public conservatory in the Western Hemisphere.

plants, flowering trees, and theme gardens grace this splendid oasis. Docents give free tours daily at 1:30pm, with an additional 10:20am tour on weekends. ⏱ *1 hr. 9th Ave. (at Lincoln Way).* ☎ *415/661-1316. www.strybing.org. Free admission. Mon–Fri 8am–4:30pm; Sat–Sun 10am–5pm.*

⑤ ★★ kids **Japanese Tea Garden.** This exquisite garden features koi ponds, Japanese maples, and bonsai. Highlights include a 1790 bronze Buddha, a Shinto wooden pagoda, a Zen Garden, and an outdoor teahouse. Kids love scaling the Drum Bridge. ⏱ *1 hr. Music Concourse (at Tea Garden Dr., off Concourse Dr. near Martin Luther King*

Jr. Dr.). ☎ 415/752-4227. *Admission $7 adults, $5 seniors & kids 6–12, free for kids under 6. Apr–Sept 9am–5pm; Oct–Mar 9am–4:45pm.*

⑥ ★★★ de Young Museum. Many highlights of this fabulous museum are free. Savor a huge Gerhard Richter painting in the lobby before ascending the observation tower for sweeping city views. Then head out to the sculpture garden for more free art appreciation—including a look skyward from within James Turrell's *Three Gems.* If you still want more, pay admission and be sure to visit the second floor Oceanic art wing. 🕐 *1 hr. 50 Hagiwara Tea Garden Dr.* ☎ *415/750-3600. www.famsf.org/deyoung. Admission $10 adults, $7 seniors, $6 college students with ID & kids 13–17, free for kids under 13. Price includes same-day admission to the California Palace of the Legion of Honor (p 87). Tues–Sun 9:30am–5:15pm; Fri 9:30am–8:45pm.*

The Japanese Tea Garden was created by Makoto Hagiwara, a wealthy Japanese landscape designer.

⑦ kids California Academy of Sciences. Following impressive renovation, this ambitious museum, aquarium, planetarium, and education/research complex reopened in 2008 as a state-of-the-art, ultra-green space. From rooftop wildflowers to splashing penguins and a coral reef ecosystem, the complex is a real showstopper. *55 Concourse Dr., Golden Gate Park.* ☎ *415/379-8000. Admission $30 adults, $25 seniors & kids 12–17, $20 kids 7–11, free for kids under 7. Mon–Sat 9:30am–5pm; Sun 11am–5pm.*

⑧ kids Stow Lake. Tool around this enjoyable man-made lake in a boat. You can also rent a bike here. *Stow Lake Boat House, 50 Stow Lake Dr.* ☎ *415/752-0347. Rowboats $19/hr.; pedal boats $24/hr. 4 passengers/boat max. Wheel Fun Rentals* ☎ *415/752-0347. Bikes $8/hr., $20/half-day, $25/all day.*

⑨ Buffalo Paddock. Visit these enormous mammals, descendants of the original creatures brought here in 1891, when the park also had elk, bears, and goats. *On John F. Kennedy Dr.*

⑩ Dutch Windmill. This was one of two windmills that pumped water to a reservoir on Strawberry Hill in the middle of the park. *Great Hwy. & Fulton St.*

⑪ Beach Chalet Brewery & Restaurant. The food here is secondary to the stunning ocean view. If you aren't hungry, hang out in the bar area to sip hot cocoa or a house-made beer—brewed on-site! On sunny days relax and dine on the lawn behind the building. *1000 Great Hwy. (btw. Fulton & Lincoln Way).* ☎ *415/386-8439. www.beachchalet.com. $$.* ●

The Best Dining

Dining Best Bets

Best **Celebrity-Chef Meal**
★★★ Gary Danko $$$$ *800 North Point St.* (p 104)

Best **Chinese Restaurant**
★ R&G Lounge $$ *631 Kearny St.* (p 111)

Best **Steak Experience**
★★ Epic Roasthouse $$$ *369 Embarcadero* (p 103)

Most **Local Ingredients**
★ Fish & Farm $$$ *339 Taylor St.* (p 104)

Best **Burger Experience**
★ Spruce $$$ *3640 Sacramento St.* (p 113)

Best **Seafood Experience**
★★ Waterbar $$$ *369 Embarcadero* (p 115)

Best **Raw Bar**
★ Bar Crudo $$ *603 Bush St.* (p 99)

Best **Bakery**
★ Tartine Bakery $ *600 Guerrero St.* (p 114)

Best **Dim Sum**
★★ Yank Sing $ *101 Spear St.* (p 116) and *49 Stevenson St.* (p 116)

Best **Pizza**
★★ Pizzeria Delfina $$ *3611 18th St.* (p 111)

Best **French Restaurant**
★★★ La Folie $$$$ *2316 Polk St.* (p 107)

Best **Cafe**
★ Mario's Bohemian Cigar Store $ *556 Columbus Ave.* (p 108)

Most **Worth the Wait**
★★ The Slanted Door $$ *1 Market St.* (p 112)

Previous page: The Ferry Building offers some high quality restaurants in addition to its food shops and farmers' markets.

Most **Romantic Experience**
★★ Café Jacqueline $$$ *1454 Grant Ave.* (p 101)

Best **Belly Dancer Experience**
★ Aziza $$ *5800 Geary Blvd.* (p 99)

Best **Outdoor Dining Area**
★ Park Chalet $$ *1000 Great Hwy.* (p 110)

Best **Neighborhood Italian**
★★ A16 $$ *2355 Chestnut St.* (p 99)

Most **Uplifting Meal**
Café Gratitude $$ *2400 Harrison St. and 1336 9th Ave.* (p 101)

Best **Brunch**
★ Ella's $ *500 Presidio Ave.* (p 103)

Best **Vegetarian**
★★ Greens $$ *Building A, Fort Mason Center* (p 105)

Best **Intimate Restaurant**
★★★ Baker & Banker $$$ *1701 Octavia St.* (p 99)

Best **Burrito**
★ La Taqueria $ *2889 Mission St.* (p 107)

Best **View**
Cliff House $$$ *1090 Point Lobos* (p 102)

Best **Business Lunch**
★★ Wayfare Tavern $$$ *558 Sacramento St.* (p 115)

The Cliff House may be pricey, but it is more than worth it for its view of the Pacific.

The Mission & Environs Dining

San Francisco Dining

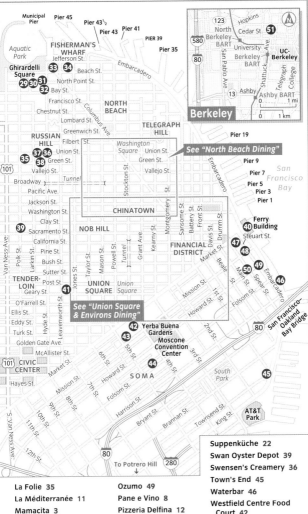

La Folie 35
La Méditerranée 11
Mamacita 3
McCormick & Kuleto's 31
Memphis Minnie's 20
Mijita 47
Okoze 37
One Market 47
Osha 6, 41
Out the Door 42

Ozumo 49
Pane e Vino 8
Pizzeria Delfina 12
Restaurant LuLu 44
Sebo 23
The Slanted Door 47
Sociale 16
SPQR 13
Spruce 1
Straits Café 42

Suppenküche 22
Swan Oyster Depot 39
Swensen's Creamery 36
Town's End 45
Waterbar 46
Westfield Centre Food
  Court 42
'wichcraft 43
Yank Sing 50
ZA Pizza 38
Zuni Café 28

BERKELEY (see inset)
Chez Panisse 51

Union Square & Environs Dining

Pacific Ave.

Jackson St.

Washington St.

Clay St.

Mason St.

Powell St.

Stockton St.

CHINATOWN

Taylor St.

Jones St.

NOB HILL

❶

Sacramento St.

Grace Cathedral

Huntington Park

❷

Joice St.

California St.

Pine St.

Stockton Tunnel

Bush St.

Waverly Pl.

Grant Ave.

❸

Sutter St.

❻ **❺**

Cosmo **❹** Pl.

❼

Shannon St.

Jones St.

Taylor St.

❽

❾

❿

O'Farrell St.

⓫

Ellis St.

Post St.

UNION SQUARE

⓭

Geary St.

Mason St.

Powell St.

⓬

C. Magnin St.

Ellis St.

⓯

⓮

Campton Pl.

Union Square

Maiden

Stockton St.

Market St.

4th St.

Grant Ave.

Michael Mina 26
Millennium 7
Naan-N-Curry 22
Nob Hill Café 1
Osha 28, 34
Perbacco 27
Puccini & Pinetti 12
R & G Lounge 20

Salt House 32
Sam's Grill 17
Sanraku 3
Sears Fine Foods 14
Sellers Markets 29, 30
Tadich Grill 28
Town Hall 33
Wayfare Tavern 19
Yank Sing 31

North Beach Dining

Café Jacqueline 7

Coi 10

Il Pollaio 3

Lichee Garden 2

L'Osteria del Forno 4

Mario's Bohemian Cigar Store 6

Maykadeh 8

Naan-N-Curry 12

Quince 9

Rose Pistola 5

Tommaso's Restaurant 11

Trattoria Contadina 1

Richmond & Sunset Dining

Aziza 3

Burma Superstar 6

Cliff House 1

Park Chalet 2

Park Chow 7

Ton Kiang 4

Troya 5

Restaurants A to Z

★★ A16 MARINA *ITALIAN* A chic crowd comes for superb wood-fired pizza and delectable offerings like ricotta gnocchi and house-cured hams. Its enticing wine list features wines from several Italian regions and small, local vintners. Named for the highway to Naples, Italy. *2355 Chestnut St. (btw. Scott & Divisadero sts.).* ☎ *415/771-2216. Entrees $10–$25. AE, MC, V. Lunch Wed–Fri, dinner daily. Bus: 22, 30x, 30. Map p 94.*

★ Absinthe HAYES VALLEY *FRENCH* This Hayes Valley hot spot is sexy, fun, reasonably priced, and frequented by everyone from the theatergoing crowd to the young and chic. *398 Hayes St. (at Gough St.).* ☎ *415/551-1590. Entrees $14–$30. AE, DC, DISC, MC, V. Lunch, dinner daily. Bus: 21. Map p 94.*

Ana Mandara FISHERMAN'S WHARF *VIETNAMESE* Palm trees, colonial architecture, and Indo-Chinese cuisine transport you to Vietnam. Have the mango soup with durian sorbet for dessert. *891 Beach St. (at Polk St.).* ☎ *415/771-6800. Entrees $22–$40. AE, DC, DISC, MC, V. Lunch Mon–Fri, dinner daily. Bus: 10, 19, 30. Cable car: Powell-Hyde. Map p 94.*

★ Aziza RICHMOND *MOROCCAN* This is my favorite spot for Moroccan food. Delicious North African cuisine is served on decorative plates under colorful arches, with friendly service and weekend belly dancers. *5800 Geary Blvd. (at 22nd Ave.).* ☎ *415/752-2222. Entrees $15–$28. MC, V. Dinner Wed–Mon. Bus: 38. Map p 98.*

B44 FINANCIAL DISTRICT *CATALAN* A Catalan-style bistro serving nine kinds of paella in a European-style pedestrian alley with outdoor tables. *44 Belden Place. (btw. Bush & Pine sts.).* ☎ *415/986-6287. Entrees $16–$22. AE, MC, V. Lunch Mon–Fri, dinner daily. Bus: 15. Streetcar: F. Map p 96.*

★★★ Baker & Banker PACIFIC HEIGHTS *CONTEMPORARY AMERICAN* Co-owners and spouses Jeff Banker (the chef) and Lori Baker (the pastry chef) keep their cozy booths full, thanks to their winning combination of superb cuisine and inviting atmosphere. You will love this restaurant. *1701 Octavia St. (at Bush St.).* ☎ *415/351-2500. Entrees $20–$28. AE, MC, V. Dinner Tues–Sun. Bus: 1, 2, 3, 47, 49, 76, 90. Map p 94.*

★ Bang San Thai TENDERLOIN *THAI* Some of the city's best Thai fare at ridiculously cheap prices. A bigger location just opened up around the corner at 791 O'Farrell St. (☎ 415/928-2772) with the same hours. *505 Jones St. (btw. Geary & O'Farrell sts.).* ☎ *415/440-2610. Entrees $7.95–$11. AE, MC, V. Lunch, dinner daily. Bus: 38. Streetcar: All Muni lines. BART: Powell St. Map p 96.*

★★ Bar Bambino MISSION *ITALIAN* Walking in the opposite direction of the main Mission dining scene, just as you start to doubt if you have the right address, you'll reach this tiny, sleek gem. Excellent seasonal, local fare—including luscious cheeses, meats, salads, and bruschette meant to be shared as you sip one of the 175 top wines. *2931 16th St. (btw. Mission St. & Van Ness Ave.).* ☎ *415/701-8466. Entrees $14–$28. AE, MC, V. Lunch & dinner Tues–Sat, dinner Sun. Bus: 22, 49. BART: to 16th St. Map p 93.*

★ Bar Crudo NOPA *SEAFOOD* SoHo meets NoHo at this hip little restaurant serving exceptional seafood, much of it raw, most of it inventively prepared, and all of it irresistible. *655 Divisadero St. (at Hayes St.).* ☎ *415/409-0679. Small plates: $12–$15. AE, DC, DISC, MC, V. Dinner daily. Bus: 5, 24. Map p 96.*

★★ **Bar Tartine** MISSION DISTRICT *AMERICAN* Sister to the ever-popular Tartine Bakery down the street, so you know the bread's good. Courses run the surf-to-turf gamut from sand dabs in brown butter to a rib steak for two with salt-roast russet potatoes. *561 Valencia St. (btw. 16th & 17th sts.).* ☎ *415/487-1600. Entrees $14–$38. AE, DISC, MC, V. Lunch Sat-Sun, dinner daily. Bus: 26, 33. Streetcar: J. Map p 93.*

★★ **Beretta** MISSION DISTRICT *ITALIAN* Packed since its debut in early 2008, one-of-a-kind pizzas and inventive small plates are what Beretta is best known for. That, and a bar that takes its cocktails seriously. *1199 Valencia St. (at 23rd St.).* ☎ *415/695-1199. Entrees $12–$18. AE, DISC, MC, V. Lunch Sat–Sun, dinner daily. Bus: 26, 33. BART: 24th St. station. Map p 93.*

★ **Betelnut** MARINA *ASIAN* After more than a decade, this Pan-Asian eatery is still a huge draw. Try Cecilia's minced chicken in lettuce cups and the Shanghai steamed dumplings. *2030 Union St. (at Buchanan St.).* ☎ *415/929-8855. Entrees $17–$21. AE, DC, DISC, MC, V. Lunch & dinner daily. Bus: 22, 41, 45. Map p 94.*

★★ **Bix** FINANCIAL DISTRICT *AMERICAN/CALIFORNIA* The martini lifestyle may now be, but it was never out of style in this glamorous retro. Bix is an utterly stylish '30s-era supper club where martinis are always *en vogue.* Chicken hash has been a menu favorite for the past 20 years. *56 Gold St. (btw. Sansome &* *Montgomery sts.).* ☎ *415/433-6300. Entrees $20–$40. AE, DC, DISC, MC, V. Dinner daily. Bus: 15, 30, 41, 45. Map p 96.*

Blue Front Café HAIGHT *MIDDLE EASTERN/BREAKFAST* This enduringly popular neighborhood spot offers terrific lunch specialties like gyros and falafels, as well as plentiful breakfast options, such as the all-American three-egg omelet. *1430 Haight St. (btw. Masonic & Ashbury sts.).* ☎ *415/252-5917. Entrees $5–$10. MC, V. Breakfast, lunch & dinner daily. Bus: 7, 66, 71. Map p 94.*

kids **Blue Mermaid Chowder House** FISHERMAN'S WHARF *AMERICAN* The simple menu of tasty chowders, salads, and a few heartier dishes ranks above other wharf choices. *495 Jefferson St. (at Hyde St.).* ☎ *415/771-2222. Entrees $15–$25. AE, DC, DISC, MC, V. Breakfast, lunch & dinner daily. Bus: 10, 30. Cable car: Powell-Hyde. Map p 94.*

★ **Bocadillos** FINANCIAL DISTRICT *SPANISH/TAPAS* Forget pricey tapas spinoffs. Bocadillos' well-priced authentic vittles are superb. Good luck getting a seat at the communal table, as they don't take reservations. *710 Montgomery St. (at Washington St.).* ☎ *415/982-2622. Small plates $6–$14. AE, DC, DISC, MC, V. Breakfast & lunch Mon–Fri, dinner Mon–Sat. Bus: 12, 15. Map p 96.*

★★ **Boulevard** SOMA *AMERICAN* The grand decor and upscale American cuisine have been attracting SF's most stylish diners for more than a decade. *1 Mission St. (at Steuart St.).* ☎ *415/543-6084. Entrees $29–$42. AE, DC, DISC, MC, V. Lunch Mon–Fri, dinner daily. Bus: 12. Streetcar: F. Map p 94.*

★★★ **Bourbon Steak** UNION SQUARE *STEAKHOUSE* Michael Mina's revamp as a steakhouse in the Westin St. Francis will knock your socks off, as expected. Less expected: It's a good place to drop in for cocktails and $10 side dishes (try black truffle mac and cheese), with complimentary duck fat fries. (*Note*: **Michael Mina** is now at 282 California St.) *335 Powell St. (at Geary St.).* ☎ *415/397-3003. Dinner entrees $16–$72. AE, DC, DISC, MC, V. Dinner daily. Bus: 2, 3, 4, or 38. Cable car: Powell–Mason or Powell–Hyde line. Map p 96.*

★ kids **Burger Joint** HAIGHT *HAMBURGERS* Burgers made with naturally raised Niman's free-range beef are best washed down with one of their awesome milkshakes. They make a decent veggie burger too. *807 Valencia St. (btw. 19th & 20th sts.).* ☎ *415/824-3494. Entrees $7–$9. No credit cards. Lunch & dinner daily.* ☎. *Bus: 14, 49. BART: to 16th St. Map p 94.*

★★ **Burma Superstar** RICHMOND *BURMESE* It'll knock your socks off! After trying the famed tea leaf salad, *nan gyi dok* (creamy coconut chicken on noodles), irresistible coconut rice, or even just one bite of the ultrarich pan-fried bread, you'll wish you had a Burmese kitchen in your home town. No reservations, but the wait is worth it. *309 Clement St. (at 4th Ave.).* ☎ *415/387-2147. Entrees $7.75–$13. AE, MC, V. Lunch & dinner daily. Bus: 2, 4, 38, 44. Map p 98.*

★ **Café Claude** FINANCIAL DISTRICT *FRENCH* Parisian bistro cheer in an enchanting alley-side nook. A very popular lunch spot. *7 Claude Ln. (off Sutter St., btw. Grant Ave. & Kearny St.).* ☎ *415/392-3505. Entrees $14–$27. AE, DC, DISC, MC, V. Lunch Mon–Sat, dinner daily. Bus: 2, 3, 4, 15, 30, 45. Cable car: Powell lines. Map p 96.*

Café Gratitude POTRERO HILL/ SUNSET *VEGAN* Even more creative than the meatless dishes are the names they are given, such as the "I Am Festive Taco Salad" or the "I Am Mahalo Hawaiian Pizza" (the pizza is made with Brazil nut parmesan). After ordering an "I Am Worthy" fruit juice, you're sure to feel uplifted. *2400 Harrison St. (at 20th Ave.).* ☎ *415/824-4652. Entrees $10–$12. Bus: 12, 27. MC, V. Breakfast, lunch & dinner daily. Map p 93.*

★★ **Café Jacqueline** NORTH BEACH *SOUFFLES* Consistently voted SF's most romantic restaurant. That said, even "just friends" will enjoy the artful, all-soufflé menu. *1454 Grant Ave. (btw. Green & Union sts.).* ☎ *415/981-5565. Soufflés for two $30–$50. AE, DISC, MC, V. Dinner*

It may look like a tourist trap on first glance, but locals are fans of the food and the kitschy party vibe at Cha Cha Cha's on Haight Street.

Chez Panisse in nearby Berkeley is considered a birthplace of California cuisine.

Wed–Sun. Bus: 15, 30, 41. Cable car: Powell-Mason. Map p 98.

★ **Canteen** UNION SQUARE *CALIFORNIA/MEDITERRANEAN* This tiny restaurant accommodates guests in two seatings per evening. You can feel the chef's love in any one of the amazing dishes from the weekly-changing menu.*817 Sutter St. (at Jones St.). ☎ 415/928-8870. Entrees $20–$25. AE, MC, V. Lunch Wed–Fri, dinner Tues–Sat, brunch Sat–Sun. Bus: 2, 3,4, 27. Map p 96.*

Cha Cha Cha's HAIGHT *CARIBBEAN* Tapas like Cajun shrimp and spicy Caribbean entrees are jazzed up with tropical decor and festive Latin rhythms. The wait is long, but the sangrias are strong. *1801 Haight St. (at Shrader St.). ☎ 415/386-7670. Lunch & dinner daily. Bus: 7, 66, 71. 2327 Mission St. (btw. 19th & 20th sts.). ☎ 415/824-1502. Dinner daily. Bus: 14, 49. BART: to 16th St. Entrees $13–$16; tapas $6–$9. MC, V. Map p 94.*

Chez Panisse BERKELEY *CALIFORNIA* Alice Waters' famous cooking is the definition of California Cuisine. The prix-fixe menu changes nightly, accordingly to what is fresh and available, and the price changes accordingly. If you can't get a

reservation at the restaurant, try the "cafe" upstairs, which is really like a second restaurant. *1517 Shattuck Ave. (btw. Cedar & Vine sts.). ☎ 510/548-5525. Restaurant prix-fixe dinners $55–$85. Cafe entrees $17–$29. AE, DC, DISC, MC, V. Lunch, dinner Mon–Sat. BART: Downtown Berkeley. Map p 95.*

Chow CASTRO *AMERICAN* Local, organic ingredients are behind the comforting victuals like chicken pot-pie, wood-fired pizzas, and roasted meats. Relaxed decor and moderate prices, too. *215 Church St. (at Market St.). ☎ 415/552-2469. Entrees $9–$15. MC, V. Breakfast, lunch & dinner daily. Bus: 8, 22, 37. Muni: J, K, L, M. Map p 93.*

★ **Citizen Cake** PACIFIC HEIGHTS *CALIFORNIA* What started as a bakery is now a pre-show destination for the symphony, opera, and ballet crowd. Leave room for dessert. *2125 Fillmore St. (at California St.). ☎ 415/861-2228. Entrees $20–$26. AE, MC, V. Lunch & dinner daily, brunch Sat–Sun. Bus: 21. Map p 94.*

Cliff House SUNSET *AMERICAN* This place is literally on a cliff overlooking the ocean. In the bistro, breathtaking views and charming early-20th-century decor make up for the high-priced basic American fare—like $16 fish and chips. You can also splurge at Sutro's restaurant in the same building, which has a more upscale menu, modern decor, and huge windows showing off the sea. *1090 Point Lobos Ave. (just west of 48th Ave. Geary Blvd. turns into Point Lobos Ave. after 43rd Ave.). ☎ 415/386-3330. Bistro entrees $13–$26. Breakfast, lunch & dinner daily. Sutro's entrees $29–$40. Lunch & dinner daily. AE, DC, DISC, MC, V. Bus: 18, 38. Map p 98.*

★★★ **Coi** FINANCIAL DISTRICT *CALIFORNIA* Lusciously elegant food in serene surroundings. Chef Daniel

Peterson changes the multicourse menu daily; the veggie options are as sublime as the rest of the dishes. *373 Broadway (btw. Montgomery & Sansome sts.).* ☎ *415/393-9000. Dinner $145 ($240 w/wine pairing). AE, MC, V. Dinner Tues–Sat. Bus: 10, 12. Map p 98.*

★★ **Delfina** MISSION *ITALIAN* Locals love this first-rate Tuscan fare with a cool, vibrant ambience. If you can't get a table, head to Pizzeria Delfina next door. *3621 18th St. (btw. Dolores & Guerrero sts.).* ☎ *415/552-4055. Entrees $18–$26. MC, V. Dinner daily. Bus: 26, 33. BART: to 16th St. Map p 93.*

★ kids **Dolores Park Cafe** MISSION *AMERICAN/BREAKFAST* Enjoy healthy sandwiches or a simple latte on the sunny deck across from Dolores Park. *501 Dolores St. (at 18th St.).* ☎ *415/621-2936. Sandwiches/ salads $5–$7.50. AE, MC, V. Breakfast, lunch & dinner daily. Fri music nights until 10pm. Bus: 33. BART: to 16th St. Map p 93.*

★★ **Dosa** MISSION/JAPANTOWN *SOUTHERN INDIAN* There's always a hip and happy crowd here; it's happy for the mouthwatering dishes based on Indian *dosas*, crispy flat breads served with a variety of spicy, succulent fillings. *995 Valencia St. (at 21st St.).* ☎ *415/642-3672. Dinner daily, brunch Sat–Sun. Bus: 33. BART: to 24th St. 1700 Fillmore St. (at Post St.).* ☎ *415/441-3672. Lunch & dinner daily. Bus: 2, 3, 4, 22, 38, 38L. Entrees $10–$15. AE, DISC, MC, V. Map p 93.*

Dottie's True Blue Cafe UNION SQUARE *AMERICAN/BREAKFAST* Ample portions of the best cornmeal pancakes, eggs, and gourmet sausages in the city. Lunch features salads and burgers. Kitschy decor. Expect to wait in line on weekends. *522 Jones St. (btw. Geary & O'Farrell sts.).* ☎ *415/885-2767. Entrees $5–$11. DISC, MC, V. Breakfast &*

lunch Wed–Mon. Bus: 2, 3, 4, 27, 38. Cable car: Powell lines. Map p 96.

★ kids **Dragon Well** MARINA *CHINESE* Here's Chinese with a California bend: super fresh ingredients and less oil. Terrific! *2142 Chestnut St. (btw. Pierce & Steiner sts.).* ☎ *415/474-6888. Entrees $8–$12. MC, V. Lunch & dinner daily. Bus: 22, 30. Map p 94.*

★ **Ella's** PRESIDIO HEIGHTS *AMERICAN/BREAKFAST* SF's best brunch, with a wait to prove it. Serving fresh breads, awesome pancakes, and appetizing omelets. *500 Presidio Ave. (at California St.).* ☎ *415/441-5669. Entrees $9.50–$13. AE, DISC, MC, V. Breakfast & lunch Mon–Fri, brunch Sat–Sun. Bus: 1, 3, 43. Map p 94.*

★★ **Epic Roasthouse** EMBARCADERO *STEAKHOUSE* Famed SF restaurateur Pat Kuleto's worked his usual magic at this upscale, updated steakhouse designed to look like a fantastical pumphouse, all with a view of the Bay Bridge. *369 Embarcadero (btw. Folsom & Harrison sts.).* ☎ *415/369-9955. Entrees $19–$42. AE, DC, DISC, MC, V. Lunch Mon–Fri, dinner daily, brunch Sat–Sun. Bus: 1, 12, 14, 41. Streetcar: F. BART: Embarcadero. Map p 94.*

What is California cuisine? It can fuse a variety of ethnic styles, but it starts with seasonal, local, and (ideally) organic produce.

★★★ Farina Focaccia & Cucina Italiana

MISSION ITALIAN It's all *farina* (wheat in Italian) here: A former bakery converted into one swanky restaurant, serving savory breads and some of the best pasta you'll ever eat. The salads, meats, and fish dishes are also divine. *3560 18th St. (btw. Valencia & Guerrero sts.).* ☎ *415/565-0360. Entrees $18–$34. AE, DC, DISC, MC, V. Dinner daily, brunch Sun. Bus: 33, 49. BART: to 16th St. Map p 93.*

★ Fish & Farm

UNION SQUARE NEW AMERICAN The emphasis here is on local foods, as much sourced from within a 100-mile (160km) radius as possible. And the dishes created with Northern California's bounty of produce, meats, and seafood are amazing. This place is small, so call to reserve. *339 Taylor St. (btw. O'Farrell & Ellis sts.).* ☎ *415/474-3474. Entrees $17–$28. AE, DC, DISC, MC, V. Dinner Mon–Sat. Bus: 27, 38. Streetcar: F. Cable car: Powell lines. Map p 96.*

★★★ Fleur de Lys

UNION SQUARE FRENCH Regal decor, unparalleled service, and superlative

The presentation at Fleur de Lys is so lovely that you may hesitate to take a bite.

French cuisine from celebrated SF chef Hubert Keller. This is the city's most traditional and classic French affair. *777 Sutter St. (btw. Jones & Taylor sts.).* ☎ *415/673-7779. Prix-fixe menu from $70. AE, DC, MC, V. Dinner Mon–Sat. Bus: 2, 3, 4, 27. Map p 96.*

★★ Flour + Water

SOMA ITALIAN Pizzas from F+W's Italian wood-fired 900-degree oven take exactly 2 minutes to cook. Small, folksy, and unassuming (think menus on butcher paper), this place has been packed since the day it opened in 2009. *2401 Harrison St. (at 20th St.).* ☎ *415/826-7000. Entrees $13–$24. AE, MC, V. Dinner daily. Bus: 14, 14L, 27, 12. Map p 93.*

★ Foreign Cinema

MISSION CALIFORNIA/MEDITERRANEAN Dine inside in the chic digs or outside under the stars (among abundant heat lamps). Oscar-quality films are projected onto the outdoor courtyard wall. A lengthy oyster list, fresh salads, and hearty entrees like a grilled natural rib-eye satisfy all tastes. *2534 Mission St. (btw. 21st & 22nd sts.).* ☎ *415/648-7600. Entrees $18–$36. AE, MC, V. Dinner daily, brunch Sat–Sun. Bus: 14, 49. BART to 24th St. Map p 93.*

★ Fresca

PACIFIC HEIGHTS PERUVIAN Exemplary ceviche and inspired Peruvian fare like braised pork in adobo sauce keep Fresca jampacked. *2114 Fillmore St. (at California St.).* ☎ *415/447-2668. Entrees $13–$24. AE, MC, V. Lunch Mon–Fri, dinner daily. Bus: 1, 22. Map p 94.*

★★★ Gary Danko

FISHERMAN'S WHARF CALIFORNIA One of the best restaurants in the country—with a sleek interior, flawless service, outstanding wines, and a superlative menu that changes daily. Reserve 4 weeks ahead, or try your luck at the bar. *800 North Point St. (at Hyde St.).* ☎ *415/749-2060.*

Prix-fixe menu from $68. AE, DC, DISC, MC, V. Dinner daily. Bus: 10, 30. Cable car: Powell-Hyde. Map p 94.

kids Ghirardelli Soda Fountain & Chocolate Shop FISHERMAN'S WHARF *ICE CREAM* The ever-present line attests to consistently great chocolate. *Ghirardelli Sq., 900 North Point St. (at Larkin St.).* ☎ *415/771-4903. Desserts $5–$9. AE, DISC, MC, V. Mon–Thurs 9am–11pm; Fri–Sat 9am–midnight; Sun 10am–11pm. Bus: 10, 30. Cable car: Powell-Hyde. Map p 94.*

★ **Grand Café** UNION SQUARE *CALIFORNIA/FRENCH* A majestic Beaux Arts interior and inspired dishes attract the theater crowd for dinner or drinks. *501 Geary St. (at Taylor St.).* ☎ *415/292-0101. Entrees $13–$28 lunch, $18–$34 dinner; Petit Café $10–$22. AE, DC, DISC, MC, V. Breakfast & lunch Mon–Fri, dinner daily, brunch Sat–Sun. Bus: 2, 3, 4, 27, 38. Cable car: Powell lines. Map p 94.*

Great Eastern Restaurant CHINATOWN *CHINESE* Order your ultrafresh seafood from the fish tanks and you'll eat well. Don't be

The main dining room at the Grand Café is set in an elegant turn-of-the-last-century ballroom.

steered to more familiar Chinese dishes. *649 Jackson St. (btw. Grant Ave. & Kearny St.).* ☎ *415/986-2500. Entrees $10–$32. AE, MC, V. Lunch & dinner daily. Bus: 12, 15, 30, 45. Map p 96.*

★★ **Greens** MARINA *VEGETARIAN* Executive chef Annie Somerville's fabulous flavors and stunning views will impress even dedicated carnivores. *Bldg. A, Fort Mason*

Gary Danko won the prestigious James Beard Foundation's "Best New Restaurant" award in 2000—and still lives up to the acclaim.

You don't have to be a vegetarian to enjoy Greens Restaurant.

Center (by Buchanan & Marina sts.). ☎ 415/771-6222. Entrees $16–$23; Sat prix fixe $48. AE, DISC, MC, V. Lunch Tues–Sat, dinner daily, brunch Sun. Bus: 28, 30. Map p 94.

Hayes Street Grill HAYES VALLEY *CALIFORNIA/SEAFOOD* Very fresh fish or naturally raised meats simply prepared with the finest ingredients. 320 Hayes St. (btw. Franklin & Gough sts.). ☎ 415/863-5545. Entrees $21–$27. AE, DC, DISC, MC, V. Lunch Mon–Fri, dinner daily. Bus: 21. Map p 94.

★ Hog Island Oyster Co. EMBARCADERO *SEAFOOD* Fans of fresh, local oysters will be in slurping nirvana at this smart little seafood spot inside the Ferry Plaza Marketplace. On weekdays, happy hour features $1 oysters and $3.50 pints of beer. Ferry Building Marketplace, 1 Ferry Building no. 11-1 (at Embarcadero & Market St.). ☎ 415/391-7117. Entrees $6–$17. AE, MC, V. Lunch, early dinner daily. Bus: All Market St. buses. Streetcar: F, N-Judah line. Map p 94.

Il Pollaio NORTH BEACH *CHICKEN* Fragrant roast chicken or other meat, salads, and a few sides are all you'll find at this simple, tasty eatery. 555 Columbus Ave. (btw. Union & Green sts.). ☎ 415/362-7727. Entrees $6.95–$17. DISC, MC, V. Lunch & dinner Mon–Sat. Bus: 15,

30, 41. Cable car: Powell-Mason. Map p 98.

★★ Incanto NOE VALLEY *ITALIAN* The most difficult part of eating at this rustic Italian outpost in Noe Valley is simply deciding what to choose off of chef Chris Cosentino's wildly inventive menu: He highlights seasonal produce, handmade pastas, and a whole lot of meat. 1550 Church St. (at Duncan St. btw. 27th and 28th sts.). ☎ 415/641-4500. Entrees $18–$25. AE, DC, DISC, MC,

Chef Chris Cosentino helms Incanto in Noe Valley and Boccalone in the Ferry Building.

V. Dinner daily. Subway: J to 24th St. Map p 93.

★ **Indian Oven** HAIGHT *INDIAN* There's always a line for the formidable curries, tandoori specials, and naan breads. *233 Fillmore St. (btw. Haight & Waller sts.).* ☎ *415/626-1628. Entrees $8–$19. AE, DC, DISC, MC, V. Lunch, dinner daily. Bus: 6, 7, 22, 66, 71. Map p 94.*

kids **In-N-Out Burger** FISHER-MAN'S WHARF *HAMBURGERS* This popular California chain serves its burgers on toasted buns with extra-thin fries. *333 Jefferson St. (btw. Leavenworth & Jones sts.).* ☎ *800/786-1000. Entrees $1.65–$2.80. No credit cards. Lunch & dinner daily. Bus: 10, 30. Streetcar: F. Map p 94.*

Isobune JAPANTOWN *JAPANESE/ SUSHI* Pluck sushi off boats on an aquatic conveyer belt. Come when it's busy; at off hours the *maguro* is limply waiting to be fished. *1737 Post St. (in the Japan Center).* ☎ *415/ 563-1030. 2 pieces of sushi $1.80– $3.75. MC, V. Lunch & dinner daily. Bus: 38. Map p 94.*

★★ **Jardiniere** HAYES VALLEY *FRENCH* Symphony and opera patrons complete a night on the town with dinner at this affluent Civic Center staple. *300 Grove St. (at Franklin St.).* ☎ *415/861-5555. Entrees $26–$40. AE, DC, DISC, MC, V. Dinner daily. Bus: 19, 21. Map p 94.*

Juban Yakiniku House JAPAN-TOWN *JAPANESE* Grill your own thin slices of beef, chicken, and shrimp right at the table. *1581 Webster St. (in the Japan Center).* ☎ *415/ 776-5822. Entrees $7.50–$20. AE, MC, V. Lunch Fri–Sun, dinner daily. Bus: 38. Map p 94.*

★★ **Kokkari** FINANCIAL DISTRICT *GREEK* Superb seasonal dishes and Greek classics prepared with an expert California touch—all in a warm, upscale setting. *200 Jackson St. (at Front St.).* ☎ *415/981-0983. Entrees $19–$39. AE, DC, DISC, MC, V. Lunch Mon–Fri, dinner Mon–Sat. Bus: 12, 15, 41, 83. Map p 96.*

★ **kids** **La Corneta Taqueria** MISSION *MEXICAN* Stand in line to choose the fillings for your mammoth burrito—or order a baby burrito you can actually finish. *2731 Mission St. (btw. 23rd & 24th sts.).* ☎ *415/643-7001. Entrees $3–$12. MC, V. Lunch & dinner daily. Bus: 14, 49. BART: to 24th St. Map p 93.*

★★★ **La Folie** RUSSIAN HILL *FRENCH* My favorite French restaurant in the city. Celebrity chef/owner Roland Passot's seared foie gras alone is worth the visit. The five-course tasting menu is a journey to culinary heaven. *2316 Polk St. (btw. Green & Union sts.).* ☎ *415/776-5577. Tasting menus $70, $80, and $90. AE, DC, DISC, MC, V. Dinner Mon–Sat. Bus: 19, 41, 45, 47, 49, 76. Map p 94.*

La Méditerranée PACIFIC HEIGHTS AND NOE VALLEY *MEDITERRANEAN* A casual, narrow storefront serving up satisfying hummus, stuffed grape leaves, and the like. The chicken cilicia in phyllo dough is a winner. *2210 Fillmore St. (at Sacramento St.).* ☎ *415/ 921-2956. Bus: 1, 22. 288 Noe St. (at Market St.).* ☎ *415/431-7210. Bus: 6, 7, 66, 71. Streetcar: F. Entrees $7.25– $14. AE, MC, V. Lunch & dinner Mon– Sat. Map p 95.*

★ **kids** **La Taqueria** MISSION *MEXICAN* SF's best taqueria has tiled floors, a colorful mural, devoted fans, and an impressive selection of taco and burrito fillings, including beef tongue, veggie, and chorizo. *2889 Mission St. (at 25th St.).* ☎ *415/285-7117. Entrees $3.50–$5.25. No credit cards. Lunch & dinner daily. Bus: 14, 22, 49. BART: to 24th St. Map p 93.*

Laurel Court Restaurant NOB HILL *AFTERNOON TEA* This opulent, domed dining room in the grand Fairmont Hotel offers a lovely afternoon tea service—a pleasant splurge after a day of sightseeing or shopping at nearby Union Square. *950 Mason St. (at California St.).* ☎ *415/772-5260. Tea service: $32–$47. AE, DISC, MC, V. Tea daily 2:30–4:30pm. Bus: 1. Cable car: California line. Map p 96.*

Le Colonial UNION SQUARE *VIET-NAMESE* Swanky colonial-style decor. Join the locals for appetizers and drinks upstairs in the sultry lounge. *20 Cosmo Place (off Post St., btw. Jones & Taylor sts.).* ☎ *415/931-3600. Entrees $12–$34. AE, DC, MC, V. Dinner daily. Bus: 2, 3, 4, 27, 38. Map p 96.*

★ **Lichee Garden** NORTH BEACH *CHINESE* Located next to Chinatown, the food's very authentic—as long as you avoid the English menu. Lunch specials aren't translated, so ask for help. I suggest the crispy chicken with shrimp chips. *1416 Powell St. (at Broadway).* ☎ *415/397-2290. Entrees $6.50–$9.95. MC, V. Dim sum, lunch & dinner daily. Bus: 12, 30, 45. Cable car: Powell-Mason. Map p 98.*

★★ **Limòn** MISSION *PERUVIAN* Peruvian is all the rage, and the *muy bueno* ceviche dishes at this hip Mission restaurant show you why. The Picante de Mariscos is divine. *524 Valencia St. (btw. 16th & 17th sts.).* ☎ *415/252-0918. Entrees $18–$27. AE, MC, V. Lunch Mon, Wed–Fri, dinner Tue-Sun. Bus: 14, 22, 33, 49. BART: to 16th St. Map p 93.*

★★ **L'Osteria del Forno** NORTH BEACH *ITALIAN* There are always as many people lined up outside as seated inside the cozy dining room that serves some of North Beach's best Italian. *519 Columbus Ave. (btw. Union & Green sts.).* ☎ *415/982-1124.*

Entrees $11–$13. No credit cards. Lunch & dinner Wed–Mon. Bus: 15, 30, 41, 45. Cable car: Powell-Mason. Map p 98.

Lovejoy's Tea Room CASTRO *AFTERNOON TEA* Enjoy crustless sandwiches, scones, and a bountiful tea selection. Lovejoy's doubles as an antiques shop, so go ahead and buy the tea set you're sipping from. *1351 Church St. (at Clipper St.).* ☎ *415/648-5895. Tea service $10–$22. MC, V. Tea service Wed–Sun 11am–5:30pm. Muni: Castro. Map p 93.*

★ **Mamacita** MARINA *MEXICAN* Ultrafresh, locally sourced dishes marry the flavors of Mexico with a new Californian sensibility; think cornmeal beer-battered mahimahi tacos with red cabbage–mango slaw or pulled pork tacos with grilled corn and avocado. The festive bar draws a trendy crowd, which comes in for the top-grade tequilas and other Latin drinks. *2317 Chestnut St. (at Divisadero St.).* ☎ *415/346-8494. Entrees $10–$18. AE, MC, V. Dinner daily. Bus: 22, 30. Map p 94.*

★ **Mario's Bohemian Cigar Store** NORTH BEACH *ITALIAN* This century-old corner cafe still cranks out the best cappuccino in the United States. The meatball focaccia sandwich and a slice of Mario's house-made ricotta cheesecake is just the picker-upper you needed. And no, they don't sell cigars. *566 Columbus Ave. (at Union St.).* ☎ *415/362-0536. Sandwiches $7.75–$11. MC, V. Lunch, dinner daily. Bus: 15, 30, 41, 45. Map p 98.*

Maykadeh NORTH BEACH *PERSIAN* Local Iranians seek Maykadeh for refined Persian fare, like eggplant with mint garlic sauce and lamb filet marinated in lime, yogurt, and saffron. *470 Green St. (btw. Grant Ave. & Kearny St.).* ☎ *415/362-8286. Entrees $14–$27. MC, V. Lunch & dinner daily.*

Bus: 15, 30, 41, 45. Cable car: Powell-Mason. Map p 98.

McCormick & Kuleto's FISHERMAN'S WHARF *SEAFOOD* The stellar view, elegant decor, and well-prepared fish compensate for the massive space and overly long menu. *900 North Point St. (in Ghirardelli Sq. at Hyde St.).* ☎ *415/929-1730. Entrees $13–$35. AE, DC, DISC, MC, V. Lunch & dinner daily. Bus: 10, 30. Cable car: Powell-Hyde. Map p 94.*

★★ Medjool MISSION *MEDITERRANEAN* This tall, airy space is usually packed with trendy diners—often in festive groups—sharing scrumptious southern European, North African, and Middle Eastern tapas. Even if it's just two of you, it's worth coming in for dishes like the lamb and fig tagine. *2522 Mission St. (btw. 21st and 22nd sts.).* ☎ *415/550-9055. Small plates $6–$19. AE, DISC, MC, V. Dinner daily. Bus: 14, 49. BART: to 24th St. Map p 93.*

★ Memphis Minnie's HAIGHT *BARBECUE* SF's best BBQ serves up slow-cooked brisket and succulent pulled pork with three kinds of sauce and a roll of paper towels at every table. *576 Haight St. (at Steiner St.).* ☎ *415/864-8461. Entrees $7.95–$14.*

AE, MC, V. Lunch & dinner Tues–Sun. Bus: 6, 7, 22, 66, 71. Map p 95.

★★ Mijita EMBARCADERO *MEXICAN* A celebrated SF chef offers inexpensive Mexican food made with top-quality, local ingredients. Order your braised pork *carnitas* or *queso fundido* at the counter and enjoy it outside with a view of the bay and maybe a cold beer, too. *1 Ferry Building no. 44 (at the Embarcadero & Market St.).* ☎ *415/399-0814. Entrees $4–$5. AE, MC, V. Lunch & early dinner Mon–Fri, breakfast, lunch & early dinner Sat, breakfast & lunch Sun. Streetcar: F. BART/ Muni: Embarcadero. Map p 94.*

Millennium UNION SQUARE *VEGAN* No animal products are used to make everything from vegetarian sausages to truffled vegetable gratin. This place proves that a meatless menu doesn't mean you have to sacrifice taste. *580 Geary St. (at Jones St.).* ☎ *415/345-3900. Entrees $20–$24. AE, DC, MC, V. Dinner daily. Bus: 2, 3, 4, 27, 38. Map p 96.*

Naan-N-Curry NORTH BEACH *INDIAN/PAKISTANI* Good, cheap Indian/Pakistani food: tandoori-oven meats, savory curries, and warm

Shop for produce or just sample delicious foods at the Ferry Building's Farmers Market. See p 12.

naan breads. *533 Jackson St. (at Columbus Ave.).* ☎ *415/693-0499. Entrees $5–$10. MC, V. Lunch & dinner daily. Bus: 15, 41. Map p 96.*

★ **Nob Hill Café** NOB HILL *ITALIAN* For down-home ambience (and prices) amidst the posh Nob Hill alternatives, squeeze into this neighborhood nook. *1152 Taylor St. (btw. Sacramento & Clay sts.).* ☎ *415/776-6500. Entrees $10–$15. DC, DISC, MC, V. Lunch & dinner daily. Bus: 1. Cable car: California line. Map p 96.*

★★ **Okoze** RUSSIAN HILL *JAPANESE* The owner shops at the fish market 5 mornings a week for ultrafresh fish. Sit at the counter and ask the chef what's best; opt for sashimi and simple sushi, as the rolls are less inspired. *1207 Union St. (at Hyde St.).* ☎ *415/567-3397. 2 pieces sushi $5–$12. AE, DC, DISC, MC, V. Dinner daily. Bus: 41, 45. Cable car: Powell-Hyde. Map p 94.*

★ **One Market** FINANCIAL DISTRICT *CALIFORNIA* It's all big here: the space, windows, view, prices, flavor, and the farm-fresh menu. Around happy hour, a corporate crowd convenes at the bar. *1 Market St. (at Steuart St.).* ☎ *415/777-5577. Entrees $19–$29. AE, DC, DISC, MC, V. Lunch Mon–Fri, dinner Mon–Sat. Bus: 20, 41. Streetcar: F. BART/Muni: Embarcadero. Map p 94.*

★★ **Osha** COW HOLLOW/EMBARCADERO/SOMA/MISSION/TENDERLOIN *THAI* We used to take out from the funky Tenderloin branch— but this place is so good and the quality so high there are now several very snazzy locations in which to enjoy the best Thai in town. *2033 Union St. (at Buchanan St.).* ☎ *415/ 567-6742. Bus: 41, 45. 4 Embarcadero Center (at Clay and Drumm sts.).* ☎ *415/788-6742. Bus: 1, 41. 149 2nd St. (btw. Mission & Howard sts.).* ☎ *415/278-9991. Bus: 10, 14.*

819 Valencia St. (btw. 19th and 20th sts.). ☎ *415/826-7738. Bus: 14, 49. BART: to 24th St. 696 Geary St. (at Leavenworth St.).* ☎ *415/673-2368. Bus: 2, 3, 4, 27, 38. Entrees $8–$18. AE, DISC, MC, V. Lunch & dinner daily (no lunch Sun at 2nd St. & Embarcadero locations; open to 3am Fri–Sat at Geary St. location). Map p 94.*

★ **Out the Door** SOMA *VIETNAMESE* Couldn't get a reservation at the Slanted Door? Grab take-out platters here or in the Ferry Building. *Westfield San Francisco Centre, 865 Market St., Concourse Level (btw. 4th and 5th sts.).* ☎ *415/541-9913. Entrees $8–$16. AE, MC, V. Lunch & dinner daily. BART/Muni: Powell. Bus: 5, 7, 9, 21, 71. Map p 94.*

Ozumo SOMA *JAPANESE* Ultrahip diners come to this sleek space for fresh sushi, creative entrees, and excellent sake. *161 Steuart St. (btw. Mission & Howard sts.).* ☎ *415/882-1333. Entrees $25–$35. AE, DC, DISC, MC, V. Dinner daily. Bus: 12. BART/ Muni: Embarcadero. Map p 94.*

★ **Pane e Vino** COW HOLLOW *ITALIAN* Exceptionally prepared, unfussy Tuscan dishes keep locals coming back for more. *1715 Union St. (at Gough St.).* ☎ *415/346-2111. Entrees $14–$29. AC, MC, V. Dinner daily. Bus: 41, 45. Map p 94.*

★ **kids Park Chalet** SUNSET *CALIFORNIA* A glass ceiling and glass walls that open onto a garden patio make this the nicest outdoor space in town, even if you're inside. Food is decent if not fabulous, but this is a great standby at the western end of Golden Gate Park. This place is an extension of the Beach Chalet (p 90). *1000 Great Hwy. (at Fulton St.).* ☎ *415/386-8439. Entrees $10– $24. AE, MC, V. Lunch & dinner daily, brunch Sat–Sun. Bus: 5, 18, 31, 38. Map p 98.*

broccoli raab with ricotta, or house-made fennel sausage. A second location is in Pacific Heights. *3611 18th St. (at Guerrero St.).* ☎ *415/437-6800. Pizzas $10–$17. MC, V. Lunch & dinner Tues–Sat, dinner Mon. Bus: 14, 33, 49. BART: to 16th St. Map p 93. 2nd location: 2406 California St. (at Fillmore St.). Lunch & dinner daily. Bus: 1, 3, 22. Map p 94.*

kids Puccini & Pinetti UNION SQUARE *ITALIAN* Kids design their own pizzas, while parents order classics like eggplant parmigiana. *129 Ellis St. (at Cyril Magnin St., btw. Mason & Powell sts.).* ☎ *415/392-5500. Entrees $12–$16 lunch, $14–$20 dinner. AE, DC, DISC, MC, V. Breakfast, lunch, dinner daily. Bus: 27, 31. Streetcar: F. Cable car: Powell lines. Map p 96.*

★★ **Quince** PACIFIC HEIGHTS *ITALIAN* Chef Michael Tusk's nightly-changing Italian-inspired menu of seasonally-shifting dishes keep the reservations booked. *470 Pacific Ave. (at Montgomery St.).* ☎ *415/775-8500. Entrees $16–$39. AE, MC, V. Dinner daily. Bus: 2, 3, 4. Map p 98.*

★ **kids R & G Lounge** CHINATOWN *CHINESE* This is SF's best Chinatown restaurant, but it helps to know what to order. The salt-and-pepper crab is the signature dish. If they have live prawns in the tank, try them split in half with minced garlic. I also recommend the filet mignon beef with snow peas and XO sauce, and Fu King fried rice (a risotto-ish starch). Try to sit upstairs. *631 Kearny St. (at Commercial St.).* ☎ *415/982-7877. Entrees $10–$50. AE, DC, DISC, MC, V. Lunch & dinner daily. Bus: 15, 30. Map p 96.*

Restaurant LuLu SOMA *CALIFORNIA/FRENCH* Savor excellent roasted meats and seasonal items like prawn risotto with summer squash in a busy, spacious dining room. *816 Folsom St. (btw. 4th & 5th*

A must for foodies: Friday night's Off the Grid food truck extravaganza, 5 to 10 pm at Fort Mason, features the Creme Brulee Cart and over 30 other vendors. See offthegridsf.com.

★ **kids Park Chow** SUNSET *AMERICAN* Like Chow (p 102) in the Castro, Park Chow balances eclectic American fare from Cobb salads to pasta to sandwich specials, a lively atmosphere, and amazing value. *1240 9th Ave. (btw. Lincoln Way & Irving St.).* ☎ *415/665-9912. Entrees $9–$14. MC, V. Breakfast Mon–Fri, lunch & dinner daily, brunch Sat–Sun. Bus: 6, 43, 44. Muni: N. Map p 98.*

★★ **Perbacco** FINANCIAL DISTRICT *ITALIAN* Stockholm native Staffan Terje makes some of the best Italian food in town, and he's not afraid to push the limits for what cuts of meat he puts on his outstanding, oft-changing menu. *230 California St. (btw. Battery & Front sts.).* ☎ *415/955-0663. Entrees $15–$28. AE, DC, DISC, MC, V. Lunch Mon–Fri, dinner Mon-Sat. Train: F, J, K, L, M, N to Embarcadero. Map p 96.*

★★ **Pizzeria Delfina** MISSION/PACIFIC HEIGHTS *ITALIAN* The owners of Delfina (p 102) have graced us with some of the best gourmet pizza anywhere. Toppings might include buffalo mozzarella,

sts.). ☎ 415/495-5775. *Entrees $17–$30. AE, DC, DISC, MC, V. Lunch & dinner daily. Bus: 30, 45. Map p 94.*

★ **Rose Pistola** NORTH BEACH *ITALIAN* Come for the always-tasty antipasti and the bustling scene. The entrees, however, are not as consistent. Ask for a sidewalk table. *532 Columbus Ave. (btw. Green & Union sts.). ☎ 415/399-0499. Entrees $19–$36. AE, DC, DISC, MC, V. Lunch & dinner daily. Bus: 15, 30, 41. Cable car: Powell–Mason. Map p 98.*

★ **Salt House** SOMA *NEW AMERICAN* SoMa and Financial District types love this chic, neo-industrial spot that invites diners to eat anywhere (dining room, bar, communal table, counter) anytime (they serve 'til midnight on weekends). The roasted pork Cubano sandwich is a don't-miss. *545 Mission St. (btw. 1st and 2nd sts.). ☎ 415/543-8900. Entrees $20–$27. AE, MC, V. Lunch Mon–Fri, dinner daily. Bus: 10, 14, 76. Map p 96.*

Sam's Grill FINANCIAL DISTRICT *ITALIAN/SEAFOOD* Grab a comfy booth and order charbroiled fish, roasted chicken, or simple pasta dishes at one of SF's oldest restaurants. *374 Bush St. (at Belden Place, btw. Kearny & Montgomery sts.). ☎ 415/421-0594. Entrees $11–$29. AE, DC, DISC, MC, V. Lunch & dinner Mon–Fri. Bus: 2, 3, 4, 30, 45. Streetcar: F. Map p 96.*

★ **Sanraku** UNION SQUARE *JAPANESE* Come in for some of the freshest sushi in town. Decor is minimal, but the fish is excellent and the service friendly. Highchairs and boosters are available. *704 Sutter St. (at Taylor St.). ☎ 415/771-0803. (Additional location in the Sony Metreon food court.) Entrees $11–$25. AE, DC, DISC, MC, V. Lunch & dinner daily. Bus: 2, 3, 4, 27. Map p 96.*

kids **Sears Fine Foods** UNION SQUARE *AMERICAN/BREAKFAST* This old-fashioned diner serves 18 dollar-size Swedish pancakes per serving, in addition to other hearty breakfast fare. At other times of day, big sandwiches and staples like fish and chips are on the menu. *439 Powell St. (at Sutter St.). ☎ 415/986-0700. Breakfast $8–$12; dinner entrees $18–$29. AE, DC, MC, V. Breakfast, lunch & dinner daily. Bus: 2, 3, 4, 38. Cable car: Powell–Mason, Powell–Hyde line. Map p 96.*

★★★ **Sebo** HAYES VALLEY *JAPANESE/SUSHI* Expect to see lines out the door at this subdued 25-seat restaurant, ranked the "best sushi in the country" by *San Francisco* magazine. Most menu items are flown in daily from Japan. *517 Hayes St. (btw. Laguna & Octavia sts.). ☎ 415/864-2122. Sushi items $7–$18; izakaya items $5–$9. AE, DC, DISC, MC, V. Dinner Tue-Sun. Bus: 19, 21, 31, 38. Map p 94.*

★ **Sellers Markets** FINANCIAL DISTRICT/SOMA *AMERICAN* Sellar's is a local favorite place for a quick, inexpensive lunch made with sustainably raised, "artisan" ingredients. The pulled free-range chicken sandwich melts in your mouth and the handmade pizzas are hard to resist. *338 Market St. (at Pine & Front sts.). ☎ 415/956-3825. Breakfast, lunch & early dinner Mon–Thurs to 7:30pm, breakfast & dinner Fri. Bus: 10. Streetcar: F. Map p 96. 595 Market St. (at 2nd St.). ☎ 415/227-9850. Lunch & dinner daily. Entrees $7.50–$12. AE, DISC, MC, V. Bus: 9, 10. Streetcar: F. Map p 96.*

★★ **The Slanted Door** FINANCIAL DISTRICT *VIETNAMESE* Despite two moves to bigger spaces, there's a perpetual crowd for Charles Phan's delectable cooking. This is SF's most popular restaurant; call ahead. *Ferry Bldg., 1 Ferry Plaza (at the*

If you can't get a booth at the Slanted Door, sip a creative cocktail and watch the ferryboats go by.

Embarcadero & Market St.). ☎ 415/861-8032. Entrees $8.50–$27 dinner. AE, MC, V. Lunch & dinner daily. Streetcar: F. BART/Muni: Embarcadero. Map p 94.

★ **Sociale** PRESIDIO HEIGHTS *ITALIAN* Locals head to this courtyard nook behind a tony shopping street for superb Tuscan fare. Outdoor tables on warm days are a plus. 3665 Sacramento St. (btw. Locust & Spruce sts.). ☎ 415/921-3200. Entrees $16–$28. MC, V. Lunch Tues–Sat, dinner Mon–Sat. Bus: 1, 4. Map p 94.

★★ **SPQR** PACIFIC HEIGHTS *ITALIAN* I love everything about this place: the interesting Roman cuisine lovingly prepared with local ingredients, the cozy space tastefully decorated with dark wood and Roman posters, and the enticing wine list. Come early, as they don't take reservations. 1911 Fillmore St. (at Bush St.). ☎ 415/771-7779. Entrees $12–$24. AE, MC, V. Dinner daily, brunch Sat–Sun. Bus: 2, 3, 4, 22, 38. Map p 94.

★ **Spruce** PACIFIC HEIGHTS *CONTEMPORARY AMERICAN* It's both a destination restaurant and neighborhood hangout—a restaurant, cafe, bar, takeout, and lounge within a beautifully restored 1930s-era auto barn. A seat at the bar while

tucking into their fantastic all-natural burger and fries is oh-so satisfying. 3640 Sacramento St. (at Spruce St.). ☎ 415/931-5100. Entrees $26–$40. AE, DC, DISC, MC, V. Lunch Mon-Fri, dinner daily. Bus: 1, 2, 4. Map p 94.

★ **Straits Café** SOMA *SINGAPOREAN* Having grown from a little place in the Richmond District to four very chic restaurants in various cities, Straits still offers delectable Singaporean cooking, a winning blend of Chinese, Malaysian, and south Indian cuisines. Westfield San Francisco Centre, 845 Market St., 4th Floor (btw. 4th and 5th sts.). ☎ 415/668-1783. Entrees $11–$34. AE, DISC, MC, V. Lunch & dinner daily. Bus: 14, 27, 30, 45. Streetcar: F. Cable car: Powell lines. Map p 94.

★ **Suppenküche** HAYES VALLEY *GERMAN* An excellent beer selection and well-prepared Bavarian classics make this an unlikely "soup kitchen" hot spot among trendy young locals. 525 Laguna St. (at Hayes St.). ☎ 415/252-9289. Entrees $12–$19. AE, DC, DISC, MC, V. Dinner daily, brunch Sun. Bus: 21. Map p 94.

★ **Swan Oyster Depot** RUSSIAN HILL *SEAFOOD* The lunch line for a cup of chowder and oysters on the half shell at this 1912 cubbyhole fortunately moves quickly. 1517 Polk St. (btw. California & Sacramento sts.).

Better than the crab at Fisherman's Wharf: The seafood at Swan Oyster Depot, in Russian Hill.

☎ 415/673-1101. Seafood cocktails $9.75–$15. Oysters $8/half dozen. No credit cards. Mon–Sat 8am–5:30pm. Bus: 1, 19. Map p 94.

kids Swensen's Ice Cream RUSSIAN HILL *ICE CREAM* This is the original Swensen's, since 1948. No exotic flavors, but three kinds of vanilla. *1999 Hyde St. (at Union St.).* ☎ 415/775-6818. Cones $2.45–$3.95. No credit cards. Sun & Tues–Thurs noon–10pm, Fri–Sat noon–11pm. Bus: 41, 45. Cable car: Powell-Hyde. Map p 94.

Tadich Grill FINANCIAL DISTRICT *AMERICAN/SEAFOOD* Suits and tourists alike appreciate the clubby feel of SF's oldest restaurant, serving traditional seafood. Prepare to stand in line. *240 California St. (btw. Battery & Front sts.).* ☎ 415/391-1849. Entrees $17–$35. MC, V. Lunch & dinner Mon–Sat. Bus: 1. Cable car: California line. Map p 96.

★ Tartine Bakery MISSION *BAKERY* While the fresh breads and flaky scones win accolades, Tartine's creative, mouthwatering

sandwiches and salads are also a hit. This tiny place is packed at lunchtime. *600 Guerrero St. (at 18th St.).* ☎ 415/487-2600. Sandwiches $6–$10. AE, MC, V. Mon 8am–7pm; Tues–Wed 7:30am–7pm; Thurs–Fri 7:30am–8pm; Sat 8am–8pm; Sun 9am–8pm. Bus: 14, 33, 49. BART: to 16th St. Map p 96.

★ Ti Couz MISSION *CREPES* Square buckwheat crepes with fillings like sausage, smoked salmon, or goat cheese. Sunny outdoor tables, too. *3108 16th St. (at Valencia St.).* ☎ 415/252-7373. Crepes $2–$12. MC, V. Lunch & dinner daily. Bus: 14, 22, 49. BART: to 16th St. Map p 93.

Tommaso's Restaurant NORTH BEACH *ITALIAN/PIZZA* Pass X-rated storefronts to sit at a communal table and have excellent wood-fired pizzas and other Italian classics. *1042 Kearny St. (btw. Broadway St. & Pacific Ave.).* ☎ 415/398-9696. Entrees $13–$22. AE, DC, MC, V. Dinner Tues–Sun. Bus: 12, 15. Map p 98.

★★ kids Ton Kiang RICHMOND *CHINESE* An excellent choice for dim sum. Sip tea and choose from trays laden with stuffed crab claws, pork buns, and snow-pea shoots. Save room for the custard pancakes. Come early to avoid the line. *5821 Geary Blvd. (btw. 22nd & 23rd aves.).* ☎ 415/387-8273. Dim sum $2–$5.50 each. AE, DC, DISC, MC, V. Lunch & dinner daily. Bus: 38. Map p 98.

★★ Town Hall SOMA *AMERICAN* The celebrated owners-chefs-brothers Mitchell and Steven Rosenthal serve up irresistible New American cuisine, with a tilt toward New Orleans. *342 Howard St. (at Fremont St.).* ☎ 415/908-3900. Entrees $19–$26. AE, MC, V. Lunch Mon–Fri, dinner daily. Bus: 10, 14, 15. Map p 96.

★ Town's End SOMA *AMERICAN/BRUNCH* Baskets of homemade

breads accompany meals at this low-key joint across the street from the bay. With a few outdoor tables, this is a great breakfast spot. *2 Townsend St. (at the Embarcadero).* ☎ *415/512-0749. Entrees $6.50–$11 brunch, $9–$17 dinner. AE, MC, V. Breakfast & lunch Tues–Fri, dinner Tues–Sat, brunch Sat–Sun. Bus: 10. Muni: T or N. Map p 94.*

★ **kids Trattoria Contadina** NORTH BEACH *ITALIAN* Escape the North Beach crowds at this ma-and-pa trattoria serving no-nonsense dishes like linguine with homemade meatballs. *1800 Mason St. (at Union St.).* ☎ *415/982-5728. Entrees $13–$25. AE, DC, DISC, MC, V. Dinner daily. Bus: 30, 41. Cable car: Powell-Mason. Map p 98.*

Troya RICHMOND *TURKISH* A new addition to the Richmond District's astounding variety of ethnic restaurants, Troya offers well-priced, hearty Turkish fare prepared with local, seasonal ingredients and served in a friendly, casual setting. *349 Clement St. (5th Ave.).* ☎ *415/379-6000. Entrees $13–$17. MC, V. Dinner Mon–Thurs, lunch & dinner Fri–Sun. Bus: 1, 2, 4, 44. Map p 98.*

★ **Universal Café** POTRERO HILL *CALIFORNIA* Glorious New American dishes in a cool, intimate locale. An out-of-the way treasure worth the detour. *2814 19th St. (btw. Bryant & Florida sts.).* ☎ *415/821-4608. Entrees $14–$27. AE, MC, V. Lunch Wed–Fri, dinner Tues–Sun, brunch Sat–Sun. Bus: 9, 27. Map p 93.*

★★ **Waterbar** EMBARCADERO *SEAFOOD* Next to the turf at Epic Roasthouse (p 103), Kuleto has put the surf. Massive aquariums, tanks full of fish destined for dinner plates, and big windows showing off the bay view decorate this exuberant restaurant. The outdoor tables are nice in the late afternoon. *369 Embarcadero (at Folsom St.).* ☎ *415/284-9922. Entrees $29–$36. AE, DC, DISC, MC, V. Lunch & dinner daily. Bus: 1, 12, 14, 41. Streetcar: F. BART: Embarcadero. Map p 94.*

★★ **Wayfare Tavern** FINANCIAL DISTRICT *AMERICAN* Celebrity chef Tyler Florence's Wayfare Tavern added a much-needed boost to the Financial District's tired food scene. Pricy plates of hearty food are served in an intimate hunting lodge–like environment. *558 Sacramento St. (at Leidesdorff Alley).* ☎ *415/772-9060. Entrees $22–$28. AE, DC, DISC, MC, V. Lunch Mon-Fri, dinner daily. Bus: 1, 10, 12, 30X, 41, 82X. Map p 96.*

Load up on dim sum for a song at Yank Sing.

San Francisco's hip, chic Zuni Café serves up Mediterranean cuisine.

kids Westfield Centre Food Court SOMA *VARIED* If you're looking for a quick, unfussy lunch and can't decide what to eat, you'll find a variety of good options at the kiosks here, including Korean, Mexican, and Southwestern fare, as well as soups, crepes, burgers, and pasta. Just pass on the Thai food; it's bland. *Westfield San Francisco Centre, 845 Market St., Concourse Level (btw. 4th and 5th sts.).* ☎ *415/512-6776. Entree prices vary by restaurant. Lunch & dinner daily. Bus: 14, 27, 30, 45. Streetcar: F. Cable car: Powell lines. Map p 94.*

★ 'wichcraft SOMA *SANDWICHES* The brainchild of chef Tom Colicchio, best known as TV's *Top Chef* host, this is the home of the perfect sandwich—be it cold, crisp-toasted, juicy and meaty, cheesy, veggie, or vegan. The open space with two-story high ceilings and windows offers a nice respite during a hectic downtown shopping trip. *868 Mission St., 4th Floor (at 5th St.).* ☎ *415/593-3895. Sandwiches $5–$9.50. AE, DISC, MC, V. Breakfast, lunch & early dinner daily. Bus: 14, 27, 30, 45. Streetcar: F. Cable car: Powell lines. Map p 94.*

★★ Yank Sing FINANCIAL DISTRICT *CHINESE/DIM SUM* Home of the best dim sum in SF, Yank Sing serves 60 varieties of excellent dim sum daily, from stuffed crab claws to steamed pork buns. *101 Spear St. (in Rincon Center, at Mission St.).* ☎ *415/957-9300. Dim sum $3.50–$7.50. AE, DC, MC, V. Lunch daily. Streetcar: F. Map p 94.*

★ kids ZA Pizza RUSSIAN HILL *PIZZA* Thin-crust pizza with sun-dried tomatoes, pesto, or more classic toppings. It's a good stop along the Powell-Hyde cable car en route to Fisherman's Wharf. *1919 Hyde St. (btw. Green & Union sts.).* ☎ *415/771-3100. Slices $3.30–$4.35. AE, DC, MC, V. Lunch & dinner daily. Bus: 41, 45. Cable car: Powell-Hyde. Map p 94.*

★ Zuni Café HAYES VALLEY *MEDITERRANEAN/CALIFORNIA* After 2 decades, acclaimed chef Judy Rodgers still creates masterpieces like her signature roast chicken with bread salad. *1658 Market St. (btw. Gough & Franklin sts.).* ☎ *415/552-2522. Entrees $15–$38. AE, MC, V. Lunch & dinner Tues–Sun. Bus: 6, 7, 71. Streetcar: F. Map p 94.* ●

The Best Nightlife

Nightlife Best Bets

Best Irish Coffee
★ The Buena Vista Café, *2765 Hyde St.* (p 121)

Best Singles Scene
★ Americano Bar, *8 Mission St.* (p 121)

Best Happy Hour Food
The Tonga Room & Hurricane Bar, Fairmont Hotel, *950 Mason St.* (p 121)

Best Speak-Easy
★★ Bourbon & Branch, *Call 415/673-1921 for address.* (p 121)

Best Beer Selection
★★ Toronado Pub, *547 Haight St.* (p 126)

Best View
★ The Top of the Mark, *InterContinental Mark Hopkins Hotel, 1 Nob Hill* (p 123)

Best Rooftop Bar
★★ Medjool Sky Terrace, *2522 Mission St.* (p 121)

Best Place to Watch European Soccer
★★ Mad Dog in the Fog, *530 Haight St.* (p 126)

Best Old-Time Bar
Perry's, *1944 Union St.* (p 121)

Best Neighborhood for Barhopping
The Mission, *various venues (see p 128 for minitour)*

Best Karaoke
★ The Mint Karaoke Lounge, *1942 Market St.* (p 125)

Best Blues Bar
★★ The Boom Boom Room, *1601 Fillmore St.* (p 122)

Previous page: Alembic's Daniel Hyatt pours you a cocktail.

Best Sports Bar
★ Greens Sports Bar, *2239 Polk St.* (p 126)

Best Wine Bar
★★ Terroir, *1116 Folsom St.* (p 127)

Biggest Martini
★ Blondie's Bar and No Grill, *540 Valencia St.* (p 128)

Best Rock Club
★★★ Fillmore Auditorium, *1805 Geary Blvd.* (p 126)

Best Beatnik Bar
★ Vesuvio, *255 Columbus Ave.* (p 122)

Best Dive Bar
★ Li Po Cocktail Lounge, *916 Grant Ave.* (p 123)

Best Gay Bar
★ Moby Dick, *4049 18th St.* (p 125)

Best Dance Club
★★ Ruby Skye, *420 Mason St.* (p 124)

Best Jazz Club
★★ Yoshi's Jazz Club, *1330 Fillmore St.* (p 125)

Most Romantic Bar
★ The Hidden Vine, *½ Cosmo Place* (p 127)

For quality cocktails, try Bourbon & Branch. Book online in advance—and remember your password.

Nightlife East of Van Ness Ave.

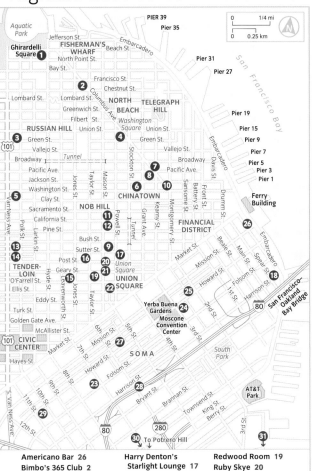

Americano Bar 26
Bimbo's 365 Club 2
Biscuits & Blues 21
Blur 14
Bottom of the Hill 30
Bourbon & Branch 15
The Bubble Lounge 10
The Buena Vista Café 1
The Cinch 5
The EndUp 28
Gold Club 25
Gordon Biersch 18
Greens Sports Bar 3

Harry Denton's
  Starlight Lounge 17
Hemlock 13
The Hidden Vine 16
Johnny Foley's
  Irish House 22
Leatherneck
  Lounge 9
Li Po 6
Mezzanine 27
O'Reilly's Irish Pub
  & Restaurant 4
The Ramp 31

Redwood Room 19
Ruby Skye 20
Slim's 29
Terroir 23
Thirsty Bear
  Brewing Co. 24
The Tonga Room &
  Hurricane Bar 11
The Top of the Mark 12
Tosca 7
Vesuvio 8

Nightlife West of Van Ness Ave.

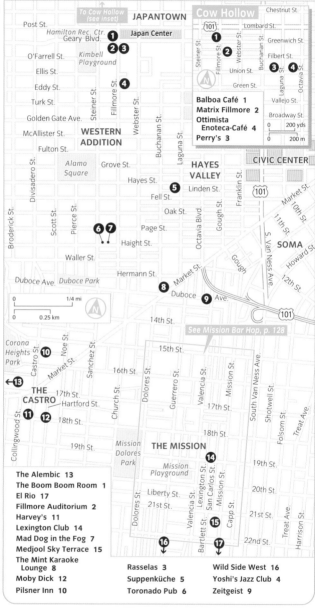

To Cow Hollow (see inset)

JAPANTOWN

Cow Hollow

Chestnut St.

Post St.

Hamilton Rec. Ctr. Geary Blvd.

Japan Center

Lombard St.

Greenwich St.

O'Farrell St.

Kimbell Playground

Filbert St.

Ellis St.

Union St.

Eddy St.

Green St.

Turk St.

Vallejo St.

Golden Gate Ave.

Broadway St.

McAllister St.

WESTERN ADDITION

Fulton St.

Balboa Café 1
Matrix Fillmore 2
Ottimista
  Enoteca-Café 4
Perry's 3

0   200 yds
0   200 m

Alamo Square

Grove St.

HAYES VALLEY

CIVIC CENTER

Hayes St.

Linden St.

Fell St.

Oak St.

Page St.

SOMA

Haight St.

Waller St.

Hermann St.

Duboce Ave. Duboce Park

Duboce   Ave.

See Mission Bar Hop, p. 128

0   1/4 mi
0   0.25 km

14th St.

Corona Heights Park

15th St.

16th St.

THE CASTRO

17th St. Hartford St.

17th St.

18th St.

18th St.

THE MISSION

19th St.

19th St.

Mission Dolores Park

Mission Playground

20th St.

Liberty St.

21st St.

21st St.

22nd St.

The Alembic 13
The Boom Boom Room 1
El Rio 17
Fillmore Auditorium 2
Harvey's 11
Lexington Club 14
Mad Dog in the Fog 7
Medjool Sky Terrace 15
The Mint Karaoke
  Lounge 8
Moby Dick 12
Pilsner Inn 10

Rasselas 3
Suppenküche 5
Toronado Pub 6

Wild Side West 16
Yoshi's Jazz Club 4
Zeitgeist 9

Nightlife A to Z

Bars

★ **Americano Bar** EMBARCADERO Although this hopping indoor/outdoor bar offers postcard views of the bay, the stylish singles who gather here in the evening hours are more interested in viewing their fellow bar patrons. *8 Mission St. (at the Embarcadero).* ☎ *415/278-3777. www.americanorestaurant.com. Bus: 1, 12, 14, 41. Streetcar: F. BART: Embarcadero. Map p 119.*

Balboa Café COW HOLLOW Filled with affluent 30- and 40-somethings from the neighborhood, this preppie bar with an old-time flair is an SF institution—except weekend nights when it's full of college kids and bridge-and-tunnel types. *3199 Fillmore St. (at Greenwich St.).* ☎ *415/921-3944. www.plumpjack.com. Bus: 22, 41, 45, 76. Map p 120.*

★ **Blur** TENDERLOIN Hidden away among the grittier Tenderloin bars is this sleek, candlelit lounge serving up excellent cocktails and decent sushi rolls. *1121 Polk St. (btw. Post & Sutter sts.).* ☎ *415/567-1918. www. blursf.com. Bus: 2, 3, 4, 19, 38, 76. Map p 119.*

★★ **Bourbon & Branch** TENDERLOIN Reserve online, get your password, and get admitted to the 1920s-style speak-easy everyone's talking about. Naturally, the location's a secret. ☎ *415/673-1921. www.bourbonandbranch.com. Bus: 2, 3, 4, 19, 38, 76. Map p 119.*

★ **The Buena Vista Café** COW HOLLOW Despite popular belief, the Buena Vista didn't invent Irish coffee, but it has served more of them than any other bar in the world. It's an SF tradition. *2765 Hyde St. (at Beach St.).* ☎ *415/474-5044. www.thebuenavista.com. Bus: 10, 20, 30. Cable car: Powell-Hyde. Map p 119.*

★ **Hemlock** TENDERLOIN Tattooed bartenders and a laid-back vibe, plus local and national bands playing every night in the back room (a separate, small cover charge applies), make for a popular place on weekend evenings. *1131 Polk St. (at Hemlock St., btw. Post & Sutter sts.).* ☎ *415/923-0923. www.hemlocktavern.com. Cover for back room varies. Bus: 2, 3, 4, 19, 38, 76. Map p 119.*

★★ **Medjool Sky Terrace** MISSION Atop the roof of the terrific Medjool restaurant (p 109) you'll find Medjool's alluring outdoor bar, as well as a panoramic view, casually stylish bar patrons, and, if you're lucky, a table waiting just for you. *2522 Mission St. (btw. 21st & 22nd sts.).* ☎ *415/550-9055. www. medjoolsf.com. Bus: 14, 49. BART: to 24th St. Map p 120.*

Perry's COW HOLLOW Immortalized in Armistead Maupin's *Tales of the City,* this bar/restaurant serving classic American fare was once the hot bar for singles from the surrounding posh neighborhoods. It's got a mellower, old-time feel about it these days. *1944 Union St. (btw. Buchanan & Laguna sts.).* ☎ *415/922-9022. www.perryssf.com. Bus: 41, 45. Map p 120.*

★★ **Suppenküche** HAYES VALLEY The best selection of German beers and food in town. *See p 120.*

The Tonga Room & Hurricane Bar NOB HILL With umbrella drinks and fake thunderstorms, it doesn't get kitschier than this. But the $9.50 happy hour—with plenty of Asian snacks—is a bargain. *Fairmont Hotel, 950 Mason St. (at California St.).* ☎ *415/772-5278.*

Boogie down to some of the best blues bands around at the Boom Boom Room.

www.tongaroom.com. Bus: 1. Cable car: all lines. Map p 119.

★ **Tosca** NORTH BEACH   This relaxed North Beach institution draws local politicos and celebrities. With a dark wood bar and red leather stools, it's a true classic. *242 Columbus Ave. (btw. Broadway St. & Pacific Ave.).* ☎ *415/986-9651. www.toscacafesf.com. Bus: 12, 20, 41. Map p 119.*

★ **Vesuvio** NORTH BEACH   Once the favored beatnik watering hole, Vesuvio still draws an artsy crowd. Order the Bohemian coffee: brandy and amaretto with a lemon twist. *255 Columbus Ave. (at Pacific Ave.).* ☎ *415/362-3370. www.vesuvio. com. Bus: 12, 20, 41. Map p 119.*

★★ **Zeitgeist** MISSION   This indie-rocker Mission staple has a spacious outdoor beer garden, a long list of microbrews on tap, and many devoted customers. *199 Valencia St. (at Duboce Ave.).* ☎ *415/255-7505. Bus: 26. Streetcar: F. Map p 120.*

Blues Bars

★ **Biscuits & Blues** UNION SQUARE   This basement nightclub is a nationally known blues venue. *401 Mason St. (at Geary St.).* ☎ *415/292-2583. www.biscuitsandblues.com. Cover during performances $12–$20. Bus: 2, 3, 4, 38, 76. Cable car: Powell lines. Map p 119.*

★★ **The Boom Boom Room** WESTERN ADDITION   This dark, steamy joint hosts some of the best blues bands in the country. *1601 Fillmore St. (at Geary Blvd.).* ☎ *415/673-8000. www.boomboomblues.com. Cover free–$15. Bus: 22, 38. Map p 120.*

Brewpubs

★ **Gordon Biersch** EMBARCADERO   Gordon Biersch is San Francisco's largest brewery/restaurant, serving hot plates and cold beer to a well-dressed crowd of mingling professionals. *2 Harrison St. (on the Embarcadero).* ☎ *415/243-8246. www.gordonbiersch.com. Bus: 1, 12, 14, 41. Streetcar: F. BART: Embarcadero. Map p 119.*

★ **Thirsty Bear Brewing Company** SOMA   The excellent house-made beers are complemented by a toothsome menu of Spanish tapas. Pool tables and dartboards are upstairs, and there's live flamenco on Sunday. *661 Howard St. (btw. New Montgomery & 3rd sts.).* ☎ *415/974-0905. www.thirstybear. com. Bus: 10, 14, 30, 45, 76. BART: Montgomery. Map p 119.*

Cocktail Lounges

★ **The Alembic** HAIGHT   One of the city's premier cocktail bars serving fine-tuned classics, unusual originals, and a tasty snack menu including lamb sliders. *1725 Haight St. (btw. Cole & Shrader sts.).* ☎ *415/666-0822; www.alembicbar. com. Bus: 14, 49. BART: to 16th St. Map p 120.*

Leatherneck Steakhouse & Lounge UNION SQUARE This sky-view restaurant and bar at the top of the Marines Memorial Club may just be the best-kept secret in town. The small rooftop lounge offers views that are big-city spectacular. No cover, and the drinks are very reasonable (especially during 4–6pm happy hour). *609 Sutter St. (at Mason St.)* ☎ *415/673-6672. www.marineclub.com. Bus: 2, 3, 4, 27, 38. Map p 119.*

★ **Li Po Cocktail Lounge** CHINA-TOWN A dim, divey, and slightly spooky Chinese bar that was once an opium den, Li Po's alluring character stems from its mishmash clutter of dusty Asian furnishings and mementos. The bartenders, who pour a mean Li Po Special Mai Tai, love to creep out patrons with tales of opium junkies haunting the joint. *916 Grant Ave. (btw. Washington and Jackson sts.).* ☎ *415/982-0072. Bus: 15, 30. Map p 119.*

Matrix Fillmore UNION SQUARE On sunny Fridays, the sidewalk tables are packed with trendy singles who apparently don't have real

The Alembic serves up some of the best cocktails in the city and is a good excuse to check out Haight Street.

jobs. *3138 Fillmore St. (btw. Greenwich & Filbert sts.).* ☎ *415/563-4180. www.plumpjack.com. Bus: 22, 30, 41, 45. Map p 120.*

Redwood Room UNION SQUARE It's worth checking out the historic Redwood Room for the cool decor given it by famed hotelier Ian Schrager—even if the scene is not as hip as it once was. *Clift Hotel, 495 Geary St. (at Taylor St.).* ☎ *415/929-2372. www.clifthotel.com. Bus: 2, 3, 4, 27, 38, 76. Map p 119.*

★ **The Top of the Mark** NOB HILL This historic lounge, with the best view in town and a 100-martini menu, has live entertainment on weekend nights. A prix-fixe sunset

The Tonga Room & Hurricane Bar is the kind of place you order fruity drinks and a giant pupu platter.

dinner's also a weekend option. *InterContinental Mark Hopkins Hotel, 1 Nob Hill (at Mason & California sts.).* ☎ *415/616-6916. www.top ofthemark.com. Cover $10. Bus: 1. Cable car: all lines. Map p 119.*

Dance Clubs

★ **The EndUp** SOMA   After 35 years in a sketchy neighborhood, this place still rocks—usually until early Monday morning. Some evenings are gayer or straighter than others, so call ahead to find out the night's theme; Fridays are "Ghetto Disco" nights. *401 6th St. (at Harrison St.).* ☎ *415/646-0999. www. theendup.com. Cover varies. Bus: 12, 27. Map p 119.*

Mezzanine SOMA   This dance hot spot is an upscale, industrial-chic nightclub and gallery in one of the grittier sections of town. *444 Jesse St. (at Mint St.).* ☎ *415/625-8880. www.mezzaninesf.com. Cover varies. Bus: 14, 27. BART: Powell. Map p 119.*

★ **The Ramp** SOMA   From May through October you can dance to live jazz, salsa, and world music Friday through Sunday evenings—with no cover charge—at this indoor/outdoor bar and restaurant. *855 China Basin St. (at Mariposa and Illinois sts.).* ☎ *415/621-2378. www.ramp restaurant.com. No cover. Bus: 22. Streetcar: T. Map p 119.*

Ruby Skye UNION SQUARE   This former Victorian movie house is SF's biggest dance space, featuring live music and DJs from around the country on weekend nights. *420 Mason St. (btw. Post & Geary sts.).* ☎ *415/ 693-0777. www.rubyskye.com. Cover free–$30. Bus: 2, 3, 4, 38, 76. Cable car: Powell lines. Map p 119.*

Gay Bars

The Cinch RUSSIAN HILL   With happy hour Monday through Friday 4 to 8pm (all night on Mon), progressive music by DJs on Thursday and Friday nights, and a host of other fun theme nights, the bar attracts a mixed crowd of gays, lesbians, and gay-friendly straights. *1723 Polk St. (near Washington St.).* ☎ *415/776-4162. Bus: 19, 41, 45, 47, 49, 76. Map p 119.*

Harvey's CASTRO   A lively bar/restaurant attracting a cross section of Castro patrons for reasonable food and plenty of drinks. *500 Castro St. (at 18th St.).* ☎ *415/431-4278. www.harveyssf.com. Bus: 24, 33, 35. Streetcar: F. Map p 120.*

The Redwood Room has real style—though it tends to draw a hipper-than-thou crowd.

The EndUp is just that—it's where both gay and straight barhoppers end up dancing at 3am.

★ **Moby Dick** CASTRO A 25-year-old Castro institution, with a low-key attitude, pool table, pinball machines, and a massive fish tank above the bar. *4049 18th St. (btw. Castro & Noe sts.).* ☎ *415/861-1199. www.mobydicksf.com. Bus: 24, 33, 35. Streetcar: F. Map p 120.*

Pilsner Inn CASTRO This mellow bar, with a good selection of on-tap beers and an outdoor garden, is more of a scene on weekend nights. *225 Church St. (btw. Market & 15th sts.).* ☎ *415/621-7058. www.pilsner inn.com. Bus: 22. Streetcar: F, J. Map p 120.*

Jazz Venues

★ **Rasselas** WESTERN ADDITION This local favorite is a casual, comfortable lounge where you can listen to jazz, Latin rhythms, R&B, or blues, or enjoy snacks from the adjacent Ethiopian restaurant. *1534 Fillmore St. (at O'Farrell St.).* ☎ *415/346-8696. www.rasselasjazzclub.com. Cover $7 Fri–Sat after 9pm. 2-drink minimum Sun–Thurs. Bus: 22, 38. Map p 120.*

★★ **Yoshi's Jazz Club** WESTERN ADDITION A swanky space to chill out to great jazz while enjoying some excellent Japanese cuisine. *1330 Fillmore St. (at O'Farrell St.).* ☎ *415/655-5600. www.yoshis.com.*

Cover $10–$32. 1 menu item minimum. Bus: 22, 38. Map p 120.

Karaoke

★ **The Mint Karaoke Lounge** MISSION This once-gay destination now draws patrons of all persuasions, who, after one of the many potent cocktails, are ready to take to the stage. *1942 Market St. (btw. Guerrero St. & Duboce Ave.).* ☎ *415/ 626-4726. www.themint.net. Bus: 22. Streetcar: F, J, N. Map p 120.*

Lesbian Bars

El Rio MISSION This eclectic club features dancing, an outdoor patio, and funky rhythms from around the world. *3158 Mission St. (south of Cesar Chavez, btw. Precita & Powers aves.).* ☎ *415/282-3325. www.elriosf. com. Bus: 12, 26, 27. Map p 120.*

Lexington Club MISSION A friendly crowd, a pool table, and cheap beers grace this ladies' club. *3464 19th St. (at Lexington St. btw. Valencia & Mission sts.).* ☎ *415/863-2052. www.lexingtonclub.com. Bus: 14, 26, 49. BART: 16th St. Map p 120.*

★ **Wild Side West** BERNAL HEIGHTS This cozily cluttered, saloon-style bar and outdoor garden area is a longtime staple in the SF lesbian community. *424 Cortland Ave. (btw. Wool & Bennington sts.).* ☎ *415/647-3099. Bus: 24. Map p 120.*

Pubs

★ **Johnny Foley's Irish House** UNION SQUARE This spacious pub serves a full menu of Irish and non-Irish fare, has a large selection of Irish whiskeys and single malts, and screens European soccer. *243 O'Farrell St. (btw. Mason & Powell sts.).* ☎ *415/954-0777. www.johnny foleys.com. Bus: 27, 38. Cable car: Powell lines. Map p 119.*

Smoking Laws

On January 1, 1998, smoking was officially banned in all California bars. This law is generally enforced and though San Francisco's police department has not made bar raids a priority, people caught smoking in bars can be ticketed and fined. If you must smoke, do it outside.

★★ Mad Dog in the Fog HAIGHT This quirky British pub is the best place to watch European soccer. It's also good for a pint of bitter and a game of darts. *530 Haight St. (btw. Steiner & Fillmore sts.).* ☎ *415/626-7279. Bus: 6, 7, 22. Map p 120.*

★ O'Reilly's Irish Pub & Restaurant NORTH BEACH You'll find your pint of Guinness at this cozy joint, along with Irish lamb stew and the less traditional "Irishman's quesadilla." *622 Green St. (btw. Powell St. & Columbus Ave.).* ☎ *415/989-6222. www.oreillysirish.com. Bus: 20, 30, 41, 45. Cable car: Powell-Mason line. Map p 119.*

★★ Toronado Pub HAIGHT A boisterous Lower Haight hangout with over 40 microbrews on tap and dozens of bottled beers. *Bonus:* Most pints are $2.50 until 6pm every day. *547 Haight St. (btw. Steiner & Fillmore sts.).* ☎ *415/863-2276. www.toronado. com. Bus: 6, 7, 22. Map p 120.*

Rock/Alternative Venues
★ Bimbo's 365 Club NORTH BEACH Swanky 1930s decor, complete with chandeliers and tux-clad servers belies the low-key atmosphere at this North Beach staple, which is more likely to feature rock and hip-hop than jazz or cabaret. *1025 Columbus Ave. (at Chestnut St.).* ☎ *415/474-0365. www.bimbos 365club.com. Tickets $15–$50; 2-drink minimum. Bus: 20, 30. Cable car: Powell-Mason. Map p 119.*

★★ Bottom of the Hill POTRERO HILL This unpretentious rock club draws a broad cross section of rock–'n'-roll fans. Happy hour takes place Friday from 3 to 7pm. *1233 17th St. (at Missouri St.).* ☎ *415/621-4455. www.bottomofthehill. com. Cover $8–$20. Bus: 10, 22. Map p 119.*

★★★ Fillmore Auditorium WESTERN ADDITION The club that featured bands like Jefferson Airplane and the Grateful Dead is once again the best rock venue in town. *1805 Geary Blvd. (at Fillmore St.).* ☎ *415/346-6000. www.thefillmore. com. Tickets $20–$90. Bus: 22, 38. Map p 120.*

★★ Slim's SOMA Co-owned by musician Boz Scaggs, this bar and restaurant plays rock and hip-hop acts almost nightly. Hot acts sell out quickly. *333 11th St. (at Folsom St.).* ☎ *415/255-0333. www.slims-sf.com. Cover free–$30. Bus: 9, 12, 47. Map p 119.*

Sports Bar
★ Greens Sports Bar RUSSIAN HILL The best sports bar in SF boasts polished dark wood, 15 TVs, 18 beers on tap, a pool table, video games, and happy hour Monday through Friday from 4 to 7pm. *2239 Polk St. (at Green St.).* ☎ *415/775-4287. Bus: 19, 41, 45. Cable car: Powell-Hyde. Map p 119.*

Supper Club

★ **Harry Denton's Starlight Lounge** UNION SQUARE This classic 1930s penthouse lounge offers stellar city views, a lengthy appetizer menu, and dancing. The Harry Denton Starlight Orchestra plays Friday and Saturday eves. Call to reserve a table, and don't wear jeans or sneakers. *Sir Francis Drake Hotel, 450 Powell St. (btw. Sutter & Post sts.).* ☎ *415/395-8595. www.harrydenton.com. Cover after 8:30pm Wed–Fri $10, Sat $15. Bus: 2, 3, 4, 38, 76. Cable car: Powell lines. Map p 119.*

Wine & Champagne Bars

★ **The Bubble Lounge** FINANCIAL DISTRICT The SF sister to the NY club is très posh. Beyond the dizzying array of champagnes, martinis, and caviars, a dress code is enforced: no sneakers, combat fatigues, or baseball caps. *714 Montgomery St. (at Washington St.).* ☎ *415/434-4204. www.bubblelounge.com. No cover. Bus: 10, 20, 41. Map p 119.*

★ **The Hidden Vine** UNION SQUARE The name says it all. Tucked into a side-alley, this is a cozy spot where the specialty is lesser-known wines from various places. *½ Cosmo Place (at Taylor St. or enter at 620 Post St.).* ☎ *415/674-3567. www.thehiddenvine.com. Bus: 2, 3, 4, 38, 76. Map p 119.*

★ **Ottimista Enoteca-Café** COW HOLLOW Warm decor, big oak barrels, Italian wines, an appetizing Mediterranean menu, and plenty of outdoor tables make this one of my favorite neighborhood haunts. *1838 Union St. (at Octavia St.).* ☎ *415/674-8400. www.ottimistasf.com. Bus: 41, 45. Map p 120.*

★★ **Terroir** SOMA This SoMa area wineshop-slash-bar shop sells a handpicked selection of natural wines that you can taste at a tiny zinc bar in the back. Owners Luc Ertoran, Guilhaume Gerard, and Dagan Ministero pour by the glass, half-bottle or bottle, and will guide you through your selections. *1116 Folsom St. (btw 7th & Langton sts.)* ☎ *415/558-9946. www.terroirsf. com. BART/Muni: Powell. Bus: 5, 7, 9, 21, 71. Map p 119.*

Harry Denton's Starlight Lounge.

Mission Bar Hop

SF's best bar hop is in the Mission—though BART is unsafe at night here. Taxi is your best bet. START: **Bus no. 26, 49. BART at 16th Street (before dark).**

1 500 Club *(500 Guerrero St.;* 415/861-2500). A huge pink neon cocktail beckons you to this classic dive bar, made festive by year-round chili lights. It's more upscale at **2 Elixir** *(3200 16th St.;* 415/552-1633), the sub-dued site of an 1875 saloon, but at neighborhood tavern **3 ★ Kilowatt** *(3160 16th St.;* 415/861-2595), you can buy a pitcher, play a rock tune on the jukebox, and sit in a weathered booth. Next stop is quirky **4 ★★ Casanova Lounge** *(527 Valencia St.;*

415/863-9328), which hosts a good mix of Mission locals and hipsters from around town. If you've got the stamina, order a 16-ounce martini at **5 ★ Blondie's Bar and No Grill** *(540 Valencia St.;* 415/864-2419). Now chill out to some African tunes at **6 ★★ Little Baobab** *(3388 19th St.;* 415/643-3558), before trying to forget it all at dark, loud, and fun **7 ★ Amnesia** *(853 Valencia St.;* 415/970-0012). Congrats! You've made it to the always buzzing, counterculture **8 ★ Revolution Cafe** *(3248 22nd St. Valencia St.;* 415/642-0474), where the crowd overflows onto the sidewalk.

Arts & Entertainment Best Bets

Expect the unexpected at Beach Blanket Babylon's comedy show.

Best **Theater Company**
★★★ American Conservatory Theater (A.C.T.), Geary Theater, *415 Geary St. (p 136)*

Longest-Running **Comedy**
★ Beach Blanket Babylon, *Club Fugazi, 678 Green St. (p 134)*

Best **Inexpensive Shows**
★★ San Francisco Conservatory of Music, *50 Oak St. (p 133)*

Best **Broadway Shows**
★ Curran Theatre, *445 Geary St. (p 136)*

Best **Uplifting Experience**
★ Glide Memorial Sunday Service, *330 Ellis St. (p 133)*

Best **Foreign & Independent Films**
★★ Embarcadero Center Cinema, *1 Embarcadero Center (p 135)*

Wackiest **Place to Watch a Film**
★★ Castro Theatre, *429 Castro St. (p 134)*; and ★ Red Vic Moviehouse, *1727 Haight St. (p 134)*

Best **Comedy Club**
★ Punch Line, *444 Battery St. (p 134)*

Best for **Visiting Virtuosos**
★★ San Francisco Performances, *various locations (p 133)*

Previous page: The San Francisco Ballet rehearses for its 2012 season.

Best **Seasonal Event**
★★★ San Francisco Ballet's *The Nutcracker, War Memorial Opera House, 301 Van Ness Ave. (p 134)*

Best **Inexpensive Show**
★★ San Francisco Conservatory of Music, *50 Oak St. (p 133)*

Best **Entertainment for the Whole Family**
★ Lamplighters Music Theatre, *various locations (p 136)*

Best **Gospel**
★ Glide Memorial Church, *330 Ellis St. (p 133)*

Best **Modern Dance**
★★ ODC/San Francisco, *351 Shotwell St. (p 134)*

The highly esteemed American Conservatory Theater has been operating since 1967.

San Francisco A & E

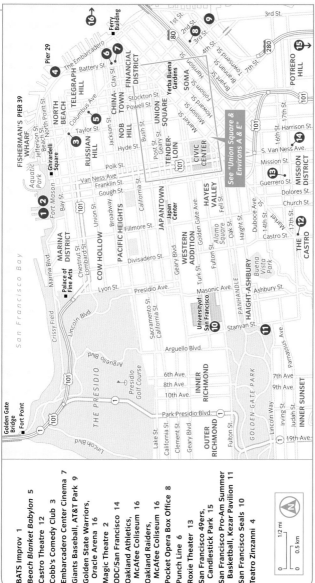

See "Union Square & Environs A & E"

BATS Improv 1
Beech Blanket Babylon 5
Castro Theatre 12
Cobb's Comedy Club 3
Embarcadero Center Cinema 7
Giants Baseball, AT&T Park 9
Golden State Warriors,
  Oracle Arena 16
Magic Theatre 2
ODC/San Francisco 14
Oakland Athletics,
  McAfee Coliseum 16
Oakland Raiders,
  McAfee Coliseum 16
Pocket Opera Box Office 8
Punch Line 6
Roxie Theater 13
San Francisco 49ers,
  Candlestick Park 15
San Francisco Pro-Am Summer
  Basketball, Kezar Pavilion 11
San Francisco Seals 10
Teatro Zinzanni 4

The Best Arts & Entertainment

Union Square & Environs A & E

American Conservatory
Theater (A.C.T.),
Geary Theatre 4
City Box Office 10
Curran Theatre 3
Davies Symphony Hall 13
Glide Memorial Church 5
Golden Gate Theater 9
Herbst Theatre 11
Lamplighters Music
Theatre 7, 11
Orpheum Theater 14
Philharmonia Baroque
Orchestra 11
San Francisco Ballet 12
San Francisco
Conservatory 15
San Francisco Opera 12
San Francisco Performances
Box Office 1
San Francisco Symphony 13
Smuin/SF Dance Company 6
Tix Bay Area,
Union Square Pavilion 2
Yerba Buena Center for
the Arts Theater 8
War Memorial
Opera House 12

Arts & Entertainment A to Z

Classical & Choir Music

★ **Glide Memorial Church** TENDERLOIN Nationally recognized Rev. Cecil Williams leads Sunday services, featuring rousing gospel choir music at 9 and 11am. Arrive at least 30 minutes early to get seats. *330 Ellis St. (at Taylor St.).* ☎ *415/674-6000. www.glide.org. Bus: 27, 31, 38. Streetcar: F. Cable car: Powell lines. Map p 132.*

★ **Philharmonia Baroque Orchestra** CIVIC CENTER Performs early music in SF and the Bay Area. *Herbst Theatre, 401 Van Ness Ave. (at McAllister St.).* ☎ *415/252-1288. www.philharmonia.org. Tickets $30–$80. Bus: 5, 21, 47, 49. BART/Muni: Civic Center. Streetcar: F. Map p 132.*

★★ **San Francisco Conservatory of Music** CIVIC CENTER Beyond educating young musicians, the conservatory also offers inexpensive and free orchestral and opera recitals. *50 Oak St. (at Franklin St.).* ☎ *415/864-7326. www.sfcm.edu. Tickets free–$20. Bus: 6, 7, 47, 49, 71. BART/Muni: Civic Center. Streetcar: F. Map p 132.*

★★ **San Francisco Performances** LOCATION VARIES Its October-through-April season includes classical music, dance, and jazz at various locations, including Herbst Theater and Yerba Buena Center for the Arts Theater. Tickets for Saturday 11am and 2pm matinees are $10 to $20. *500 Sutter St., Ste. 700 (at Powell St.).* ☎ *415/392-2545. www.performances.org. Tickets $25–$81. Map p 132.*

★★★ **San Francisco Symphony** CIVIC CENTER Founded in 1911 and directed by internationally acclaimed conductor Michael Tilson Thomas. Music for Families matinees are $10 to $45. *Davies Symphony Hall, 201 Van Ness Ave. (btw. Grove & Hayes sts.).* ☎ *415/864-6000. www.sfsymphony.org. Tickets $10–$125. Bus: 6, 7, 47, 49, 71. BART/Muni: Civic Center. Streetcar: F. Map p 132.*

Comedy & Cabaret

★ **BATS Improv** MARINA DISTRICT Combining improvisation with competition, BATS performs hilarious improvisational tournaments in which teams of actors compete against each other in scenes, songs, and games, based on suggestions from the audience. *Bayfront Theatre at the Fort Mason Center, Building B no. 350, 3rd floor.* ☎ *415/474-6776. www.improv.org. Tickets $5–$15. Bus: 49. Map p 131.*

Even non-believers will enjoy a morning of soul-stirring gospel music at Glide Memorial Church.

Where to Score Tickets

Tix Bay Area (Union Square Pavilion, Powell St.; ☎ 415/430-1140; www.tixbayarea.org), sells advance and full-price tickets with a service charge of $1.75 to $6, plus half-price theater, dance, and music tickets on show days (Sun–Mon tickets are sold Sat–Sun). Try **City Box Office** (180 Redwood St., Ste. 100; ☎ 415/392-4400; www.cityboxoffice.com), for tickets to most theater and dance events. **Tickets.com** (☎ 800/225-2277; www.tickets.com) sells computer-generated tickets (with a hefty service charge of $3–$19 per ticket!) to concerts, sporting events, plays, and special events. **Ticketmaster** (☎ 415/421-TIXS [8497]; www.ticketmaster.com) also offers advance ticket purchases (also with a service charge). **Craigslist** (www.craigslist.org) also connects people with tickets (especially to 49ers games).

★ Beach Blanket Babylon

NORTH BEACH For more than 30 years, *BBB* has spoofed popular culture with updated parodies of well-known figures. *Club Fugazi, 678 Green St. (at Columbus Ave.).* ☎ *415/421-4222. www.beachblanketbabylon.com. Tickets $25–$80. Bus: 20, 30, 41, 45. Cable car: Powell-Mason. Map p 131.*

Cobb's Comedy Club NORTH

BEACH Cobb's features touring comics Thursday through Saturday; local comedians on Wednesday nights for $10. *915 Columbus Ave. (at Lombard St.).* ☎ *415/928-4320. www.cobbscomedyclub.com. Tickets $15–$35. Bus: 20, 30. Cable car: Powell-Mason. Map p 131.*

★ Punch Line Comedy Club

EMBARCADERO The largest comedy nightclub in SF; it features both locally and nationally known comedians. *444 Battery St. (at Clay St.).* ☎ *415/397-7573. www.punchlinecomedyclub.com. Tickets from $13–$20. Bus: 1, 10, 20, 41. BART/Muni: Embarcadero. Map p 131.*

Dance

★★ ODC/San Francisco MISSION

This renowned modern dance company's last few seasons have sold out. They perform *The Velveteen Rabbit* in November and December. *ODC Theater, 351 Shotwell St. (btw. 17th and 18th sts.).* ☎ *415/863-6606. www.odcdance.org. Tickets $10–$90. Bus: 27. BART: 16th St. Map p 131.*

★★★ San Francisco Ballet

CIVIC CENTER The first and one of the finest professional ballet companies in the U.S. The season runs February through May, plus *The Nutcracker* in December. *War Memorial Opera House, 301 Van Ness Ave. (at Grove St.).* ☎ *415/865-2000. www.sfballet.org. Tickets $20–$205. Bus: 5, 21, 47, 49. BART/Muni: Civic Center. Streetcar: F. Map p 132.*

★ Smuin Ballet LOCATION VAR-

IES The Smuin presents theatrical ballet performances, featuring tango, rock, or other music for a modern spin, at various venues throughout the city. ☎ *415/556-5000. www.smuinballet.org. Tickets $40–$55.*

Film

★★ Castro Theatre CASTRO

This Art Deco theater plays classic motion pictures and hosts film

A game at AT&T Park has the added bonus of unobstructed views of the Bay.

festivals—often accompanied by a Mighty Wurlitzer Organ. Get advance tickets through Ticketweb. com. *429 Castro St. (at 17th St.).* ☎ *415/621-6120. www.castro theatre.com. Tickets $10 adults, $7.50 seniors & kids. Bus: 24, 33. Muni: L, K, M. Streetcar: F. Map p 131.*

★★ **Embarcadero Center Cinema** EMBARCADERO   A cineplex featuring excellent foreign and indie films, plus award-winning documentaries. *1 Embarcadero Center (Battery & Clay sts.).* ☎ *415/267-4893. www.landmarktheatres.com. Tickets $11 adults, $8.25 seniors & kids. Bus: 1, 10, 20, 41. BART: Embarcadero. Map p 131.*

★ **The Roxie** MISSION   San Francisco's oldest continually operating theater (since 1909) is home to cutting-edge films and fests, including IndieFest, DocFest, and Noise Pop. Now serving beer. *3117 16th St.* ☎ *415/863-1087. www.roxie.com. Tickets $10 adults, $6.50 seniors and kids (and all on Mon), $7 matinees. Bus: 22. Map p 131.*

★★ **San Francisco International Film Festival** LOCATION VARIES Every April, films from new and established directors hit several SF venues. ☎ *925/866-9559. www.sffs.org. Tickets $15; 10 films $120. Varying ticket prices for each event. Tickets can be ordered on the website.*

Opera

★ **Pocket Opera** LOCATION VARIES   Since 1978, the Pocket Opera has presented comical operas staged with a small cast, simple sets, and a chamber orchestra. *469 Bryant St. (btw. 2nd & 3rd sts.).* ☎ *415/972-8930. www.pocketopera.org. Tickets $20–$37. Map p 131.*

★★ **San Francisco Conservatory of Music.** *See p 132.*

★★★ **San Francisco Opera** CIVIC CENTER   North America's second-largest opera company is among the finest. *Tip:* On the day of show $10 standing-room tickets are sold (cash only; one per person). The season runs from September through December and June and July. *War Memorial Opera House, 301 Van Ness Ave. (at Grove St.).* ☎ *415/864-3330. www.sfopera.com. Tickets $15–$250. Bus: 5, 21, 47, 49. BART/ Muni: Civic Center. Map p 132.*

Spectator Sports

★★ **Giants Baseball** SOMA   Dramatic views of the bay and Treasure Island and excellent food—from traditional baseball fare to sushi and other ethnic cuisine—make a day at AT&T Park well spent. Check the Giants website or Craigslist for tickets. *AT&T Park, 24 Willie Mays Plaza (King & 2nd sts.).* ☎ *415/972-2000. www.giants.mlb.com. Tickets*

$10–$120. Bus: 10, 30, 45, 76. Muni: N, T. Map p 131.

Golden State Warriors OAKLAND
Even if you're not a Warriors fan, trek to Oakland to see the NBA's best teams in action. Regular games rarely sell out. *Oracle Arena, 1011 Broadway, Oakland.* ☎ *510/986-2200. www.nba.com/warriors. Tickets: $15–$55. BART: Oakland. Map p 131.*

Oakland Athletics OAKLAND
The "other" Bay Area baseball team plays in the American League. Whatever. *McAfee Coliseum, 7000 Coliseum Way, Oakland.* ☎ *510/568-5600. http://oakland.athletics.mlb.com. Tickets: $9–$55. BART: Oakland. Map p 131.*

Oakland Raiders OAKLAND   See what "Raider Nation" is all about. The Raiders maintained a solid Bay Area fan base even when they were in Southern California in the '80s and early '90s. Single-game tickets are available through Ticketmaster. *McAfee Coliseum, 7000 Coliseum Way, Oakland.* ☎ *800/724-3377. www.raiders.com. Tickets: $36–$161. BART: Oakland. Map p 131.*

San Francisco 49ers CANDLE-STICK POINT   Because there are so many season ticket holders, single tickets to see SF's pro football team are hard to come by. All single tickets are sold through Ticketmaster. Check Craigslist, too. *Monster Park, Candlestick Point.* ☎ *415/464-9377. www.sf49ers.com. Tickets $59–$113. Map p 131.*

Theater

★★★ **American Conservatory Theater (A.C.T.)** UNION SQUARE
The Tony Award–winning theater troupe is among the top in the U.S. and performs in a world-class theater. *Geary Theater, 415 Geary St. (btw. Mason & Taylor sts.).* ☎ *415/749-2228. www.act-sf.org. Tickets*

$14–$82. Bus: 2, 3, 4, 38, 76. BART/Muni: Powell St. Cable car: Powell lines. Map p 132.

★ **Curran Theatre** UNION SQUARE
Established in 1922 to host European and East Coast productions. Along with the **Orpheum Theater** *(1192 Market St. Bus: 5. BART/Muni: Civic Center. Streetcar: F. Map p 132),* and the **Golden Gate Theater** *(1 Taylor St. Bus: 5 or 31. Streetcar: F. Map p 132),* its Best of Broadway series brings NY hit plays and musicals to SF for 2- to 6-week runs. *445 Geary St. (btw. Mason & Taylor sts.).* ☎ *415/551-2000. www.shnsf.com. Tickets $30–$99. Bus: 2, 3, 4, 38, 76. BART/Muni: Powell St. Cable car: Powell lines. Map p 132.*

★ **Lamplighters Music Theatre**
LOCATION VARIES   Brings the works of Gilbert & Sullivan plus other comic operas to Bay Area stages. Good family fun staged at Yerba Buena Gardens or Herbst Theatre. ☎ *415/227-4797. www.lamplighters.org. Tickets through Yerba Buena Center for the Arts* ☎ *415/978-2787. Tickets $34–$97 adults, $11–$18 kids. Yerba Buena: Bus: 30, 45, 76. BART/Muni: Powell St. Streetcar: F. Herbst Theatre: Bus: 5, 21, 47, 49. BART/Muni: Civic Center. Map p 132.*

★ **Magic Theatre** MARINA   This prominent national theater is dedicated to developing and producing new playwrights' works. *Bldg. D, Fort Mason Center, Marina Blvd. (at Gough St.).* ☎ *415/441-8822. www.magictheatre.org. Tickets $25–$75. Bus: 10, 20, 19, 28, 30, 76. Map p 131.*

Teatro Zinzanni EMBARCADERO
Circus artists, a five-piece band, and a five-course meal come together for a 3-hour show/dinner extravaganza. *Pier 29, the Embarcadero (at Battery St.).* ☎ *415/438-2668. www.teatrozinzanni.org. Tickets $117–$167. Bus: 10. Streetcar: F. Map p 131.* ●

The Best **Lodging**

Lodging Best Bets

Most **Luxurious**
★★★ Four Seasons $$$$
757 Market St. (p 143)

Most **Ecofriendly Hotel**
★★ Orchard Garden Hotel $$$
466 Bush St. (p 148)

Best **Views**
★★★ InterContinental Mark Hopkins $$$$ *1 Nob Hill (p 147)*; and
★★★ Mandarin Oriental $$$$
222 Sansome St. (p 148)

Most **Impeccable Service**
★★★ St. Regis $$$$ *125 3rd St.
(p 150)*

Most **Historic**
★★ The Palace $$$$ *2 New Montgomery St. (p 149)*

Hippest Hotel
★★ Clift Hotel $$ *495 Geary St.
(p 142)*

Best **Fisherman's Wharf Hotel**
★★ The Argonaut $$$ *495 Jefferson St. (p 142)*

Best **For Starving Artists**
★★ Hotel des Arts $ *447 Bush St.
(p 145)*

The lobby at the ultrahip Triton.

Best **Union Square Bargain**
★ Hotel Bijou $ *111 Mason St.
(p 144)*

Best **Family Hotel**
★ Hotel Del Sol $$ *3100 Webster
St. (p 145)*

Best **Cheap Bed**
★ Hostelling International—
Fisherman's Wharf $ *Fort Mason,
Bldg. 240 (p 144)*

Most **Romantic**
★★ Hotel Drisco $$$ *2901 Pacific
Ave. (p 145)*; and ★ Hotel Boheme
$$ *444 Columbus Ave. (p 145)*

Best **Boutique Hotel**
★★★ Harbor Court $$ *165 Steuart
St. (p 144)*

Best **Rock-'n'-Roll Hotel**
★★ Hotel Triton $$ *342 Grant Ave.
(p 146)*

Best **Spa**
★★ The Huntington Hotel $$$$
1075 California St. (p 147)

Best **Under $100**
★ Marina Inn $ *3110 Octavia St.
(p 148)*

Best **Hidden Gem**
★★ Jackson Court $$ *2198 Jackson
St. (p 148)*

Best **Pool**
★★★ St. Regis $$$$$ *125 3rd St.
(p 150)*

Best **Bed & Breakfast**
★ The Golden Gate Hotel $ *775
Bush St. (p 143)*

Best **Place to Pretend the
Summer of Love Never Ended**
★ Red Victorian B&B $
1665 Haight St. (p 149)

*Previous page: The pool at the Phoenix
Hotel.*

CHINATOWN

Washington St.

Clay St.

Sacramento St.

California St.

NOB HILL

Pine St.

Bush St.

Sutter St.

Cosmo Pl.

Post St.

UNION SQUARE

Geary St.

O'Farrell St.

Ellis St.

Eddy St.

Turk St.

Grace Cathedral

Huntington Park

Portsmouth Square

Transamerica Pyramid

Commercial St.

St. Mary's Square

Dashiell Hammett St.

Harlan Pl.

Campton Pl.

Crocker Galleria

Union Square

Maiden Ln.

SOMA

Yerba Buena Lane

SFMOMA

Yerba Buena Center for the Arts

Yerba Buena Gardens

Metreon

Pedestrians only

Hotel	No.	Hotel	No.	Hotel	No.
Campton Place Hotel	16	Hotel Bijou	27	King George Hotel	24
Chancellor Hotel	14	Hotel des Arts	11	Orchard Garden	6
Clift Hotel	22	Hotel Monaco	21	Orchard Hotel	9
Fairmont Hotel	2	Hotel Nikko	26	Ritz-Carlton	4
Four Seasons	29	Hotel Palomar	28	Serrano Hotel	23
Galleria Park Hotel	17	Hotel Rex	12	Sir Francis Drake	15
Golden Gate Hotel	8	Hotel Triton	10	St. Regis	30
Grant Plaza	5	The Huntington Hotel	1	Westin St. Francis	20
The Handlery Union Square	25	The Inn at Union Square	13	White Swan Inn	7
Hotel Adagio	19	InterContinental Mark Hopkins	3		
Hotel Beresford Arms	18				

San Francisco Lodging

The Argonaut 12

Best Western 15

Cow Hollow Motor Inn
& Suites 2

The Good Hotel 11

Harbor Court Hotel 23

Hostelling International–
Fisherman's Wharf 5

The Hotel Boheme 17

Hotel Carlton 18

Hotel Del Sol 3

Hotel Drisco 6

The Hotel Griffon 22

Hotel Metropolis 25

Hotel Milano 26

Hotel Tomo 9

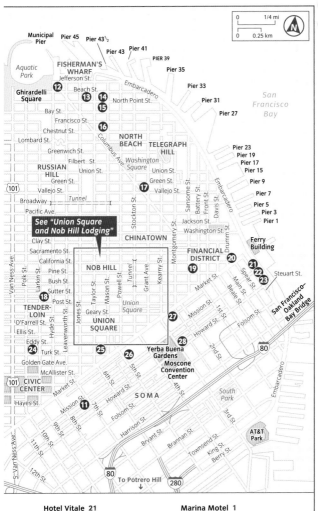

Hotels A to Z

★★ **kids** **The Argonaut** FISHERMAN'S WHARF   This beautifully restored 1907 building has vibrant decor, a great location, and some bay views. It's the best choice at the wharf. *495 Jefferson St. (at Hyde St.).* ☎ *866/415-0704 or 415/563-0800. www.argonauthotel.com. 252 units. Doubles $189–$389. AE, DC, DISC, MC, V. Bus: 10, 30. Cable car: Powell-Hyde. Map p 140.*

★★ **Best Western Tuscan Inn** FISHERMAN'S WHARF   A pleasant wharf option with nicely furnished guest rooms, lots of amenities, free morning coffee and evening wine, and a friendly staff. *425 N. Point St. (at Mason St.).* ☎ *800/648-4626 or 415/561-1100. www.tuscaninn.com. 221 units. Doubles $149–$269. AE, DC, DISC, MC, V. Bus: 10, 15. Streetcar: F. Map p 140.*

★★ **Campton Place Hotel** UNION SQUARE   Refined opulence and exclusivity. Bathrooms, with Portuguese limestone and deep soaking tubs, are a dream. *340 Stockton St. (btw. Post & Sutter sts.).* ☎ *866/332-1670 or 415/781-5555. www.camptonplace.com. 110 units. Doubles $250–$685. AE, DC, DISC,*

The nautical feel of the Argonaut is fitting, given its location on the wharf.

MC, V. Bus: 2, 3, 4. BART/Muni: Montgomery St. Cable car: Powell lines. Map p 139.

Chancellor Hotel UNION SQUARE   A prime location makes up for the plain decor, as do nice touches like free coffee, apples, and cookies, plus a menu of 12 pillows. *433 Powell St. (btw. Sutter & Post sts.).* ☎ *800/428-4748 or 415/362-2004. www.chancellorhotel.com. 137 units. Doubles $180. AE, DC, DISC, MC, V. Bus: 2, 3, 4. BART/Muni: Montgomery St. Cable car: Powell lines. Map p 139.*

★★ **Clift Hotel** UNION SQUARE   Hotelier Ian Schrager and designer Philippe Starck created this überhip hotel with very modern furnishings and a cool attitude. Most rooms scream minimalism, and bathrooms are stylish but small. The in-house Redwood Room is a hopping lounge. *495 Geary St. (at Taylor St.).* ☎ *800/697-1791 or 415/775-4700. www.clifthotel.com. 363 units. Doubles $215–$275. AE, DC, DISC, MC, V. Bus: 2, 3, 4, 27, 38. Map p 139.*

★ **kids** **Cow Hollow Motor Inn & Suites** MARINA   The motel has spacious rooms, but avoid those on noisy Lombard Street. The suites on quieter Chestnut Street are like well-furnished apartments—ideal for longer stays. *2190 Lombard St. (at Steiner St.).* ☎ *415/921-5800. www.cowhollowmotorinn.com. 129 units. Doubles $82–$150. AE, DC, MC, V. Bus: 22, 30, 76. Map p 140.*

★★ **The Fairmont San Francisco** NOB HILL   This 1907 landmark's exterior and lobby impress. The Historic Building rooms and closets are very large. For great bathrooms and views, opt for the Tower Building. *950 Mason St. (at California St.).* ☎ *866/540-4491 or 415/772-5000. www.fairmont.com.*

Enjoy a drink on the ultramodern terrace of the Clift Hotel.

591 units. Doubles $229–$469. AE, DC, DISC, MC, V. Bus: 1. Cable cars: all lines. Map p 139.

★★★ **Four Seasons Hotel San Francisco** SOMA SF's most luxurious hotel has top furnishings and large marble bathrooms. The impeccable service and access to the massive Sports Club/LA add to the wonders. Ask for a corner room. *757 Market St. (at 3rd St.).* ☎ *415/633-3000. www.fourseasons.com. 277 units. Doubles $355–$855. AE, DC, DISC, MC, V. BART/Muni: Montgomery St. Map p 139.*

★ **Galleria Park Hotel** FINANCIAL DISTRICT Unique features here include a rooftop jogging track/garden, an easy-access garage, and a shopping center next door. *191*

Sutter St. (at Kearny St.). ☎ *800/792-9639 or 415/781-3060. www.jdv hotels.com. 177 units. Doubles $179–$299. AE, DC, DISC, MC, V. Bus: 15, 30, 45. BART/Muni: Montgomery St. Map p 139.*

★ **Golden Gate Hotel** UNION SQUARE This B&B's petite rooms have wicker furniture and floral prints. Nice touches include an antique bird-cage elevator and afternoon cookies. *775 Bush St. (btw. Powell & Mason sts.).* ☎ *800/835-1118 or 415/392-3702. www.golden gatehotel.com. 25 units, some with shared bathrooms. Doubles $95–$165 w/breakfast. AE, DC, MC, V. Bus: 2, 3, 4. BART/Muni: Powell St. Cable car: Powell lines. Map p 139.*

★ **The Good Hotel** SOMA This "socially conscious" budget hotel is designed to give back to the environment (hybrid car drivers, for example, get free parking). The neighborhood, however, is one of San Francisco's more interesting (to put it delicately). *112 7th St. (btw. Minna and Mission sts.). 800/444-5819 or 415/621-7001. www.thegood hotel.com.* ☎ *117 units. Doubles $89–$139. AE, DC, DISC, MC, V. Bus: 6, 7, 9, 19, 21, 27, 31, 71. BART: Civic Center, Powell St. Cable car: Powell–Hyde, Powell–Mason line (2 blocks west). Map p 140.*

The Fairmont is a San Francisco institution.

The Harbor Court is located in the historic Embarcadero YMCA spa building.

Grant Plaza CHINATOWN This no-frills bargain has compact rooms and bathrooms. Sixth-floor rooms are newer and a bit quieter. The hotel does not have a kitchen. *465 Grant Ave. (at Pine St.).* ☎ *415/434-3883. www.grantplaza.com. 72 units. Doubles $89–$109. AE, DC, DISC, MC, V. Bus: 30, 45. Map p 139.*

★ The Handlery Union Square UNION SQUARE The central location and outdoor pool are the draws. Poolside club rooms are nice, but the dark lobby and long hallways detract. *351 Geary St. (btw. Powell & Mason sts.).* ☎ *800/995-4874 or 415/781-7800. www.handlery.com. 377 units. Doubles $115–$269. AE, DC, DISC, MC, V. Bus: 2, 3, 4, 38. BART/Muni: Powell St. Cable car: Powell lines. Map p 139.*

★★★ Harbor Court Hotel FINANCIAL DISTRICT Boutique hotel with chic decor and fine bay views. A YMCA fitness center and pool are next door, and its slick restaurant, Ozumo (p 110) is downstairs. *165 Steuart St. (btw. Mission & Howard sts.).* ☎ *866/792-6283 or 415/882-1300. www.harborcourt hotel.com. 131 units. Doubles $87–$295. AE, DC, DISC, MC, V. Bus: 12, 14. BART/Muni: Embarcadero. Map p 140.*

★ Hostelling International— Fisherman's Wharf FISHERMAN'S WHARF/MARINA Free breakfast, woodsy location, bay views, free parking, and cheap rates make up for the bunk beds, dorm rooms, and shared showers. (A handful of private rooms are available.) *Fort Mason, Bldg. 240 (North on Franklin St. past Bay St. Franklin St. ends at the hostel).* ☎ *415/771-7277. www.sfhostels.com. 164 beds, 8–12 beds per room. Singles $26–$30 w/breakfast. AE, MC, DISC, V. Bus: 10, 28. Map p 140.*

★★ Hotel Adagio UNION SQUARE Sleek charm for a good price. Double queen rooms are a great deal for families. Adjacent Bar Adagio is a hip spot for cocktails, wines by the glass, and pizzettas, paninis, and burgers. *550 Geary St. (btw. Jones & Taylor sts.).* ☎ *800/228-8830 or 415/775-5000. www.jdvhotels.com/hotels/adagio. 171 units. Doubles $139–$349. AE, DC, DISC, MC, V. Bus: 2, 3, 4, 38. BART/Muni: Powell St. Map p 139.*

Hotel Beresford Arms UNION SQUARE Not much style, but definitely a good value for families, since most rooms have two full queen beds, and the "Jacuzzi suites" have kitchens or kitchenettes. *701 Post St. (at Jones St.).* ☎ *800/553-6533 or 415/673-2600. www.beresford.com/arms. 95 units. Doubles $99–$289. AE, DC, DISC, MC, V. Bus: 2, 3, 4. Map p 139.*

★ Hotel Bijou UNION SQUARE This 1911 building has vibrantly hued, tiny rooms and screens movies shot in SF nightly in the lobby. Stay on a higher floor, away from street level noise. *111 Mason St. (at Eddy St.).* ☎ *800/771-1022 or 415/771-1200. www.hotelbijou.com. 65 units. Doubles $109–$159. AE, DC, DISC, MC, V. BART/Muni: Powell St. Map p 139.*

★ **The Hotel Boheme** NORTH BEACH This inn has an intimate feel and extras like afternoon sherry, but the tiny bathrooms have showers only. Get a room at the back, off noisy Columbus Avenue. *444 Columbus Ave. (btw. Vallejo & Green sts.).* ☎ *415/433-9111. www.hotel boheme.com. 15 units. Doubles $174–$214. AE, DC, DISC, MC, V. Bus: 15, 30, 41. Map p 140.*

Hotel Carlton UNION SQUARE You'll find hip decor with cool indigenous touches and great rates, but the neighborhood's not ideal. *1075 Sutter St. (btw. Larkin & Hyde sts.).* ☎ *800/ 922-7586 or 415/673-0242. www. jdvhotels.com/carlton. 161 units. Doubles $89–$199. AE, DC, DISC, MC, V. Bus: 2, 3, 4. Map p 140.*

★★ **Hotel des Arts** UNION SQUARE This bargain Euro-style hotel distances itself from the competition by including a visually stimulating dose of artistic license. You'll love the lively location as well: right across the street from the entrance to Chinatown and 2 blocks from Union Square. There's even a French brasserie right downstairs. For the money it's quite possibly the best budget hotel in the city. *447 Bush St. (at Grant St.).* ☎ *800/956-4322 or 415/956-3232. www.sfhoteldesarts.com. 51 units. Doubles $79–$159 double with bathroom, $59–$79 without. Rates include continental breakfast. AE, DC, MC, V. Cable car: Powell–Hyde, Powell–Mason line. Map p 139.*

★ **kids Hotel Del Sol** COW HOLLOW A 1960s motel livened up with paint and palm trees. Rooms are compact, but it's on a quiet street, has a small pool, and parking is free. *3100 Webster St. (at Greenwich St.).* ☎ *877/433-5765 or 415/921-5520. www.jdvhotels.com. 57 units. Doubles $139–$199 w/breakfast. AE, DC, DISC, MC, V. Bus: 30. Map p 140.*

★★ **Hotel Drisco** PACIFIC HEIGHTS Stylish exclusivity in an elegant neighborhood. The 1903 building has the amenities of a top-tier hotel, except parking. *2901 Pacific Ave. (at Broderick St.).* ☎ *800/634-7277 or 415/346-2880. www.hoteldrisco.com. 48 units. Doubles $169–$259 deluxe king, suite $351–$519. Rates include breakfast. AE, DC, DISC, MC, V. Bus: 1, 3, 41, 45. Map p 140.*

★★ **The Hotel Griffon** FINANCIAL DISTRICT Highlights at this boutique inn include mahogany headboards, marble vanities, white-washed exposed brick walls, and some stellar views. *155 Steuart St. (btw. Mission & Howard sts.).* ☎ *800/321-2201 or 415/495-2100.*

Rooms at the Hotel des Arts are designed by graffiti artists. Pictured: a room by Damon Soule.

You won't want to leave your room at the Hotel Monaco.

www.hotelgriffon.com. 62 units. Doubles $166–$599. AE, DC, DISC, MC, V. Bus: 12. BART/Muni: Embarcadero. Map p 140.

kids **Hotel Metropolis** UNION SQUARE   The family suite has a special kids' room with bunk bed and toys. Decor is nice, but rooms are small and the location iffy. *25 Mason St. (at Turk St.).* ☎ *877/628-4412 or 415/775-4600. www.hotel metropolis.com. 105 units. Doubles $99–$289; suite $159–$369. AE, DC, DISC, MC, V. BART/Muni: Powell St. Map p 140.*

Hotel Milano SOMA   Location is the top draw at this small, modern hotel. The upholstery is fading, but rates are attractive. Room sizes vary. *55 5th St. (btw. Market & Mission sts.).* ☎ *415/543-8555. www. hotelmilanosf.com. 108 units. Doubles $109–$199. AE, DC, DISC, MC, V. BART/Muni: Powell St. Map p 140.*

★★ **Hotel Monaco** UNION SQUARE   Vivid Art Deco design and many amenities, like a renovated spa, L'Occitane products, and evening wine tasting. Pets welcome. The majestic Grand Café (p 105) is downstairs. *501 Geary St. (at Taylor St.).* ☎ *866/622-5284 or 415/292-0100. www.monaco-sf.com. 201 units.*

Doubles $139–$279 double; suite $279–$539. AE, DC, DISC, MC, V. Bus: 2, 3, 4, 27, 38. BART/Muni: Powell St. Cable car: Powell lines. Map p 139.

★★ **Hotel Nikko** UNION SQUARE   Rooms are large, light, and well furnished. The atrium houses a large pool, fitness center, and hot tubs. Good weekend rates at this biz hotel. *222 Mason St. (btw. Ellis & O'Farrell sts.).* ☎ *800/248-3308 or 415/394-1111. www.hotelnikkosf. com. 532 units. Doubles from $350. AE, DC, DISC, MC, V. Bus: 27, 38. Cable car: Powell lines. Map p 139.*

★★ **Hotel Palomar** SOMA   On the top five floors of a historic building, Palomar is big, but feels like a small boutique luxury hotel. *12 4th St. (at Market St.).* ☎ *866/373-4941 or 415/348-1111. www.hotelpalomar. com. 198 units. Doubles $179–$429; suite $379–$679. AE, DC, DISC, MC, V. BART/Muni: Powell St. Map p 139.*

★★ **Hotel Rex** UNION SQUARE   Plush 1930s decor in the lobby and rooms. Request a room overlooking the courtyard; it will be quieter than the Sutter-side rooms. *562 Sutter St. (btw. Powell & Mason sts.).* ☎ *800/433-4434 or 415/433-4434. www.thehotel rex.com. 94 units. Doubles $139–$265. AE, DC, DISC, MC, V. Bus: 2, 3, 4. BART/Muni: Powell St. Map p 139.*

Hotel Tomo JAPANTOWN   With each guest room decorated in unique Japanese pop-art style, you get good rates without the bland decor that often comes with them. *1800 Sutter St. (at Buchanan St.).* ☎ *800/738-7477 or 415/921-4000. www.jdvhotels.com/tomo. 125 units. Doubles $139–$189. AE, DC, DISC, MC, V. Bus: 2, 3, 4. Map p 140.*

★★ **Hotel Triton** UNION SQUARE   A rock–'n'-roll themed hotel with suites designed by famous musicians, ecofriendly floors, complimentary Friday-night wine parties (with DJ, tarot-card readings, and chair massages!). Rooms are tiny. Free Wi-Fi. *342 Grant Ave. (at Bush St.).* ☎ *800/800-1299 or 415/394-0500. www.hoteltriton.com. 140 units. Doubles $95–$269; suite $329–$369. AE, DC, DISC, MC, V. Bus: 2, 3, 4, 15, 30. BART/Muni: Montgomery St. Map p 139.*

★ **Hotel Vitale** FINANCIAL DISTRICT   Subtle elegance and expansive bay views make this hotel shine. While its Americano Bar (p 121) is always hopping, the rooms are quiet. Free Wi-Fi. *8 Mission St. (at Steuart St.).* ☎ *888/890-8688 or 415/278-3700. www.hotelvitale.com. 199 units. Doubles $329–$399. AE, DC, DISC, MC, V. Bus: 12, 14. BART/Muni: Embarcadero. Map p 140.*

★★ **The Huntington Hotel** NOB HILL   A discreet but upscale Nob Hill choice. Rooms are sizable and seven suites have kitchens. The hotel's spa is magnificent. *1075 California St. (at Powell St.).* ☎ *800/227-4683 or 415/474-5400. www. huntingtonhotel.com. 136 units. Doubles $350–$500; suite $600–$1,350. AE, DC, DISC, MC, V. Bus: 1. Cable cars: all lines. Map p 139.*

★ **kids Hyatt at Fisherman's Wharf** FISHERMAN'S WHARF   Best of the wharf chain hotels. Nice outdoor pool, but, with 28 TVs, the restaurant is like a sports bar. *555 N. Point St. (btw. Jones & Taylor sts.).* ☎ *888/591-1234 or 415/563-1234. www.fishermanswharf.hyatt.com. 313 units. Doubles $168–$268. AE, DC, DISC, MC, V. Bus: 10, 30. Streetcar: F. Map p 140.*

★ **Hyatt Regency San Francisco** FINANCIAL DISTRICT   This corporate hotel has a 17-story atrium, spacious rooms, some fine views, and the Embarcadero Center next door. *5 Embarcadero Center (at Market St. by the Embarcadero).* ☎ *888/591-1234 or 415/788-1234. www.hyatt.com. 802 units. Doubles $159–$299. AE, DC, DISC, MC, V. BART/Muni: Embarcadero. Map p 140.*

★★ **The Inn at Union Square** UNION SQUARE   An intimate inn with airy rooms, attentive staff, snacks throughout the day, and many repeat customers. *440 Post St. (btw. Mason & Powell sts.).* ☎ *800/288-4346 or 415/397-3510. 30 units. Doubles $171–$224; suite $219–$379. Rates include breakfast. AE, DC, DISC, MC, V. Bus: 2, 3, 4. Cable car: Powell lines. BART/Muni: Powell St. Map p 139.*

★★★ **InterContinental Mark Hopkins** NOB HILL   The plush rooms have stellar views and the

The Mark Hopkins sits on the former site of the mansion of Mark Hopkins, one of the founders of the Southern Pacific Railroad.

Top of Mark is a stunning place to dine. An extra $60 per day grants access to the club lounge and free food. *1 Nob Hill (at Mason & California sts.).* ☎ *888/424-6835 or 415/392-3434. www.markhopkins.net. 380 units. Doubles $399–$599. AE, DC, DISC, MC, V. Bus: 1. Cable cars: all lines. Map p 139.*

★★ **Jackson Court** PACIFIC HEIGHTS   Rooms in this brownstone mansion, set in SF's most posh neighborhood, are furnished with antique pieces, and four rooms have fireplaces. *2198 Jackson St. (at Buchanan St.).* ☎ *415/929-7670. www.jacksoncourt.com. 10 units. Doubles $160–$225 w/breakfast. AE, DC, DISC, MC, V. Bus: 12, 22. Map p 140.*

★ **Kabuki** JAPANTOWN   This serene hotel overlooking Japan Center offers Western-style rooms and a few suites with Eastern tatami mats and futons. Free passes (worth $22+) to nearby Kabuki Springs spa (p 81). *1625 Post St. (at Laguna St.).* ☎ *800/533-4567 or 415/922-3200. www.jdvhotels.com/hotels/kabuki. 218 units. Doubles $99–$224; suite $219–$249. AE, DC, DISC, MC, V. Bus: 2, 3, 4, 38. Map p 140.*

★ **King George Hotel** UNION SQUARE   Popular with European tourists, this 1912 hotel offers modern amenities and handsome, albeit petite, rooms. On weekends and holidays, English afternoon tea is served in the hotel's Windsor Tea Room. *334 Mason St. (btw. Geary & O'Farrell sts.).* ☎ *800/288-6005 or 415/781-5050. www.kinggeorge.com. 153 units. Doubles $66–$188. AE, DC, DISC, MC, V. Bus: 2, 3, 4, 38. Cable car: Powell lines. BART/Muni: Powell St. Map p 139.*

★★ **The Laurel Inn** PACIFIC HEIGHTS   This inn is great for longer stays. Many rooms have kitchens, and bus lines are convenient. A major bonus is the free parking and access to the enormous JCC gym across the street at $10 per day. *444 Presidio Ave. (at California St.).* ☎ *800/552-8735 or 415/567-8467. www.jdvhotels.com/hotels/laurel_inn. 49 units. Doubles $159–$209 w/breakfast. AE, DC, DISC, MC, V. Bus: 1, 3, 4, 43. Map p 140.*

★★★ **Mandarin Oriental** FINANCIAL DISTRICT   Atop one of SF's tallest buildings, the Mandarin affords jaw-dropping views from every room and regal service. *222 Sansome St. (btw. Pine & California sts.).* ☎ *800/622-0404 or 415/276-9600. www.mandarinoriental.com. 158 units. Doubles $395–$640; suites from $875. AE, DC, DISC, MC, V. BART/Muni: Montgomery St. Cable car: California. Map p 140.*

★ **The Marina Inn** MARINA   Personal feel and friendly staff make this the best low-priced option. Inside rooms are quieter than Lombard Street rooms. No parking. *3110 Octavia St. (at Lombard St.).* ☎ *800/274-1420 or 415/928-1000. www.marinainn.com. 40 units. Double $59–$69 w/ continental breakfast. AE, DC, DISC, MC, V. Bus: 28, 30, 43. Map p 140.*

★ **Marina Motel** MARINA   The updated rooms have pleasant decor and fridges and coffeemakers. Kitchenette units are rented by the week. Avoid rooms facing noisy Lombard Street. *2576 Lombard St.* ☎ *800/346-6118 or 415/921-9406. www.marinamotel.com. 38 units. Doubles $75–$165; suite $109–$199. AE, DISC, MC, V. Bus: 28, 30, 43. Map p 140.*

★★ **Orchard Garden Hotel** UNION SQUARE   The only hotel built to national green building standards offers soothing decor, high-def TVs, organic bath products, and smoke-free air. *466 Bush St. (at Grant Ave.).* ☎ *888/717-2881 or 415/399-9807. www.theorchardgardenhotel.com. 86 units. Doubles*

$169–$499. AE, DC, DISC, MC, V. Bus: 2, 3, 4, 15, 30. BART/Muni: Montgomery St. Map p 139.

★ **Orchard Hotel** UNION SQUARE   Spacious, quiet rooms, free continental breakfast, and eco-friendly design make this a good no-nonsense choice. *665 Bush St. (at Stockton St.).* ☎ *888/717-2881 or 415/362-8878. www.theorchard hotel.com. 104 units. Doubles $139–$419 w/breakfast. AE, DC, DISC, MC, V. Bus: 2, 3, 4, 15, 30. BART/Muni: Montgomery St. Map p 139.*

★★ **The Palace Hotel** SOMA   The over-the-top decor includes the landmark Garden Court Restaurant (p 13). The large rooms have 14-foot ceilings and marble bathrooms. *2 New Montgomery St. (at Market St.).* ☎ *888/627-7196 or 415/512-1111. www.sfpalace.com. 553 units. Doubles $199–$399; suites from $775. AE, DC, DISC, MC, V. BART/Muni: Montgomery St. Map p 140.*

The Phoenix Hotel CIVIC CENTER   A So Cal rocker hotel with palm trees and a pool. Its Bambuddha

The Marina Inn offers Victorian, vintage charm at budget prices.

Kick back amid the '60s style decor of the Flower Child Room at the Red Victorian B&B.

Lounge is great for a party, but not a quiet sleep. Iffy neighborhood. *601 Eddy St. (at Larkin St.).* ☎ *800/248-9466 or 415/776-1380. www.the phoenixhotel.com. 44 units. Doubles $119–$149; suites $219–$399. AE, DC, DISC, MC, V. Bus: 19, 31. Map p 140.*

★ **Red Victorian B&B** HAIGHT   There should be a sign in front of this lovely and eccentric Haight-Ashbury inn that reads WELCOME BACK TO 1967. Each room has its own theme, such as the Flower Child Room. *1665 Haight St. (at Belvedere St.).* ☎ *415/864-1978. www.redvic.com. 18 units, 4 with private bathroom. Doubles $89–$149 w/ continental breakfast. AE, DC, DISC, MC, V. Bus: 6, 7, 43, 66, 71. Muni: Carl & Cole. Map p 140.*

★★★ **Ritz-Carlton** NOB HILL   The Ritz has impeccable service, regal decor, and prices to match. Even by local standards, the $62 valet parking fee is high. *600 Stockton St. (at California St.).* ☎ *800/241-3333 or 415/296-7465. www.ritzcarlton.com. 336 units. Doubles $445 & up; suites $569 & up. AE, DC, DISC, MC, V. Cable car: all lines. Map p 139.*

San Remo Hotel FISHERMAN'S WHARF   A budget European-style *pensione* with period furnishings and beveled glass. No phones, TVs,

Sausalito

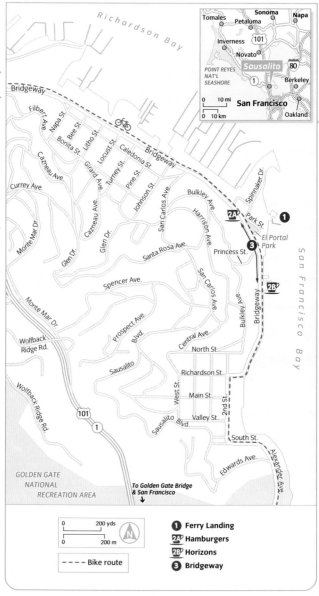

Richardson Bay

Bridgeway

Filbert Ave.

Napa St.
Bee St.
Bonita St.
Litho St.
Locust St.
Caledonia St.

Cazneau Ave.

Currey Ave.

Girard Ave.
Turney St.
Pine St.
Johnson St.

Bridgeway

San Carlos Ave.

Bulkley Ave.

Harrison Ave.

Spinnaker Dr.

Park St.

Monte Mar Dr.

Glen Dr.

Glen Dr.

Cazneau Ave.

Santa Rosa Ave.

Princess St.

El Portal
Park

San Francisco Bay

Spencer Ave.

Prospect Ave.

Blvd.

San Carlos Ave.

Bulkley Ave.

Bridgeway

Wolfback
Ridge Rd.

Central Ave.

North St.

Richardson St.

Monte Mar Dr.

Sausalito

West St.

Main St.

2nd St.

Wolfback Ridge Rd.

101

1

Sausalito Blvd.

Valley St.

South St.

Edwards Ave.

Alexander Ave.

GOLDEN GATE
NATIONAL
RECREATION AREA

**To Golden Gate Bridge
& San Francisco**
↓

Inset map:
Tomales
Sonoma
Napa
Petaluma
Inverness
101
Novato
Sausalito
80
POINT REYES
NAT'L
SEASHORE
1
Berkeley
San Francisco
Oakland

0   10 mi
0   10 km

0   200 yds
0   200 m

N

- - - - Bike route

1 Ferry Landing
2A Hamburgers
2B Horizons
3 Bridgeway

Previous page: Wine Country is just a 60- to 90-minute drive north of San Francisco.

Eclectic Sausalito, a relaxed, quaint neighbor to San Francisco, contains fewer than 8,000 residents. Although this is a town with a fair quota of paper millionaires, they rub their permanently sun-tanned shoulders with a good number of hard-up artists, struggling authors, shipyard workers, and fishermen. This is a great excursion to admire the view of the lofty hills of Marin County that so stunningly frame the San Francisco Bay and to stroll Bridgeway, the offbeat, boutique-lined main drag in town. **START: SF Ferry Building Downtown at the Embarcadero and Mission Street or Pier 41. Streetcar. F. BART/Muni at the Embarcadero or Pier 41 (Fisherman's Wharf). Bus no. 30.**

1 kids ★★ Ferry from San Francisco. Bundle up and skim across the bay from SF on the scenic ferry. Grab your camera and snap a perfect shot of **Alcatraz** (p 11), the Golden Gate Bridge, and downtown San Francisco. ⏲ *30 min. one-way. From downtown at the SF Ferry Bldg. (p 12), take the Golden Gate Ferry Service.* ☎ *415/923-2000. www. goldengateferry.org. Tickets one-way $9.25 adults, $4.50 seniors, disabled & kids 6–18, free for kids 5 and under. Daily schedule varies. Streetcar: F. BART/Muni: Embarcadero. Bus: 30. From Pier 41 (Fisherman's Wharf), take the Blue & Gold Fleet.* ☎ *415/705-5555. www.blueandgoldfleet.com. Tickets one-way $11 adults, $6.75 kids 5–11, free for kids under 5. Daily schedule varies. Bus: 10, 30, 47 to Van Ness Ave. & N. Point St. or 19 to Polk & Beach sts. Cable car: Powell-Hyde line to Fisherman's Wharf or Powell-Mason line to Taylor & Bay sts. Streetcar: F to Jones & Beach sts. Note: To reach Sausalito by bus, bike, or car (via the Golden Gate Bridge), see p 38.*

Pick up lunch at tiny eatery
2A Hamburgers (737 Bridgeway, near the Marina; ☎ 415/332-9471; $), and enjoy it in the park by the Marina. Besides the popular burgers, chicken sandwiches and vegetarian burritos are on offer, as well as to-die-for fries. Hamburgers is open daily until 5pm. Alternatively, head to

2B Horizons (558 Bridgeway; ☎ 415/331-3232; $$), and grab a bite (or a Bloody Mary) at this seafood-oriented fave. Try to sit on the alfresco waterside terrace, which boasts stellar views of the city skyline and the bay. Horizons is open for lunch and dinner daily.

3 Bridgeway. Stroll along Bridgeway and pop into some of the dozens of fine galleries and boutiques. **Capture Fine Art** (589 Bridgeway; ☎ 415/331-7031) features furniture and fabulous photographs. **Petri's Gallery** (675 Bridgeway; ☎ 415/332-2225), chock-full of handblown glass and delicate jewelry, is always popular.

Sunny Sausalito's steep, picturesque hills flank the sparkling San Francisco Bay.

Point Reyes National Seashore

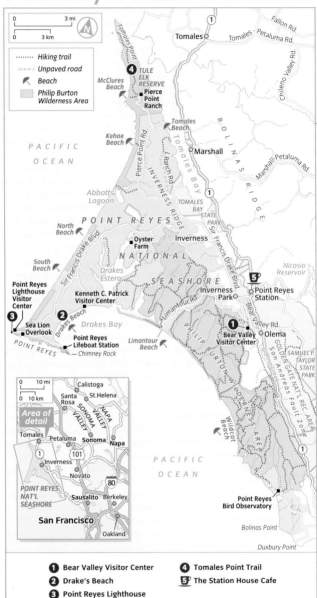

0 ········· 3 mi	
0 ········· 3 km	

········· Hiking trail
≍≍≍≍ Unpaved road
🔻 Beach
▨ Philip Burton Wilderness Area

PACIFIC OCEAN

Tomales
Fallon Rd.
Tomales - Petaluma Rd.
Chileno Valley Rd.
Tomales Point
McClures Beach
❹ TULE ELK RESERVE
■ Pierce Point Ranch
Kehoe Beach
Pierce Point Rd.
L Ranch Rd.
Tomales Beach
Marshall
B O L I N A S   R I D G E
Marshall-Petaluma Rd.
Abbotts Lagoon
INVERNESS RIDGE
Tomales Bay
TOMALES BAY STATE PARK
North Beach
P O I N T   R E Y E S
Oyster Farm ■
Inverness
Sir Francis Drake Blvd.
Nicasio Reservoir
South Beach
N A T I O N A L
Drakes Estero
S E A S H O R E
Inverness Park
❺ Point Reyes Station
Sir Francis Drake Blvd.
Point Reyes Lighthouse Visitor Center
Kenneth C. Patrick Visitor Center ■
Drakes Beach
Limantour Rd.
Bear Valley Rd.
❸ ■ Sea Lion Overlook
❷
Point Reyes Lifeboat Station
Chimney Rock
Drakes Bay
Limantour Beach
P O I N T   R E Y E S
P H I L I P   B U R T O N   W I L D E R N E S S   A R E A
❶ ■ Bear Valley Visitor Center
Olema
SAMUEL P. TAYLOR STATE PARK
GOLDEN GATE NAT'L REC AREA
San Andreas Fault Zone
Wildcat Beach
Point Reyes Bird Observatory ■
Bolinas Point
Duxbury Point
PACIFIC OCEAN

0 ────── 10 mi	
0 ────── 10 km	

Area of detail

Calistoga
Santa Rosa
St. Helena
SONOMA VALLEY
NAPA VALLEY
Tomales
Petaluma
Sonoma
Napa
(1)
(101)
Inverness
Novato
(80)
POINT REYES NAT'L SEASHORE
Sausalito
Berkeley
San Francisco
Oakland

❶ Bear Valley Visitor Center   ❹ Tomales Point Trail
❷ Drake's Beach   ❺ The Station House Cafe
❸ Point Reyes Lighthouse

Point Reyes National Seashore was created to protect rural and undeveloped stretches of the coast and is part of the National Park system. It's a rugged mix of wild coastline and forest of unequivocal appeal to hikers, nature lovers, and wildlife enthusiasts. The rocky shore is a direct result of earthquake activity. In fact, Point Reyes is moving toward Alaska at the rate of 2 inches (5cm) a year— during the 1906 earthquake, it jumped north 20 feet (6m)! This tour takes all day. START: **Rent a car (p 40), cross the Golden Gate Bridge, and head north on U.S. 101. Exit onto Sir Francis Drake Boulevard and take Hwy. 1 north to Olema. Driving time is around 90 minutes.**

❶ The Bear Valley Visitor Center, a visitor center for Point Reyes National Seashore, has eco-logical and historical exhibits, as well as a seismograph and weather station. Pick up a detailed trail map and chat with the helpful, friendly park rangers. You can take a ranger-led guided tour (call ahead) or inquire about activities like biking, horseback riding, and wildlife viewing. *Bear Valley Rd. (look for the sign north of Olema on Hwy. 1).* ☎ *415/ 464-5100. www.nps.gov/pore. Mon– Fri 9am–5pm; Sat–Sun 8am–5pm. Free admission. Best time: weekdays.*

❷ Drake's Beach. Take a walk along this sublime beach backed by white sandstone cliffs. Just don't swim—the water is frigid and the undertow dangerous. And never turn your back on the sea, as occasional powerful "sneaker waves" can suddenly come to shore.

❸ ★★ Point Reyes Light-house. You'll drive by dairy farms and pastures to reach this dramatic vista point. The walk down to, and back up from, the lighthouse is not for the faint of heart—it's steep, long, and often windy. But the view of the rugged rocks and rough seas far below is mind-blowing. Look for the sea lions and harbor seals; in winter, you may catch sight of gray whales on their 5,000-mile (8,050km) journey north from Mexico. ☎ *415/669-1534. Free admission.*

Thurs–Mon 10am–4:30pm. Stairs to lighthouse closed when winds exceed 40 mph (64kmph). Lighthouse is 300 steps down from center; no wheelchair ramp. On busy winter weekends, a shuttle takes visitors from Drake's Beach to the light-house. Shuttle ☎ *415/464-5100. $5 adults, free for kids 16 & under.*

❹ Tomales Point Trail. The northern tip of Point Reyes boasts sweeping views of the rocky coast. In spring, it also contains a breath-taking array of wildflowers, and July to October offer the best viewing of the 500 elk living on a protected reserve on this peninsula. Bring bin-oculars. *Take Pierce Point Rd. to the end—the trail head is just beyond the Pierce Point Ranch.*

❺ The Station House Cafe is a low-key favorite, where the daily specials draw on organic, local ingredients with a selection of fine California wines and beer. *11180 State Rte. 1.* ☎ *415/663-1515. $.*

Point Reyes Lighthouse is a great lookout point for whales and sea lions.

Bohemian Berkeley

1. University of California, Berkeley– Visitors Center
2. Sather Tower
3. UC Botanical Garden
4. Lawrence Hall of Science
5. Berkeley Art Museum
6. Telegraph Avenue
7. Chez Panisse
7. Cheeseboard Pizza Collective

Across the bay from San Francisco is the warm, woodsy, left-leaning city of Berkeley. Plan to arrive in the late morning and stay for dinner. START: **BART to Downtown Berkeley exit. (Change at Oakland City Center to Richmond train.) Driving (45 min.–1 hr.): Cross Bay Bridge to I-80 northbound; exit University Avenue and drive east.**

① ★★ **University of California, Berkeley.** Stroll the attractive, wooded campus on your own or reserve a spot on the free 90-minute tour. *Visitors Center, 101 University Hall, 2200 University Ave. (at Oxford St.)* ☎ *510/642-5215. www.berkeley.edu/visitors. Reserved tours Mon–Sat 10am, Sun 1pm. Mon–Fri tours start at Visitors Center, Sat–Sun at Sather Tower.*

② **Sather Tower.** Get a bird's-eye view from this 307-foot (92m) tower. It contains 61 bells weighing up to 5 tons. Carillon concerts at 7:50am, noon, and 6pm daily; extended concerts on Sunday at 2pm. **Note:** There are 38 stairs from the top of elevator to viewing platform. *Elevator ride $2 adults, $1 seniors & kids under 18. Mon–Fri 10am–4pm; Sat 10am–5pm; Sun 10am–1:30pm & 3–5pm.*

③ ★★ **UC Botanical Garden.** Enjoy more than 9,600 different species, including cacti and orchids you've never even imagined. *200 Centennial Dr.* ☎ *510/643-2755. www.botanicalgarden.berkeley.edu. Admission $9 adults, $7 seniors & kids 13–17, $2 kids 5–12, free for kids under 5. Daily 9am–5pm (redwood grove & greenhouses close at 4pm). H-line shuttle bus from Hearst Mining Circle.*

④ ★★ kids **Lawrence Hall of Science.** Learn while having a ton of fun at the world-class planetarium and in the earthquake simulator. Superb views. *1 Centennial Dr.* ☎ *510/642-5132. www.lhs.berkeley.edu. Admission $17 adults, $14 seniors & kids 7–18, $11 kids 3–6, free for kids under 3. Planetarium shows*

$3 adults, $2.50 kids under 19. Daily 10am–5pm. H line shuttle bus.

⑤ ★★ **Berkeley Art Museum.** Asian, early American, avant-garde, and international contemporary art, with works by masters like Mark Rothko and Jackson Pollock. *2626 Bancroft Way.* ☎ *510/642-0808. www.bampfa.berkeley.edu. Admission $10 adults, $7 seniors & kids 13–17, free for kids under 12. Free for all 1st Thurs. Wed–Sun 11am–5pm. P-line bus from Hearst Mining Circle.*

⑥ **Telegraph Avenue.** Rastafarian street vendors, independent booksellers, music shops, funky clothing stores, and a diverse crowd. *Telegraph Ave. (from Bancroft Way to Dwight Way).*

The crowning glory of this "Gourmet Ghetto" is 7A **Chez Panisse** (p 102). A less-expensive alternative is the 7B **Cheeseboard Pizza Collective** *(1217 Shattuck Ave.;* ☎ *707/549-3055; www.cheeseboardcollective.coop; $$).*

Telegraph Avenue in Berkeley.

The Best of Napa in One Day

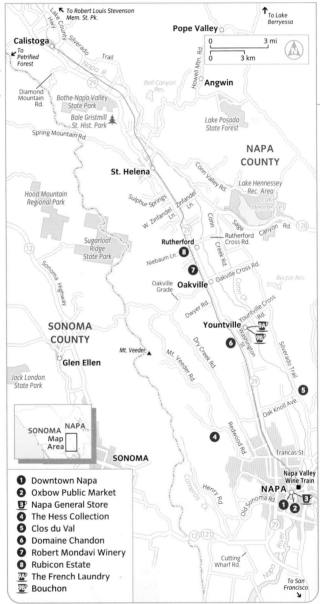

To Robert Louis Stevenson Mem. St. Pk.

To Lake Berryessa

Pope Valley

Calistoga

To Petrified Forest

Lake County Hwy.

Silverado Trail

Napa R.

Diamond Mountain Rd.

Bothe-Napa Valley State Park

Bale Gristmill St. Hist. Park

Spring Mountain Rd.

Bell Canyon Res.

Angwin

Howell Mtn. Rd.

Lake Posada State Forest

NAPA COUNTY

Hood Mountain Regional Park

St. Helena

Sulphur Springs

W. Zinfandel Ln.

Zinfandel Ln.

Conn Valley Rd.

Lake Hennessey Rec. Area

Lake Hennessey

Sugarloaf Ridge State Park

Sonoma Highway

Rutherford ❽

Niebaum Ln.

❼

Conn

Conn Creek Rd.

Sage Canyon Rd.

Rutherford Cross Rd.

Rector Res.

128

SONOMA COUNTY

Mt. Veeder

Oakville Grade

Oakville

Oakville Cross Rd.

Conn Ck.

Dwyer Rd.

Mt. Veeder Rd.

Dry Creek Rd.

Yountville

❻

Washington

Yountville Cross Rd.

❾ᴬ
❾ᴮ

Silverado Trail

Glen Ellen

Jack London State Park

SONOMA Map Area

NAPA

Redwood Rd.

Oak Knoll Ave.

❺

SONOMA

❹

Henry Rd.

Carneros Ck.

Trancas St.

Napa Valley Wine Train

NAPA

❶ ❷

❸

Old Sonoma Rd.

12 121

Cutting Wharf Rd.

Napa River

To San Francisco

0   3 mi
0   3 km

❶ Downtown Napa
❷ Oxbow Public Market
❸ Napa General Store
❹ The Hess Collection
❺ Clos du Val
❻ Domaine Chandon
❼ Robert Mondavi Winery
❽ Rubicon Estate
❾ᴬ The French Laundry
❾ᴮ Bouchon

All you have is a day to make the most of Napa? That's a tall order because the valley is so rich with delightful towns, wineries, sights, and activities, but it can be done—and done well. This full-day itinerary, manageable in a day by car (designate a driver), introduces you to the region's fundamental character. (This tour is from *Napa & Sonoma Day by Day*, by Avital Binshtock.) START: **Rent a car (p 40), cross the Golden Gate Bridge, and head north on U.S. 101. Exit at Hwy. 37; after 10 miles (16km) turn north onto Calif. 121. Driving time is just over an hour.**

❶ ★★ **Downtown Napa.** Not long ago, the actual town of Napa would never have been listed in a "best of Napa Valley" tour—but times have changed, and the town's recent redevelopment merits it a spot right at the top. Hit Napa Town Center to get a feel for everyday life here, as well as the striking Italianate-style Opera House. Pick up a picnic lunch at one of the town's upscale markets. *Napa Valley Conference & Visitors Bureau, 1310 Napa Town Center, Napa.* ☎ *707/226-7459. www.napavalley.org. Mon–Sat 9am–5pm; Sun 11am–5pm.*

❷ ★ **Oxbow Public Market.** A foodie's dream destination that lets you discover the best of the region all under one roof. Vendors sell artisanal cheeses, exotic spices, bottles from micro-wineries, and much more. Free parking is available. *600 1st St., Napa.* ☎ *707/963-1345. www.oxbowpublicmarket.com. Open Mon–Sat 10am–6pm, Sun 10am–5pm (closed Thanksgiving, Christmas, & New Year's Day).*

❸ ★ **Napa General Store.** End your downtown Napa visit at the Historic Napa Mill for sandwiches, salads, pan-Asian specialties, and hand-tossed pizzas, to stay or to go. Or pick up a box lunch ($15), which must be ordered a day in advance. *540 Main St., Napa.* ☎ *707/259-0762. $$.*

Take Hwy. 29 north and exit at Trancas St. Turn left on Redwood Rd., a four-lane road that narrows into a two-lane road. Turn left at the Hess Collection's sign.

❹ ★★★ **The Hess Collection.** The beautiful drive up provides a good example of the pristine scenery that characterizes much of Northern California. The winery itself includes art galleries, a garden that fully blooms in summer, and an impressive stone-walled tasting room in the original 1903 winery for sipping Hess's current releases, including superb cabernet sauvignon and chardonnay. *4411 Redwood Rd., Napa.* ☎ *877/707-4377.*

Wind back down Redwood Rd. and stay straight onto Trancas St., then turn left on Silverado Trail.

Stop into the tasting room at the Hess Collection.

5 ★ **Clos du Val.** You can't say you've done Napa's best without having seen at least one small, exclusive winery in the Stags Leap District along the scenic Silverado Trail. Marked with both French and American flags to affirm that this estate is French-owned, Clos du Val's tasting room is behind ivy-covered walls. In it, try Ariadne, the winery's proprietary blend of sauvignon blanc and Sémillon. Ask tasting room staff for a tour of the demonstration vineyard, where you can learn about trellising techniques and how to identify different kinds of grapes. After trying the wines, settle into Clos du Val's beautiful olive grove and break out the food you bought earlier for a picnic lunch. *5330 Silverado Trail, Napa.* ☎ *707/259-2200.*

Head southeast on Silverado Trail and turn right at Oak Knoll Ave., then left on Big Ranch Rd. Turn right to get back onto Oak Knoll Ave., and right again to get on Hwy. 29 N. Exit toward Yountville and turn left on California Dr. and head up the long, vineyard-flanked driveway.

6 ★ **Domaine Chandon.** Cross a small footbridge over a life-filled pond (keep an eye out for egrets) and past some interestingly placed sculptures (including a faux mushroom field) to enter the educational visitor center, complete with a 28-seat large-screen theater, a wall made entirely of bottles, and interactive exhibits. Domaine Chandon specializes in sparkling wine. The knowledgeable staff explains the nuances of effervescent wine. *1 California Dr. (at Hwy. 29), Yountville.* ☎ *707/944-2280.*

Take California Dr. northeast to merge onto Hwy. 29.

7 ★★ **Robert Mondavi Winery.** This mission-style winery gives the valley's most varied and comprehensive tours. Given today's time constraints, however, opt for the basic tour or simply visit the art gallery before or after tasting in the Appellation Room, an outdoor tasting area that's open in summer. If it's winter, taste in the upscale ToKalon Room. *7801 St. Helena Hwy. (Hwy. 29), Oakville.* ☎ *707/226-1395.*

Keep following Hwy. 29 northwest.

8 ★★★ **Rubicon Estate.** Sometimes better known by its former name, Niebaum-Coppola, Rubicon is film director Francis Ford Coppola's ivy-draped 1880s stone winery that exudes momentous grandeur. The Centennial Museum chronicles the winemaking estate's rich history, as well as Coppola's filmmaking. On display are Academy Awards and memorabilia from *The Godfather* and *Bram Stoker's Dracula.* Sample estate-grown blends, cabernet franc, and merlot—all made from organic grapes, but note the caveat: a $25 admission fee. For the price, you'll get a tour and a five-wine tasting flight. *1991 St. Helena Hwy., Rutherford.* ☎ *707/968-1100.*

9A ★★★ **The French Laundry.** If you want the best of Napa dining, there's only one place to go: the once-in-a-lifetime experience that is the French Laundry. Reservations required, at least 2 months in advance. *6640 Washington St., Yountville.* ☎ *707/944-2380. $$$$$.*

If you've still got next month's rent to pay, dine at Chef Thomas Keller's humbler **9B** ★★ **Bouchon.** *6534 Washington St.* ☎ *707/944-8037. $$$.* ●

The
Savvy Traveler

Before You Go

Tourist Office

Contact the **San Francisco Convention and Visitors Bureau,** 900 Market St., Lower Level, Hallidie Plaza, San Francisco, CA 94102-2804 (☎ 415/391-2000; www.only insanfrancisco.com), for a free visitors' information kit by mail.

The Best Times to Go

September and October are "Indian summer" months and are a great time to visit the city—the weather is warm and the fog disappears. The summer months from June to August are busy with fun fairs and festivals, but it's cold and foggy. Winter is beautiful and mild, plus, the city is decked out between November and January for Thanksgiving, Christmas, and New Year's. Spring is pleasant but can be rainy.

Festivals & Special Events

SPRING Mid- to late April is the time for the **Cherry Blossom Festival** (☎ 415/563-2313) in Japantown. Watch traditional drumming, flower arranging, origami, or a parade celebrating the cherry blossom and Japanese culture. Mid-April to early May is when the **San Francisco International Film Festival** (☎ 415/561-5000; www.sffs.org) takes place around San Francisco, with screenings at the Sundance Kabuki Cinemas (Fillmore and Post sts.), and at many other locations. Started in 1957, this is America's oldest film festival. The Sunday before May 5 brings the **Cinco de Mayo Celebration** in the Mission District (☎ 415/206-0577; www. sfcincodemayo.com). This is when the Latino community celebrates the victory of the Mexicans over the

French at Puebla in 1862; mariachi bands, dancers, food, and a parade fill the streets of the Mission. The parade starts at 10am at 24th and Bryant streets and ends at the Civic Center. The **Bay to Breakers 12K** (☎ 415/359-2800; www.zazzlebay tobreakers.com; 3rd Sun of May) starts at the Embarcadero and travels through Golden Gate Park to Ocean Beach. More than 60,000 entrants gather—many dressed in wacky, innovative, and sometimes X-rated costumes—for the 7.5-mile (12km) run. The Mission District's largest annual event, **Carnaval** (☎ 415/920-0125; www.carnaval. com/sf/sf_carn.htm), is a day of festivities that culminates in a parade on Mission Street. More than half a million spectators line the route, and samba musicians and dancers continue to entertain on 14th Street, near Harrison, at the end of the march. It takes place on Sunday during Memorial Day (last Mon in May) weekend.

SUMMER During the first weekend of June, the outdoor **Union Street Festival** celebrates San Francisco with plenty of food booths, music, entertainment, and booths featuring ecofriendly products. Contact the **Union Street Association** (☎ 415/441-7055; www.union streetfestival.com) for more information. A far cry from the chic Union Street festival, the grittier **Haight-Ashbury Street Fair** (☎ 415/863-3489; www.haight ashburystreetfair.org) in June features alternative crafts, ethnic foods, rock bands, and a healthy number of hippies and street kids whooping it up and slamming beers in front of the blaring rock-'n'-roll stage. Organizers claim the **North Beach Festival** (☎ 415/989-2220;

Previous page: The F Market & Wharves historic streetcars run from Fisherman's Wharf to the Castro.

www.sfnorthbeach.org) is the oldest urban street fair in the country. Close to 100,000 city folk meander along Grant Avenue, between Vallejo and Union streets, to eat, drink, and enjoy the arts and crafts booths, poetry readings, swing dancing, and *arte di gesso* (sidewalk chalk art). It usually takes place on Father's Day weekend in mid-June, but call to confirm. Free concerts take place every Sunday at 2pm between mid-June and late August at the annual **Stern Grove Mid-summer Music Festival** (☎ 415/252-6252; www.sterngrove.org), in the Sunset District. Head out early to join the thousands who come here to lie in the grass and enjoy classical, jazz, and ethnic music, and dance. Bring warm clothes—the Sunset District can be one of the coldest parts of the city. Usually the third or last weekend of June, the **San Francisco Lesbian, Gay, Bisexual, Transgender Pride Parade & Celebration** (☎ 415/864-3733; www.sfpride.org) draws up to half a million participants who celebrate all of the above—and then some. The parade proceeds west on Market Street to Market and 8th streets. The first weekend in July starts with a bang, when the upscale portion of Fillmore closes to traffic and several blocks of arts and crafts, gourmet food, and live jazz fill the street for the **Fillmore Street Jazz Festival** (☎ 510/970-3217; www.fillmorejazzfestival.com) in Pacific Heights. Call or visit the website for more information. The **Fourth of July Celebration & Fireworks** at Fisherman's Wharf (www.fishermanswharf.org) can be something of a joke—more often than not, fog rolls into the city. Sometimes it's almost impossible to view the million-dollar pyrotechnics from PIER 39 on the northern waterfront. Still, it's a party, and if the skies are clear, it's a darn good

show. The **San Francisco Marathon** (usually the 2nd or 3rd weekend in July) is one of the largest marathons in the world. For entry information, log onto www.runsfm.com.

AUTUMN On Labor Day weekend is the **Sausalito Art Festival** (☎ 415/331-3555; www.sausalitoartfestival.org), a juried exhibit of more than 180 artists which includes music and international cuisine, enhanced by local wine. Parking is impossible; take the **Blue & Gold Fleet** ferry (☎ 415/705-8200; www.blueandgoldfleet.com) from Fisherman's Wharf or the Golden Gate Ferry Service (☎ 415/921-5858; www.goldengateferry.org) from downtown at the SF Ferry Building to the festival site. Each year in early September, the San Francisco Opera (☎ 415/861-4008; www.sfopera.com) launches its season with **Opera in the Park** (usually in Sharon Meadow, Golden Gate Park), a free concert featuring a selection of arias. At the end of September, the **Folsom Street Fair** (www.folsomstreetfair.com) in SoMa is a local favorite for its kinky, outrageous, leather-and-skin gay-centric blowout celebration. It's hard-core, so only open-minded and adventurous types need head this way. During **Fleet Week** (☎ 650/599-5057; www.fleetweek.us) in October, residents gather along the bay front to watch aerial performances by the Blue Angels, flown in tribute to the U.S. Marines. On the first Sunday in October, the **Castro Street Fair** (☎ 415/841-1824; www.castrostreetfair.org) celebrates life in the city's most famous gay neighborhood. On a Sunday near October 12, the **Italian Heritage Parade** (☎ 415/587-8282; www.sfcolumbusday.org) celebrates Columbus's landing in the Americas. The festival includes a parade along Columbus Avenue and sporting events, but

Useful Websites

- **SFGate.com:** The *San Francisco Chronicle*.
- **SFBG.com:** The *San Francisco Bay Guardian,* a local free weekly.
- **SFist.com:** A news blog with a healthy dose of snark. All the stories the cool kids are talking about.
- **511.org:** Everything you need to know to take public transport in the city.
- **OpenTable.com:** Restaurant reservations.
- **Chowhound.com:** Where to eat in San Francisco.
- **GoCityKids.com:** A city guide for parents.
- **SFKids.org:** San Francisco's official family resource guide.
- **Funcheapsf.com:** A great guide to free and dirt-cheap events in the Bay Area.
- **Flavorpill.com/sanfrancisco:** Cultural happenings in the city are found here—art exhibits, book readings, and more.
- **Goldstar.com:** An events newsletter offering half-price or better tickets.
- **Laughingsquid.com:** A curated compilation of art, culture, and tech events in the Bay Area.
- **Yelp.com:** User reviews to just about everything in San Francisco.

mainly, it's a great excuse to hang out in North Beach and people-watch. In late October and early November, the 2-week **San Francisco Jazz Festival** (☎ 415/398-5655; www.sfjazz.org) presents eclectic programming in an array of fabulous jazz venues throughout the city.

WINTER Each December, the **San Francisco Ballet** (☎ 415/865-2000; www.sfballet.org) performs the holiday classic, *The Nutcracker.* Order tickets to this Tchaikovsky tradition well in advance. **Chinese New Year** celebrations (☎ 415/982-3000; www.chineseparade.com) spill onto every street in Chinatown, including parades of marching bands, rolling floats, barrages of fireworks, and a block-long dragon writhing in and out of the crowds. The revelry runs for several weeks and wraps up with a memorable parade through Chinatown that starts at Market and 2nd streets and ends at Kearny Street. Chinese New Year begins with the New Moon on the first day of the new calendar year and ends on the full moon 15 days later—thus, dates vary between January and February each year. On the Sunday before March 17, everyone's an honorary Irish person at the **St. Patrick's Day Parade** (☎ 415/675-9885; www.sfstpatricksdayparade.com), which starts at 12:45pm at Market and 2nd streets and continues to City Hall.

The Weather

San Francisco has a temperate, marine climate, which means relatively mild weather all year-round. Summers bring dense fog and low

SAN FRANCISCO'S HIGH & LOW DAILY TEMPERATURE & MONTHLY RAINFALL

	JAN	FEB	MAR	APR	MAY	JUNE
High (°F/°C)	58/14	61/16	62/17	65/18	65/18	68/20
Low (°F/°C)	46/8	48/9	49/9	50/10	51/11	53/12
Rain (in.)	4.7	4.2	3.4	1.3	0.5	0.1

	JULY	AUG	SEPT	OCT	NOV	DEC
High (°F/°C)	68/20	69/21	71/22	70/21	64/18	59/15
Low (°F/°C)	53/12	54/12	56/13	55/13	52/11	47/8
Rain (in.)	0.1	0.1	0.3	1.2	3.3	3.2

temperatures with highs only in the 70s (20s Celsius). The "Indian summer" of September and October bring temperatures up to the 90s (30s Celsius) but can drop down significantly. Always bring layers, as it could be warm in one neighborhood and cold in the next. For up-to-the-minute weather reports, log on to www.sfgate.com/weather.

Cellphones (Mobile Phones)

One good wireless rental company is **InTouch USA** (☎ 800/872-7626). **Triptel Mobile Rental Phones,** 1525 Van Ness Ave., between California and Pine streets. (☎ 415/474-3330), and **SFO International Terminal** (☎ 650/821-8000; www.triptel.com), rents cellular phones at $3 per day, or $15 per week. Airtime rates are 95¢ per minute for domestic calls, with an additional $2.50 per minute for international calls. Triptel also sells SIM cards for foreign travelers bringing their own phones.

The **GSM (Global System for Mobile Communications) wireless network,** used by much of the rest of the world, has poor reach in the U.S. GSM phones will probably work in most major U.S. cities, but not in many rural areas. To see

where GSM phones work in the U.S., check out www.t-mobile.com/coverage.

If you're not from the U.S., you'll be appalled at the poor reach of our **GSM** (Global System for Mobile Communications) **wireless network,** which is used by much of the rest of the world. Your phone will probably work in most major U.S. cities; it definitely won't work in many rural areas.

Car Rentals

For booking rental cars online, the best deals are usually found on rental-car company websites. U.K. visitors should check **HolidayAutos** (www.holidayautos.co.uk).

Major car rental companies operating in San Francisco include **Alamo** (☎ 800/327-9633; www.alamo.com), **Avis** (☎ 800/331-1212; www.avis.com), **Budget** (☎ 800/527-0700; www.budget.com), **Dollar** (☎ 800/800-4000; www.dollar.com), **Enterprise** (☎ 800/325-8007; www.enterprise.com), **Hertz** (☎ 800/654-3131; www.hertz.com), **National** (☎ 800/227-7368; www.nationalcar.com), and **Thrifty** (☎ 800/367-2277; www.thrifty.com).

Getting **There**

By Plane

Two major airports serve San Francisco: San Francisco International (SFO) and Oakland International Airport, which is across the Bay Bridge off I-880. SFO is closer to downtown and more airlines fly into this major hub—most international flights arrive here. Oakland is smaller and easier to navigate, but fares for cabs and shuttle buses into the city will be about 50% higher. It's worth checking your options flying into either airport, as you'll sometimes find a cheaper or more convenient flight arriving in Oakland; it also often enjoys better weather than San Francisco, where flights can be delayed due to foggy conditions.

Getting to & from the Airport

Taxis: From SFO, the approximate fare is $35 to $40, plus tip, for the 20- to 30-minute trip (depending on traffic). From Oakland the fare is about $60 and takes 30 to 40 minutes.

Airport Shuttles SFO: SuperShuttle (☎ 800/258-3826 or 415/558-8500), **Bay Shuttle** (☎ 415/564-3400), and **Quake City Shuttle** (☎ 415/255-4899) charge around $16 per adult and $8 per child. **Oakland International Airport: Bayporter Express** (☎ 877/467-1800 or 415/467-1800) charges $29 for the first adult and $15 for each additional adult; $10 per child.

Public Transportation (BART, a commuter train) From SFO: From any terminal, take the free, 5- to 10-minute AIRTRAIN to the BART SF International Airport station, and transfer to the BART train. A one-way ticket from the airport to downtown San Francisco is $6 and takes about 35 minutes. This is the cheapest option of getting into the city.

From Oakland International Airport: Catch the **AirBART shuttle** (☎ 510/465-2278), which runs every 10 minutes, in front of either terminal. The fare is $2 for adults and $1 for children and seniors for the 15-minute ride to the Oakland Coliseum BART station. From there, you'll transfer to a BART train San Francisco. The trip to downtown takes about 25 minutes; the fare is $3.15.

By Car

You can get to San Francisco along three major highways. I-5 runs through the center of the state and intersects with I-80, which goes to the Bay Bridge. The drive from Los Angeles to San Francisco on I-5 is about 6 hours. The drive from Los Angeles to San Francisco on Hwy. 101, a slower option, takes 7 hours.

Drivers arriving from the east will cross the Bay Bridge ($5 toll) and head toward downtown on 5th Street or toward North Beach and Fisherman's Wharf on Fremont Street. Cars coming from the south on Hwy. 101 will see the city skyline on their left a few miles past Monster Park (the former Candlestick Park). Downtown exits here are either 7th or 4th streets. If you're driving from the coast heading south, you'll enter San Francisco by the Golden Gate Bridge. Once you pass the tollbooth ($6 toll), exit along the bay to Van Ness Avenue.

By Train & Bus

Amtrak (☎ 800/872-7245 or 800/USA-RAIL (872-7245); www.amtrak.com) doesn't stop in San Francisco proper, but lands in Emeryville, just south of Berkeley in the East Bay. From the station, an Amtrak bus takes passengers into downtown

San Francisco. The buses stop at the Ferry Building at the foot of Market Street, and at the Cal Train station, where you can catch the streetcar to Embarcadero Station and thus into town. The Ferry Building is more convenient to most of the hotels listed in this book, as long as you can manage to hail a cab.

The **Greyhound Lines** (☎ 415/495-1569; www.greyhound.com) terminal is located at 425 Mission St. (3rd floor) in the Transbay Terminal and is open from 5:30am to 1am daily.

Getting **Around**

By Car

Driving in San Francisco can be frustrating. Along with aggressive local drivers, one-way streets, no right or left turns when you really need one, and dead ends, there's a lack of parking, period. Fortunately, it isn't necessary to drive to most of the places you'll want to go. When driving is imperative, rent a car for the day. For those of you who are driving to SF, park at your hotel and use public transportation.

By Taxi

You have to call for a cab in San Francisco unless you are boarding one from your hotel. **Taxi companies** are **Veteran's Cab** (☎ 415/552-1300), **Luxor Cabs** (☎ 415/282-4141), **De Soto Cab** (☎ 415/970-1300), and **Yellow Cab** (☎ 415/626-2345). Rates are around $3.10 for the first 1/5 mile and 45¢ each fifth of a mile thereafter.

By Muni (Bus, Streetcar, Cable Car & Subway)

The Bay Area has a hodgepodge of transit systems that are all managed by the county. San Francisco's Municipal Railway (☎ 415/673-6864; www.sfmuni.com), known simply as "Muni," operates the city's buses, streetcars, and cable cars. For detailed route information, call Muni or visit its website. Most routes run from 6am to midnight and some busy routes have night-owl services. Another helpful website is www.511.org, which also lists schedules and route maps for all Bay Area transit systems.

Muni Passports can be a bargain for visitors who plan to take buses, streetcars, or cable cars often. A 1-day passport is $13, a 3-day passport is $20, and a 7-day passport is $26. Passports and a Muni map (a necessary item) can be purchased at the Visitor Information Center on Hallidie Plaza, at Tix Bay Area on Union Square, at the baggage-level information booths at SFO, and at bookstores and periodical vendors. Passes and passports can be found at the cable car ticket booths at Powell and Market or Beach and Hyde streets. Single-day passports are available onboard the cable cars as well. For more information see "Passes," in the "Fast Facts" section, later in this chapter.

By BART

BART, an acronym for **Bay Area Rapid Transit** (☎ 415/989-2278; www.bart.gov), connects San Francisco with the East Bay—Oakland, Richmond, Concord, and Fremont. Fares range from $1.75 to $10.90, depending on how far you go. Machines in the stations dispense tickets that are magnetically encoded with a dollar amount. Computerized exits automatically deduct the correct fare. Children 4 and under ride free. Trains run every

15 to 20 minutes, Monday through Friday from 4am to midnight, Saturday from 6am to midnight, and Sunday from 8am to midnight.

On Foot

Seeing the city on foot is a fantastic way to get around—but remember, the steep hills can suck the wind out of you.

Fast **Facts**

APARTMENT RENTALS   For short-term rentals, your best bet is www.craigslist.org. You'll most likely negotiate a rental directly from the unit's owner (or the person subletting). **American Marketing Systems** (www.amsires.com) and **Executive Suites** (www.executivesuites-sf.com) offer furnished apartments for rent for a few days or more, although rates can be high. To research house exchanges, check out **Homelink International** (www.homelink.org), which has more than 14,000 listings in several countries, and **Homebase Holidays** (www.homebase-hols.com).

ATMs/CASHPOINTS   As in most cities these days, obtaining money is a simple matter of lining up at the nearest ATM and plugging in your bankcard. Unless you go to one of your bank's ATMs, you will be charged a fee of $3 to $4. The **Mastercard Cirrus** (☎ 800/424-7787; www.mastercard.com) and **Visa PLUS** (☎ 800/843-7587; www.visa.com) networks span the globe; look at the back of your bankcard to see which network you're on, then call or check online for ATM locations at your destination. Find out your daily withdrawal limit before you depart.

BABYSITTING   Most hotel concierges will simply provide referrals to a babysitting service, which guests must then call on their own. Local companies supplying short-term sitters are: **American Child-Care Service** (☎ 415/285-2300;

www.americanchildcare.com), **Bay Area 2nd Mom** (☎ 888/926-3666; www.2ndmom.com), and **Town & Country Resources** (☎ 800/398-8810 or 415/567-0956; www.tandcr.com).

BANKING HOURS   Most banks are open Monday through Friday from 9am to 5pm, although some branches may stay open until 6pm weekdays and have limited hours on Saturday. Most banks also have ATMs for 24-hour banking.

B&BS   Go to **Bed & Breakfast Inns Online** (www.bbonline.com) or **Pamela Lanier's Bed & Breakfast Inns** website (www.lanierbb.com).

BIKE RENTALS   If you want to bike along the Golden Gate Promenade over the Golden Gate Bridge to Sausalito, your best bet is **Blazing Saddles,** 1095 Columbus Ave. and Pier 41, Fisherman's Wharf (☎ 415/202-8888; www.blazingsaddles.com). Rental prices ($32 per day) include helmets, locks, front packs, rear racks, maps, and advice. Tandems, kids' trailers, and baby seats are available. At **Bike and Roll,** 899 Columbus Ave. (☎ 415/229-2000; www.bikeandroll.com), in addition to bike rentals, you'll get the info you need for self-guided tours to Muir Woods and similar locations. Rental rates are $8 per hour or $32 per day.

CLIMATE   See "The Weather," above.

CONCERTS   See "Tickets," later in this chapter.

CONSULATES & EMBASSIES All embassies are located in the nation's capital, Washington, D.C. Some consulates are located in major U.S. cities, and most nations have a mission to the United Nations in New York City. For a directory of embassies in Washington, D.C., call ☎ 202/555-1212 or log on to www. embassy.org/embassies. The following are consulate addresses for a selection of countries: The embassy of **Australia** is at 1601 Massachusetts Ave. NW, Washington, DC 20036 (☎ 202/797-3000; www.usa. embassy.gov.au). Consulates are in New York, Honolulu, Houston, Los Angeles, and San Francisco. The embassy of **Canada** is at 501 Pennsylvania Ave. NW, Washington, DC 20001 (☎ 202/682-1740; www.canada international.gc.ca/washington). Other Canadian consulates are in Buffalo (New York), Detroit, Los Angeles, New York, and Seattle. The embassy of **Ireland** is at 2234 Massachusetts Ave. NW, Washington, DC 20008 (☎ 202/462-3939; www. embassyofireland.org). Irish consulates are in Boston, Chicago, New York, San Francisco, and other cities. See website for complete listing. The embassy of **New Zealand** is at 37 Observatory Circle NW, Washington, DC 20008 (☎ 202/328-4800; www.nzembassy.com). New Zealand consulates are in Los Angeles, Salt Lake City, San Francisco, and Seattle. The embassy of the **United Kingdom** is at 3100 Massachusetts Ave. NW, Washington, DC 20008 (☎ 202/588-6500; www.ukinusa. fco.gov.uk). Other British consulates are in Atlanta, Boston, Chicago, Cleveland, Houston, Los Angeles, New York, San Francisco, and Seattle.

CREDIT CARDS Credit cards are a safe way to "carry" money; they provide a convenient record of all your expenses, and they generally offer good exchange rates. You can also withdraw cash advances from your credit cards at banks or ATMs, provided you know your PIN.

CUSTOMS Visitors arriving by air, no matter what the port of entry, should cultivate patience and resignation before setting foot on U.S. soil. Getting through immigration control can take as long as 2 hours on some days, especially on summer weekends. People traveling by air from Canada, Bermuda, and certain countries in the Caribbean can sometimes clear Customs and Immigration at the point of departure, which is much quicker.

DENTISTS If you have dental problems, a nationwide referral service known as **1-800-DENTIST** (☎ 800/ 336-8478; www.1800dentist.com) will provide the name of a nearby dentist or clinic.

DINING Dining in SF, as in most of California, is generally casual and a jacket is rarely required, unless you are at one of the most upscale restaurants in town. **Restaurant reservations:** Call the restaurant directly or try the website www.opentable. com, a free and convenient way to make reservations online.

DOCTORS See "Emergencies," below.

ELECTRICITY Like Canada, the United States uses 110 to120 volts AC (60 cycles), compared to 220 to 240 volts AC (50 cycles) in most of Europe, Australia, and New Zealand. If your small appliances use 220 to 240 volts, you'll need a 110-volt transformer and a plug adapter with two flat parallel pins to operate them here. Downward converters that change 220 to 240 volts to 110 to120 volts are difficult to find in the United States, so bring one with you.

EMBASSIES See "Consulates & Embassies," above.

EMERGENCIES Dial ☎ 911 for fire, police, and an ambulance.

The **Poison Control Center** (www. poison.org) can be reached at ☎ 800/222-1222, toll-free from any phone. If you encounter serious problems, contact **Traveler's Aid International** (☎ 202/546-1127; www.travelersaid.org).

EVENT LISTINGS See "Useful Websites," earlier in this chapter.

HOLIDAYS Banks, government offices, post offices, and many stores, restaurants, and museums are closed on the following legal national holidays: January 1 (New Year's Day), the third Monday in January (Martin Luther King Day), the third Monday in February (Presidents' Day, Washington's Birthday), the last Monday in May (Memorial Day), July 4 (Independence Day), the first Monday in September (Labor Day), the second Monday in October (Columbus Day), November 11 (Veterans Day/Armistice Day), the fourth Thursday in November (Thanksgiving Day), and December 25 (Christmas Day). Also, the Tuesday following the first Monday in November is Election Day and is a federal government holiday in presidential-election years held every 4 years (the next is in 2012).

INSURANCE For Domestic Visitors: Trip-cancellation insurance helps you get your money back if you have to back out of a trip, if you have to go home early, or if your travel supplier goes bankrupt. Allowed reasons for cancellation can range from sickness to natural disasters to the State Department declaring your destination unsafe for travel. (Insurers usually won't cover vague fears, though, as many travelers discovered who tried to cancel their trips in Oct 2001 because they were wary of flying.) In this unstable world, trip-cancellation insurance is a good buy if you're getting tickets well in advance—who knows what the state of the world, or of your airline, will be in 9 months! Insurance policy details vary, so read the fine print—and make sure that your airline or cruise line is on the list of carriers covered in case of bankruptcy. For information, contact one of the following insurers: **Access America** (☎ 800/284-8300; www.access america.com), **Travel Guard International** (☎ 800/826-4919; www. travelguard.com), **Travel Insured International** (☎ 800/243-3174; www.travelinsured.com), or **Travelex Insurance Services** (☎ 800/228-9792; www.travelex-insurance.com).

Medical Insurance: Insurance policies can cover everything from the loss or theft of your baggage to trip cancellation to the guarantee of bail in case you're arrested. Good policies will also cover the costs of an accident, repatriation, or death. Packages such as **Europ Assistance's "Worldwide Healthcare Plan"** are sold by European automobile clubs and travel agencies at attractive rates. **Worldwide Assistance Services, Inc.** (☎ 800/821-2828; www.worldwideassistance. com) is the agent for Europ Assistance in the United States. Although it's not required of travelers, health insurance is highly recommended. Unlike many European countries, the United States does not usually offer free or low-cost medical care to its citizens or visitors. Doctors and hospitals are expensive, and in most cases will require advance payment or proof of coverage before they render their services. Though lack of health insurance may prevent you from being admitted to a hospital in non-emergencies, don't worry about being left on a street corner to die: The American way is to fix you now and bill the living daylights out of you later.

For British Travelers: Most big travel agents offer their own insurance and will probably try to sell you their package when you book a holiday. Think before you sign. The **Consumers' Association** recommends that you insist on seeing the policy and reading the fine print before buying travel insurance. The **Association of British Insurers** (☎ 020/7600-3333; www.abi.org.uk) gives advice by phone and publishes *Holiday Insurance,* a free guide to policy provisions and prices. You might also shop around for better deals.

For Canadian Travelers: Canadians should check with their provincial health plan offices or call **Health Canada** (☎ 613/957-2991; www.hc-sc.gc.ca) to find out the extent of your coverage and what documentation and receipts you must take home in case you are treated in the United States.

For Lost Luggage: On domestic flights, checked baggage is covered up to $2,500 per ticketed passenger. On international flights (including U.S. portions of international trips), baggage is limited to approximately $9 per pound, up to approximately $635 per checked bag. If you plan to check items more valuable than the standard liability, see if your valuables are covered by your homeowner's policy, get baggage insurance as part of your comprehensive travel-insurance package, or buy Travel Guard's "BagTrak" product. Don't buy insurance at the airport, as it's usually overpriced. Be sure to take any valuables or irreplaceable items with you in your carry-on luggage, since many valuables (including books, money, and electronics) aren't covered by airline policies.

If your luggage is lost, immediately file a lost-luggage claim at the airport, detailing the luggage contents. For most airlines, you must report delayed, damaged, or lost baggage within 4 hours of arrival. The airlines are required to deliver luggage, once found, directly to your house or destination free of charge.

INTERNET San Francisco is totally wired. You'll find that many cafes have wireless access, as do many hotels. Check www.wififreespot.com for a huge list of free Wi-Fi hotspots—including every Peet's coffee shop, Panera, or McDonald's—or stop by one of the following locations around town: **Brainwash,** 1122 Folsom St., between 7th and 8th streets (☎ 415/861-FOOD [3663]; www.brainwash.com); **Quetzal,** 1234 Polk St., at Bush Street (☎ 415/673-4181); **Copy Central,** 110 Sutter St., at Montgomery Street (☎ 415/392-6470; www.copycentral.com); **Kinko's,** 1967 Market St., near Gough Street (☎ 415/252-0864; www.kinkos.com). To find a comprehensive list of public Wi-Fi hotspots in San Francisco, go to www.jiwire.com; its Hotspot Finder holds the world's largest directory of public wireless hotspots. To find a list of cybercafes in San Francisco, log onto www.cybercaptive.com and www.cybercafe.com.

LIMOS Try **Allstate** (☎ 800/453-4099; www.allstatelimos.com), or **Bauer's Intelligent Transport** (☎ 800/546-6688 or 415/522-1212; www.bauersit.com).

MAIL & POSTAGE Dozens of post offices are located around the city. The closest to Union Square is inside Macy's department store, 170 O'Farrell St. (☎ 800/275-8777). Another convenient location is Sutter Street Postal Store at 150 Sutter. You can pick up mail addressed to you and marked "General Delivery" (Poste Restante) at the Civic Center Post Office Box Unit, PO Box

429991, San Francisco, CA 94142-9991 (☎ 800/275-8777). The street address is 101 Hyde St.

MONEY It's always advisable to bring money in a variety of forms on a vacation: a mix of cash, credit cards, and ATM cards. You should also have enough petty cash upon arrival to cover airport incidentals, tipping, and transportation to your hotel before you leave home. You can always withdraw money upon arrival at an airport ATM, but you'll still need to make smaller change for tipping.

The most common bills in the U.S. are the $1 (a "buck"), $5, $10, and $20 denominations. There are also $2 bills (seldom encountered), $50 bills, and $100 bills. (The last two are usually not welcome as payment for small purchases.)

Coins come in seven denominations: 1¢ (1 cent, or a penny); 5¢ (5 cents, or a nickel); 10¢ (10 cents, or a dime); 25¢ (25 cents, or a quarter); 50¢ (50 cents, or a half dollar); the gold-colored Sacagawea coin, worth $1; and the rare silver dollar.

PARKING Most city parking meters take nickels, dimes, and quarters and have time limits of anywhere from 15 minutes to 4 hours. Legal street-parking spaces do exist, and curb colors also indicate parking regulations. *Red* means no stopping or parking; *blue* is reserved for drivers with disabilities who have a disabled plate or placard; *white* means there's a 5-minute limit and driver must stay in the vehicle; *green* indicates a 10-minute limit; and *yellow* and *yellow-and-black* curbs are for stopping to load or unload passengers or luggage only. Also, don't park at a bus stop or in front of a fire hydrant, and watch out for street-cleaning signs. If you violate the law, you might get a hefty ticket or your car might be towed; to get your car back, you'll have to get a release

from the nearest district police department and then go to the towing company to pick up the vehicle.

PASSES The **San Francisco City-Pass** is the best way to experience all the color and culture of the city. The CityPass features a book of admission tickets to a variety of attractions. You also get 7 days of unlimited transportation on the cable cars, new Embarcadero streetcars, and all Muni services. CityPasses can be purchased online or throughout SF—ask at your hotel or visit www.citypass.com.

PASSPORTS Always keep a photocopy of your passport with you when you're traveling. If your passport is lost or stolen, having a copy significantly facilitates the reissuing process at a local consulate or embassy. Keep your passport and other valuables in your room's safe or in the hotel safe. See "Consulates & Embassies," above, for more information.

PHARMACIES **Walgreens,** the Starbucks of drugstores, has stores just about everywhere. Phone ☎ 800/WALGREEN (925-47336) for the address and phone number of the nearest store.

SAFETY Don't walk alone at night, stay in well-lighted areas, and carry a minimum of cash and jewelry. Although San Francisco isn't crime ridden, it is not a 24-hour town, and you are putting yourself at risk if you venture out at 2am. There are some dodgy neighborhoods you might consider avoiding: The Tenderloin isn't great, although it is home to a huge immigrant population that manages to live side by side with the drug addicts, hookers, and vagrants. Evenings are particularly rough; daytime is okay. Parts of Van Ness Avenue, from Civic Center to Broadway, are grimy. Sixth and 7th streets from Market east to Harrison are home to an assortment of folk that are iffy; this is another area to avoid any time day or night.

SENIOR TRAVELERS   Nearly every attraction in San Francisco offers a senior discount; age requirements vary, and specific prices are listed in chapter 7. Public transportation and movie theaters also have reduced rates. Don't be shy about asking for discounts, but always carry some kind of identification, such as a driver's license, that shows your date of birth.

Members of **AARP,** 601 E St. NW, Washington, DC 20049 (☎ 888/687-2277; www.aarp.org), get discounts on hotels, airfares, and car rentals. AARP offers members a wide range of benefits, including *AARP The Magazine* and a monthly newsletter. Anyone 50 and over can join.

SMOKING   California law prohibits smoking in public buildings, restaurants, and bars. Many hotels are completely nonsmoking, and others have limited floors for smokers.

SPECTATOR SPORTS   The **San Francisco Giants** play baseball at AT&T Park, 24 Willie Mays Plaza, 2nd and King sts. (☎ 415/972-2000; www.giants.mlb.com). The city's football team, the **San Francisco 49ers,** play at Monster Park, Candlestick Point (☎ 415/464-9377; www.sf49ers.com).

TAXES   Sales tax of 8.5% is added to all purchases except snack foods. The hotel tax is 14%.

TAXIS   See "Getting Around," earlier in this chapter.

TELEPHONES   For directory assistance, dial ☎ **411.** Pay phones are getting difficult to find. If you find one, local calls cost 35¢ to 50¢.

TICKETS   **Theater tickets:** Ticket Web (www.ticketweb.com) is a popular online box office with an easy-to-use interface and relationships with most clubs and entertainment

venues. Other sources include **City Box Office,** 180 Redwood St., Ste. 100, San Francisco, CA 94102 (☎ 415/392-4400; www.cityboxoffice.com), and box offices at the individual theaters and concert halls. **TIX Bay Area** (www.tixbayarea.com) is a walk-up box office selling half-price tickets on the day of performance and full-price tickets in advance to select events. It's open Tuesday to Thursday 11am to 6pm, Friday 11am to 7pm, Saturday 10am to 7pm, and Sunday 10am to 3pm. The TIX Pavilion is located in Union Square on Powell Street, between Geary and Post.

TIPPING   In hotels, tip **bellhops** at least $1 per bag, the **chamber staff** $2 to $3 per day (more if you've left a disaster area), and the **doorman** or **concierge** $1 to $5 only if he or she has provided you with some specific service (for example, calling a cab for you or obtaining difficult-to-get theater tickets). Tip the **valet-parking attendant** $1 every time you get your car. In restaurants, bars, and nightclubs, **service staff** expect 15% to 20% of the check, **bartenders** 10% to 15%, **checkroom attendants** $1 per garment, and **valet-parking attendants** $1 per vehicle. Tip **cabdrivers** 15%, **skycaps** at airports at least $1 per bag, and **hairdressers** and **barbers** 15% to 20%.

TOILETS   Public toilets can be hard to find in San Francisco. A handful of fancy French-style pay toilets are strategically placed on high-volume streets, and a few small stores may allow you access to their facilities. Large hotels and fast-food restaurants are probably the best bet for good, clean facilities. Museums, department stores, shopping malls, and, in a pinch, gas stations all have public toilets. If possible, avoid the toilets at parks and beaches, which tend to be dirty and may even be unsafe.

TOURIST INFORMATION San Francisco Convention and Visitors Bureau is located at 900 Market St., Lower Level, Hallidie Plaza, San Francisco, CA 94142-2809 (☎ 415/391-2000; www.onlyinsanfrancisco.com).

TOURIST TRAPS Around Fisherman's Wharf and elsewhere, you may see manned booths with signs proclaiming themselves tourist information centers. These booths are operated by private businesses such as tour companies, boat lines, or other attractions, and, as such, are not the best sources of unbiased advice.

TOURS Gray Line (☎ 888/428-6937; www.sfsightseeing.com) is SF's largest bus-tour operator.

TRAVELERS WITH DISABILITIES Travelers in wheelchairs can request special ramped taxis by calling

Yellow Cab (☎ 415/333-3333), which charges regular rates for the service. Travelers with disabilities can also get a free copy of the *Muni Access Guide,* published by the San Francisco Municipal Railway, Accessible Services Program, 949 Presidio Ave. (☎ 415/923-6142 customer service, or 415/701-4485 accessible services info; www.sfmta.com/cms/mcust/access.htm), which is staffed weekdays from 8am to 5pm. Many travel agencies offer customized tours and itineraries for travelers with disabilities. Two of them are **Flying Wheels Travel** (☎ 877/451-5006 or 507/451-5005; www.flyingwheelstravel.com) and **Accessible Journeys** (☎ 800/846-4537 or 610/521-0339; www.disabilitytravel.com). From the U.K. **Access Travel** (☎ 01942/888844; www.access-travel.co.uk) offers a variety of holidays for persons with disabilities.

San Francisco: **A Brief History**

1542 Juan Rodriguez Cabrillo sails up the California coast.

1579 Sir Francis Drake lands near San Francisco, missing the entrance to the bay.

1769 The Spanish expedition led by Gaspar de Portolá becomes the first Europeans to see San Francisco Bay.

1775 The *San Carlos* is the first European ship to sail into San Francisco Bay.

1776 Captain Juan Bautista de Anza establishes a presidio (military fort); San Francisco de Asis Mission opens.

1821 Mexico wins independence from Spain and annexes California.

1835 The town of Yerba Buena develops around the port; the United States tries unsuccessfully to purchase San Francisco Bay from Mexico.

1846–48 War between the United States and Mexico.

1847 Americans annex Yerba Buena and rename it San Francisco.

1848 Gold is discovered near Sacramento. San Francisco's population swells from about 900 to 26,000.

1851 Lawlessness becomes acute before attempts to curb it.

1869 The transcontinental railroad reaches San Francisco.

1873 Andrew S. Hallidie invents the cable car.

1906 The Great Earthquake strikes; the resulting fire levels the city.

1915 The Panama-Pacific International Exposition celebrates San Francisco's restoration and the completion of the Panama Canal.

1936 The Bay Bridge is completed.

1937 The Golden Gate Bridge is completed.

1945 The United Nations Charter is drafted in San Francisco and adopted by the representatives of 50 countries.

1950 The Beat Generation moves into North Beach.

1967 A free concert in Golden Gate Park attracts 20,000 people, ushering in the Summer of Love and the hippie era.

1974 BART's high-speed transit system opens the tunnel linking San Francisco with the East Bay.

1978 Harvey Milk (a city supervisor and America's first openly gay politician) and Mayor George Moscone are both assassinated by political rival Dan White.

1989 An earthquake registering 7.1 on the Richter scale hits San Francisco just before a World Series baseball game (100 million watch it on TV).

1991 Fire rages through the Berkeley and Oakland hills, destroying 2,800 homes.

1993 Yerba Buena Center for the Arts opens.

1995 The new SF MOMA opens.

1996 Former assembly speaker Willie Brown is elected mayor of San Francisco.

1998 El Niño deluges San Francisco with its second-highest rainfall in recorded history.

2000 Pacific Bell Park opens as the new home of the San Francisco Giants baseball team.

2003 Gavin Newsome is elected mayor of San Francisco.

2004 Mayor Newsom issues over 4,000 same-sex marriage licenses, which are later annulled by the state's Supreme Court.

2005 The de Young opens in a dramatic new home in Golden Gate Park.

2006 Thousands gather before dawn on April 18 to mark the 100th anniversary of the "greate quake," falling silent at 5:12am. Eleven survivors of the original quake attend.

2008 The California Academy of Sciences opens as one of the most ecofriendly buildings of its kind. The state supreme court declares same-sex marriages constitutional.

2010 The San Francisco Giants win the World Series against the Texas Rangers; thousands of fans fill Civic Center Plaza for the parade and celebration.

2011 Ed Lee is elected mayor of San Francisco.

Index

Accommodations

Photo **Credits**